OUTFOXED

ALEX BEN BLOCK

OUTFOXED

MARVIN DAVIS, BARRY DILLER, RUPERT MURDOCH, JOAN RIVERS, and the INSIDE STORY of AMERICA'S FOURTH TELEVISION NETWORK

ST. MARTIN'S PRESS   NEW YORK

Design by Glen M. Edelstein

Library of Congress Cataloging-in-Publication Data

Block, Alex Ben.
    Outfoxed : Marvin Davis, Barry Diller, Rupert Murdoch, Joan Rivers and the inside story of America's fourth television network / Alex Ben Block.
        p. cm.
    ISBN 0-312-03904-2
    1. Television broadcasting—United States.   2. Fox Broadcasting Company.   I. Title.
    HE8700.8.B55   1990
    384.55'065'73—dc20   89-24112
                                                                                CIP

First Edition
10 9 8 7 6 5 4 3 2 1

To my sweet daughter
Hayley
who makes it all worthwhile,
and to my beautiful
wife Jodi, who makes
it all happen

CONTENTS

Contents · viii

ACKNOWLEDGMENTS

A NONFICTION BOOK of this scope would not be possible without the cooperation and aid of a large number of people, both as contributors of information and as supporters of the author. The first and biggest thank you must go to Barry Diller, the chairman of the board of Twentieth Century–Fox and Fox Incorporated and Fox Broadcasting Company, who gave generously of his own time and allowed access to employees at all three of the companies he runs—the movie studio, the TV station group, and the TV network. Although he knew this would be a completely independent book, Mr. Diller was incredibly open, candid, and helpful at every step of the process. While this book would have been written in any case, it has been incalculably enriched by Barry Diller's active assistance.

I also received help from many others in the Fox family. Rupert Murdoch, chairman of the board of News Corp. and News America, the parent organization of Fox, granted an interview by phone and another in person, and granted access to others in his organization, including Richard Sarazan, William O'Neil, Stanley Shulman, and Sir James Carruthers.

At the Fox Broadcasting Company help was generously provided by many, many people, including Jamie Kellner, Garth Ancier, Kevin Wendle, David Johnson, Scott Sassa, Michael Binkow, Brad Turell, Marion Davis, Jim McKay, John Lazurus, Brenda Mutchnick Farrier, Alan Sternfeld, Michael Lansbury, Cindy Ronzoni, Andrew Fessel, Thomas Herwitz, Paul Slagle, and Stephen Chao.

At Twentieth Century–Fox still other employees past and present were helpful and deserve thanks, including Jon Dolgen, Leonard Goldberg, Thomas Sherak, Lawrence Gordon, Ruth Haley, John DeSimio, Sherry Lansing, Norman Levy, Harris Katleman, Jeffrey C. Kramer, Scott Rudin, Richard Zanuck, Dennis Stanfill, C. Joseph La Bonte, Alan Horn, John De Simio, Alan Ladd, Jr., Edward Gradinger, Robert Kreig, Dirk Zimmerman, and David Simon.

Thanks also to Marvin Davis, who granted a face-to-face interview and then answered additional questions through his representatives Lee Solters and Jerry Greenberg. Mr. Davis also made others close to him available, including his son John Davis and Burton I. "Buddy" Monash.

At Paramount Pictures and Paramount Communications, thanks are due to Martin Davis and Jerry Sherman. Also, for providing general help over several years, to Frank Mancuso, Deborah Rosen, Sid Ganis, and Barry London.

Special thanks to Joan Rivers and to those who contributed to the telling of her story, including Courtney Conti, Bill Sammeth, Richard Grant, Mark Hudson, Peter Dekom, Stephanie Levine, Richard Meryman, Rona Barrett, and Jim Mahoney.

Others who have provided information, support, or advice and who deserve thanks include J. Ira Harris, Daniel Melnick, Frank Price, Michael Eisner, Jeffrey Katzenberg, Rich Frank, Bill Mechanic, Dawn Steel, Ricardo Mestres, Michael Fuchs, Garth Drabinsky, Jerry Belson, Terry Melcher, Jack Valenti, Sandy Gallin, Liz Fell, Clay Felker, Ginny Munger Kahn, Allan Sloan, Stephen J. Cannell, John Aggolia, Robert Fell, Paul Wilner, Louis Chunovic, Charles Bachrach, Sandy Kenyon, Stephen Bochco, Warren Littlefield, Bernie Brillstein, Richard Dreyfuss, Michael Moye, Ron Leavitt, Chuck Bowman, Patrick Hasburgh, Chris Lemmon, John Ashley, Ed O'Neill, Gary Brandt, Kevin O'Brien, Martin Colby, Gary Shandling, Brad Grey, I. Martin Pompadur, Michael Linder, Andrew J. Schwartzman, Stanley S. Hubbard, Richard Mahler, David Levy, Art Lanhan, Arnold Semsky, Fred Wray, Steve Beers, Ron Krueger, Rene Golden, Irwin Gottlieb, Alec Gerster, Gordon Weaver, Richard Natale, Ed Michaelow, Leonard Goldenson,

Barry Glasser, Jonathan Powell, the Museum of Broadcasting (New York City), and AT & T.

This book would not have been possible without the hard work and dedication of my agent, Barbara Lowenstein, and her fine staff. At St. Martin's Press I thank my patient editor Charles Spicer, former editor Felica Eth, Bill Thomas, and the rest of the excellent staff.

I also wish to acknowledge the love, patience, and understanding of my friends and family, who lived through three years of research and writing. I am especially grateful to my wife, Jodi Taylor Block; my daughter, Hayley Taylor Block; my parents, Anne and Robert Block; my sisters, Rita Block Chouinard and Paula M. Block; my mother-in-law, Anne Golub; and my sister and brother-in-law, Barbara and Murray Postal, and their children and family.

Many friends provided help and support along the way. Among them are Lawrence Minard, Kathleen Wiegner, Norman Lear, David Appelbaum, Mark Baron, Richard Melcombe, Merrill Brown, Neal Koch, Peter Burrell, Jeffrey Cheen, Henry Gellis, Andrew Jaffe, Leonard Maltin, Kathy Morlock, Paul Maxwell, Frank Swertlow, Jeanne Wolf, and Stella Zadeh.

PROLOGUE:
BIRTH OF A NETWORK

THE MANDARIN CLASS in prerevolutionary China were the aristocrats, the educated elite. They were known for living well, and in exquisite luxury. In the terms of modern advertising, they had the greatest disposable income of any demographic group in their society. Any smart merchant knew to go after them first. They were the ones who loved "literature, art, philosophy, and stylish living," according to the notes on the back of the tall gray-hewed menu at the Mandarin. The elegant, dimly lit Chinese restaurant in Beverly Hills is entered through smoke-glass doors. On the left is a small bar, and down the hall is a warren of rooms set with the finest silver, crystal, and polished wooden chopsticks. It is just the kind of place a mandarin would go to for dinner and liquid refreshment after a stimulating day of commerce.

Thus it was a fitting setting on Thursday evening, March 27, 1986, when a group of seven men, most strangers until several days earlier, gathered around a long rectangular table in the deepest recesses of the Mandarin for a leisurely repast. These seven men, ranging in age from twenty-six to fifty-five, were newly joined in a most extraordinary business venture, and they had just concluded an exciting and successful day that had burned into each of them one purpose. From that moment forward, they were agreed that they would do what no one else had been able to accomplish in four decades of frustrated efforts: create a new network of affiliated broadcasting stations to reach the approximately ninety million U.S. homes with television sets. They didn't yet know which nights it would broadcast, what shows it would carry, or what TV audience ratings it might command, but they did know that the resources were in place to launch the Fox Broadcasting Company into America's living rooms.

The last successful launch of a television network had occurred in 1948, when Leonard Goldenson pieced together the American Broadcasting Company out of the remnants of what had been the weaker of the National Broadcasting Company's two networks. RCA had originally created two National Broadcasting Company networks. When the Federal Communications Commission (FCC) forced it to divest one of them in 1943, to comply with guidelines designed to foster network competition, RCA kept the far more successful of the two as NBC. The weaker network was renamed the American Broadcasting Company. It then took ABC more than twenty-five years to achieve parity with the two dominant broadcasters of television's first generation, RCA's National Broadcasting Company and William Paley's Columbia Broadcasting System (CBS).

Now, the oldest of those assembled for dinner, Rupert Murdoch, was moving uninvited into the uncharted future of broadcasting. With the help of the forty-six-year-old head of the Twentieth Century–Fox movie studio, Barry Diller, Murdoch proposed to install a fourth player in the three-network oligopoly. He stood poised to underwrite about $150 million in losses to create a network, which, if even moderately successful, would be worth over $1 billion. The potential reward was great, but so was the risk. Murdoch's network would have to attract a large viewer audience at a time when the market shares of the existing networks were shrinking.

Murdoch, a tall, lean man with dark hair and deep-set eyes, and Diller, solidly built and slightly balding, weren't asking anyone's permission. They were simply pursuing the American dream with a vengeance. They were seizing the initiative at a time when a series of momentous events in broadcasting, the convergence of some powerful personalities, and a dazzling series of technological innovations all coalesced to make this audacious attempt possible.

Diller, in a tan suit, white shirt, and off-white tie, conducted the proceedings at dinner, even though all present knew that Murdoch wielded the ultimate clout as owner. It was Diller who would lead the effort to crack television's longtime triopoly. It was Diller who had the unique combination of experience and talent to orchestrate the construction of a network and to create the popular programming that would be necessary to feed its voracious appetite for new stimulation. It was Diller who ordered dinner for them all and around whom most of the conversation flowed.

As he looked along the row of bright, clean-cut, sharp-minded executives, Diller couldn't help but be pleased. He hadn't gotten all of his first choices, but it was a team that fit his style. They were a little younger, a bit more inexperienced than might be ideal, but to Diller that meant not being burdened with the old ideas and concepts about what composed a TV network.

On one side of Diller was Jamie Kellner, at forty-two still surprisingly boyish looking, like the apple-cheeked kid next door. Diller appreciated his intelligence and constantly tested it. Diller insistently made demands and Kellner enthusiastically tried to produce. While Kellner held the title of president of the new network, his position was, at best, difficult. Everyone present knew that Barry Diller would have final say and Murdoch ultimate authority, meaning that Kellner would be his own man only insofar as he pleased Diller.

Next to Kellner was David Johnson, an often-brilliant, analytical financial executive who had spent most of his career at ABC. He was looking for an opportunity that would propel him back into broadcasting's big leagues. He was one of the few around the table with real network television business experience, and it would be his numbers, forecasts, and projections, sometimes drawn from imaginative sources, that would become the fragile foundation of the new network.

Beyond Johnson was Scott Sassa, the youngest member of the team and, in some ways, the oddest fit. His sturdy Asian heritage set him apart physically from the others, but so did his youth. He had progressed quickly through a rising tide of executive positions, the last having been at the faltering Playboy cable TV channel, to join Fox as a jack-of-many-trades. He would work with Johnson to create the economic model by which Fox initially would be shaped and sold to the Hollywood creative community, TV viewers, and advertisers. He would work with Diller and others on start-up advertising, promotion, and publicity for the new, as yet unnamed, venture. And he would work with the creative and development executives on programming ideas. Sassa was the executive errand boy on whom fell many duties that no one else was ready to shoulder—affiliate relations, corporate publicity, special projects. He would burn brightly as one of the midwives of the new network, but from the start there were questions about whether his flame would burn long.

On Diller's immediate right were the two newest members of the Fox team, Garth Ancier and Kevin Wendle. They were so new, in fact, that officially they were still employees of the competition, NBC. Bursting with excitement, they were still astounded at where events in so short a period had propelled them. Ancier, with longish light-brown hair and a toothy smile, and Wendle, with flashing blue eyes and a narrow face, were to be the heart of the programming department. Considering their positions at NBC, in organizational terms they were leapfrogging from underling to superior. They were instantly joining the mandarins of broadcasting.

Ancier had been a vice president of comedy at NBC, where he helped shape such hits as "The Cosby Show" and "The Golden Girls." They hadn't been his ideas, but he had worked well with the creative personnel as the shows grew into successes. Some had seen Ancier as the heir apparent to Brandon Tartikoff, the brilliant programmer who had engineered the NBC network's rise to number one in the ratings the previous year. Ancier himself had seen several other executives waiting in the wings alongside him, and after much thought, had decided to hitch his star to Murdoch and Diller instead.

Wendle, a native of New Jersey, had literally grown up in local TV news broadcasting. At NBC he had been on a much lower rung than Ancier. He had been recruited by Jamie Kellner and had come along only after helping engineer the hiring of Ancier as his boss. Ancier acted as Wendle's mentor and partner. Each felt that the presence of the other would provide an important part of the support system they would need to flourish in the new environment. Their friendship would develop into a complex relationship with many dark overtones, but that was all in the future. On this evening Ancier and Wendle, feeling like best friends, were simply enjoying rubbing elbows with Diller and Murdoch.

Diller asked Ancier and Wendle their thoughts on a new movie he was thinking of financing, to be produced by and star the actor Warren Beatty. It was to be a big-budget, live-action version of the Dick Tracy comic strip about a tough cop with a high-tech wristwatch. Sassa mentioned that it would provide some natural promotional tie-ins, because the character was so well known. Diller wondered aloud what kind of programs their network might create with similar appeal. The ideas flowed quickly, with everyone contributing. They were like enthusiastic youths in a late night bull session. Wendle talked about ways to reach the audience that were different than those employed by the existing networks. He recalled a supermarket sweepstakes when he was a kid in which viewers could stop by and pick up a special card that allowed them to bet on televised horse races. The sense of camaraderie among the men was as thick as the black bean sauce over the lobster. It was like the first day of spring training in baseball. Each and every one of them felt that he was about to experience a winning season.

Murdoch was soft spoken and interested in what each man had to say. Only once did he call for everyone's attention. He wanted to make a toast. He raised his glass and let his eyes wander around. "This is really the core group, the beginning," he said in his strong Australian accent. "Look around and let us wish each other success, for tonight is the start of something. It is a night we shall long remember."

For Murdoch, there already had been many memorable moments. In a remarkably short time, he had risen from proprietor of an obscure regional Australian newspaper into an important media baron in Australia, the United Kingdom, and the United States. His American stable of publications included the *New York Post,* the *Boston Herald,* and *New York* magazine. However, he now sensed that his future in the United States was in broadcasting, tied to the biggest gamble of his high-risk career. Murdoch's holding company, News Corp., had only months before purchased seven television stations in major American cities from Metromedia at one of the highest prices ever paid for a similar property. It had been much more than an economic decision for Murdoch, even though the size of the deal, in essence, mortgaged everything he owned. Murdoch also had had to give up his Australian citizenship in order to comply with FCC regulations concerning ownership of broadcast outlets. He had sworn an oath of allegiance to the United States and recommitted his life to a new land, one with unlimited horizons.

Murdoch had bought the already-successful Metromedia stations knowing that even if their earnings and profits remained at the same level, they would not generate enough income to cover the interest and carrying costs of his acquisition debt. To make his purchase worthwhile—sane, even, in business terms—he had to find some way to jack up the value of those properties dramatically. That was what the network was all about. It not only would provide better programming for those stations, but would also allow them to charge a higher rate for each second of advertising time.

Murdoch, weaned in the tradition of English and Australian journalism, also was keenly aware of the political power that could flow from ownership of a major television network. He knew it would be a huge investment of time, money, and energy, but that was acceptable as long as he was convinced of the wisdom of the venture. In Australia he had started the *Australian,* the first national newspaper, based in the capital, and then absorbed more than twenty years of losses before it became established. To Murdoch, the red ink had been at least partly compensated for by the access his national newspaper gave him to the inner sanctum of government. As long as he could afford to keep the doors open, his media—meaning Murdoch himself—could not be ignored.

Those who knew Murdoch only from the lurid headlines on the front of the *New York Post,* those who saw him as a repellent corporate raider, those who were sure he represented the lowest, basest instinct in man, all misunderstood a great deal about Murdoch. He might be all of those things, but he was also a builder of businesses with a global view of commerce. He bought, but he rarely sold. He was willing to pay a premium, but then he usually stayed around as an operator long enough to prove he'd been right.

The one lesson that cut across all of Murdoch's media empire was that good content, good programming, and the right popular product could open all kinds of doors. It could make the government grant a licensing franchise for a TV system. It could convince advertisers to spend millions of dollars. It could create giant reputations for those who created the shows that wafted through their neighborhood electronic pipeline. And now Murdoch would have the two vehicles most likely to produce a constant flow of such programming—a movie studio and a broadcast network. Instinct told him that once the dual flow was in place, he would find myriad ways to sell it, use it, and ride it to rising fame and fortune.

As was the case with so many things in his life, Murdoch had not carefully mapped out all of his plans in advance. Rather, he was poised each time to take advantage of opportunities as they arose. He could not have foreseen that Marvin Davis would hire Barry Diller to run his movie studio and then have a falling out with him. But when it happened, Murdoch was there to buy first half and then all of Twentieth Century–Fox. He could not have predicted that John Kluge would decide to make Metromedia a private company, running up such a huge debt that his only out was to sell his lucrative independent TV station chain. But when it happened, Murdoch was ready. And he could not have known that the landscape of broadcasting would be shifted unalterably beginning in the 1980s by an increase in the number of independent TV stations and by such new broadcast media as cable TV and the VCR. But he was poised to exploit the opportunities in this new environment more daringly than anyone else.

Murdoch knew he was putting himself into debt up to, and perhaps even beyond, his eyeballs, but he had been taking extraordinary risks in his own conservative way for most of his life, and he wasn't about to stop now.

As the glasses emptied, Murdoch decided that the moment was right to reveal something else to the new members of the group. It was the most important secret of the new venture, the news that would begin to turn an idea into reality in the mind of the world.

The men grew quiet, hanging on each of Murdoch's softly spoken words. Even Diller felt a chill go up his spine. It was a secret, Murdoch warned, and they were all sworn not to breathe a word of it to anyone in advance. Joan Rivers, the most popular comedienne in America, was about to sign on as host of a late night talk show on their new network. The response was electrifying. Ancier smiled broadly. Now he knew why Rivers had been stalling on signing a new one-year contract with NBC, where she was the official alternate guest host for their incredibly lucrative, long-running late night talk program "The Tonight Show Starring Johnny Carson."

David Johnson was thinking about how he would use Rivers's fame to help sign on independent TV stations as affiliates of the new network. Sassa thought about how they might promote it for the greatest effect. Diller, who had been negotiating the deal for weeks, thought about Rivers's extraordinary $15 million contract with Fox.

Rivers was perfect for their new network. They couldn't hope to reach the broad audiences of CBS, NBC, or even ABC, but they could go after a target group. They would zero in on the upper-income audience, people who are light viewers but who have the most money to spend, the modern-day version of the mandarins of old China. They would reach out to this audience with situation comedies and creative dramas and with action shows and horror movie–type programming. They would go into the dark and make their own light and become true mandarins themselves, and they would prove once more their right to be members of the ruling class of broadcasters.

Would they make it? Could they do what no other person or company had been able to do for over forty years? Those questions lay ahead. That evening at the Mandarin, there was only the good feeling of having been chosen for an important mission. All things seemed possible; all dreams were attainable. What began on a pleasant evening in Beverly Hills over shrimp and snow peas would forever change broadcast history. The Fox was loose in the hen-house of American broadcasting.

INTRODUCTION: THE FOUNDING FOX

WILLIAM FOX, THE Fox in Twentieth Century–Fox and the man whose name now symbolizes America's newest television network, is the unsung pioneer of Hollywood. While other early moguls have been elevated to the status of legends, Fox has been systematically forgotten despite his huge contributions to the motion picture industry.

Today, few in Hollywood, or elsewhere for that matter, have even heard of William Fox. They may know that Adolph Zukor founded Paramount, that Louis B. Mayer and Irving Thalberg founded Metro-Goldwyn-Mayer (MGM), or that Jack and Harry Warner started Warner Brothers, but Fox is practically an unknown. If pressed they will tell you that Twentieth Century–Fox was the creation of Darryl F. Zanuck, the brilliant executive who ran the company from 1935 until the early 1970s.

Yet there is no question that William Fox—who usually referred to himself in the third person as "The Fox"—played a vital role in shaping the business, technological, and creative direction of the movie business. Short and stocky with a thick Hungarian accent, Fox was a true eccentric. Despite a gimpy arm, he became an expert golfer—using one arm. He never wore a watch, because he felt it limited how much time he would spend on any one project, and he always wore white socks, because he felt they were more hygenic.

The only thing that wasn't odd about The Fox was his ability to make movies and money. During his highly productive thirty-five-year tenure, Fox may not have made the most prestigious A pictures, but his business was profitable and prolific. Fox oversaw or produced some 750 feature films.

It was Fox who, around 1910, stood up to the trust created by Thomas Alva Edison and others (which was formed by pooling all of the important motion picture technology patents) to monopolize the distribution and exhibition of motion pictures. In those days, the Edison trust insisted that all theater owners pay a license fee for every foot of film shown. In many cities it also demanded that film exchange operators (wholesalers who sold movies to theater owners) sell their businesses to the trust for a very low price. In New York City, where there were more than 115 movie exchanges, only one owner refused to sell—William Fox. Instead, to outfox the trust, he began making movies first in New Jersey, then in southern California. The Fox went on to succeed as a movie producer and distributor. He also was victorious over the Edison trust in court. In 1914, acting on Fox's challenge, the U.S. Supreme Court broke up the Edison trust.

Fox was one of the first genuine showmen who recognized the role of advertising, marketing, and ballyhoo in the selling and distribution of movies. He learned his lesson early. The first theater he ever bought, in New York City, was sold to him by a con man who had filled the place with fake customers the day Fox went to look it over. When Fox opened for business, nobody showed up. So he hired a magician to stand out front and do tricks, and then lead the crowd inside. Once they learned of the movies playing in the second-floor theater, they clamored for more. Soon his business was booming. Later Fox pioneered many of the modern techniques of print and poster advertising and created one of the first publicity departments.

The Edison trust had a rule that forbade anyone from mentioning the name of a performer on screen, a ploy to keep actors' salaries low. Fox, however, believed that creating an identity for his performers helped sell tickets; and, of course, history would prove him right. He was also the first to invent a star. In 1914, Fox turned a Jewish girl from Cincinnati named Theodosia Goodman into the mysterious Theda Bara (the reverse spelling of *Arab*). He had her photographed in flamboyant costumes, alongside human skulls, snakes, and other props, and made up a completely fictional biography, which the press quickly accepted as fact. He put her in movies with historical contexts or exotic locales, including *Cleopatra,* and she was a smash hit.

Fox, who, along with his wife Eve Leo, also functioned as the studio's story and script development department for many years, was one of the very first to see the importance of the film director. Fox developed a strong stable of directors who went on to glorious careers in Hollywood, including Raoul Walsh, Howard Hawks, and John Ford.

It was Fox who first elevated the lowly Western from short, poorly made features into full-length films with production values as good as the finest dramas. Fox's biggest success was Tom Mix, who became a silent screen superstar in a series of films that featured fast-moving action, lots of stunts, and a bit of comedy.

Fox pioneered numerous modern production techniques, such as making movies on location. In the late 1920s he conceived the first wide-screen 70-mm movie-projection process, Grandeur, although financial troubles kept him from fully exploiting it.

While the Warner brothers are credited with producing the first "talkie" (*The Jazz Singer,* 1927), using a crude sound-on-disc system, it was the competing sound system pushed by Fox around the same time that actually became the industry standard. It led Fox in 1928 to open the world's first all-sound movie studio in Westwood, California, an area now called Century City (and still home to Twentieth Century–Fox studios). At one time he held the patents on all of the sound technology in movies, but during the Great Depression the U.S. Supreme Court, under intense political pressure, reversed its own earlier ruling and stripped Fox of his sound-technology patents, claiming that his powerful position was not in the public interest.

Fox relentlessly built one of the world's first and finest international film distribution operations, traveling the globe personally in the early years to hire personnel and establish field offices. He was determined that his movies be handled and released overseas as efficiently as they were in the United States.

Fox created the largest, most-watched newsreel operation—the first to send camera crews roaming the globe—and established the role model for what was to become broadcast television journalism. His *Movietone Newsreel* was already in operation when sound arrived in the mid-1920s. Fox immediately understood the power of using sound and film for journalism. *Movietone* became the first news gathering operation to bring Americans talking pictures of leading scientists, political figures, and others from around the world.

Fox helped pioneer the financial structure of the film industry as well, becoming among the first to tap the public markets for capital to make movies and build theaters. He went public in 1925 and used the $6 million he raised to build up his company and to construct what would become some of the most famous movie theaters in the world.

While few remember Fox, many have marveled at the fabulous Fox theaters in Atlanta, Detroit, Denver, San Francisco, Los Angeles, and elsewhere. William Fox himself oversaw the construction of most of those theaters between 1925 and 1928, while his wife Eve did the decorating and consulted on the elaborate, ornate designs. At one point, Fox had a circuit of over eight hundred of the finest theaters in the United States.

Fox was also among the first to see the economic efficiency of a large-scale entertainment-oriented enterprise. His ambition reached an apex for a time in 1929 and 1930. Fox, who already owned one movie studio, purchased enough stock to take over Loews, the movie-theater company that also owned Metro-Goldwyn-Mayer, the largest, best-known, most-successful movie studio of that era. Fox intended to combine Fox and MGM into the most important movie production, distribution, and theater operation in the world. Instead, his empire began to unravel.

First, Fox was in an automobile accident that put him out of action at a crucial moment, just before the 1929 stock market crash. As the value of his Fox and Loews stock fell, he became a victim of the national economic collapse. He lost Loews, in part because of back-room political maneuvering that used the antitrust laws to deny him a chance to merge Fox and MGM. In the end he was done in by the greed of Wall Street and his own bankers. In 1930 Fox was forced out of the studio he had founded. His bankers and investment brokers froze his account at a crucial moment, which made it impossible for him to borrow money to repay loans representing only a fraction of what he and the studio were actually worth.

The bankers and other creditors who took over the Fox Film Corporation said that the loss of William Fox wouldn't make any difference, that it wasn't really William Fox who was responsible for the studio's long run of economic success. They soon found out how wrong they were. During all of The Fox's years at the helm, the studio never lost money, but the year after he left, the studio recorded its first loss and subsequently fell on hard times.

Eventually the only salvation for Fox Film was to merge with a small production company, Twentieth Century Pictures, which was run primarily by a brilliant young studio executive who had spent most of his career at Warner Bros., Darryl F. Zanuck. The newly merged enterprise, which really consisted of what Fox had built and Zanuck's ideas, was called Twentieth Century–Fox.

William Fox's name and contribution have been systematically forgotten by the very industry he helped create. His crime was that he had become an embarrassment during an era when Hollywood desperately needed a clean image. For a few months in 1941, William Fox was incarcerated in a minimum-security federal prison. He had foolishly allowed a lawyer to talk him into attempting to bribe a crooked federal bankruptcy court judge, and then had gotten caught.

From the time he emerged from prison until he died in 1952, Fox tried to claw his way back into the motion picture business, but the industry turned its back on him. Hollywood already had enough image problems. Only a short time before Fox went to prison, a Twentieth Century–Fox executive had gone to jail for income-tax violations stemming from illegal payoffs made on behalf of the major studios to crooked union bosses. The industry also was embroiled in a decade of antitrust litigation designed to force moviemakers to sell off any ownership interest in movie theaters. The last thing Hollywood wanted or needed during World War II and the years immediately following was an aging, blustering old orthodox Jew with a gimpy arm and German accent whose name was tainted by personal scandal.

Now the Fox name has been resurrected for another bold experiment, the Fox Broadcasting Company. Although little reference has been made to William Fox in the process, it is certainly the kind of audacious, visionary idea that he would have been likely to champion.

Rupert Murdoch is similar in many ways to The Fox. He, too, is a foreign-born naturalized American citizen and essentially self-made; he is a visionary and a builder; he has on occasion been accused of being a ruthless corporate raider; he is quick to use the newest technology but understands that the market is really driven by strong, seductive, well-marketed programming; he is a risk taker who willingly borrows many millions of dollars, betting that he can succeed before his highly leveraged position catches up with him.

As this book is written, there is no assurance that Rupert Murdoch will succeed with the Fox Broadcasting Company, although after nearly three years of operation it is off to a very promising start.

This book is not an attempt to predict what lies ahead. Rather, it is a broad look at one of Hollywood's major movie studios—how its near bankruptcy led to a change in management, and how in 1987 that infusion of new people and new capital directly resulted in the launching of a fourth television network in the United States.

Our story will span the decade of the 1980s and bring to life a slice of broadcast history as it was being made. The first years of the Fox Broadcasting Company have been the stuff of both dreams and nightmares. It turned out to be more difficult, more expensive, more exasperating a task than any of its backers ever imagined. It tested the people and the institutions involved and pushed them to their limits. Some of the people who were there at the creation didn't survive the infancy of the new venture, but the most important players remained firm in their conviction that it was possible.

As you will see, those involved had many different reasons for making the effort. Some were driven by money, others by ambition. All found themselves caught up in a high-stakes drama that was played out on the TV sets of America and in the news media of the world. If the Fox network someday becomes truly competitive with NBC, CBS, and ABC, it will be because those most deeply involved were not willing to be stopped by short-term failure. If it fails, it still will have carved out its own little piece of broadcast history as the most spectacular particle in the explosive fragmentation of the media in the decade of the 1980s.

The first part of this book deals with what happened to Twentieth Century–Fox under the ownership of Marvin Davis, whose shrewd business practices made him rich even as the businesses he operated faltered. The middle portion is about the rebirth of the studio after the arrival of Barry Diller. And the final portion is about the creation of the new TV network under the ownership of Rupert Murdoch.

Like William Fox, each of the participants had a brilliant, and unique approach to attaining his goal. However, if there is a lesson common to all it is that money alone is not enough to guarantee success. It can't buy an audience for a movie, as Davis learned, and it can't insure a large TV audience, as Murdoch came to realize. Nor can it make unpopular executives well liked. Money *can* open windows of opportunity.

This is a book about people, television, and technology. It's about a changing society and, most of all, it's about money. But it is also a cautionary tale about the limitations of money and the dangers to those who wield the power money bestows.

OUTFOXED

MARVIN JUST WANTS
TO HAVE FUN

MARVIN DAVIS ALWAYS loved going to the movies. He just hated standing in line. So during the late 1970s, after an international oil crisis had made him one of the richest men in America, Davis built a private screening room in his home. When he couldn't always get the films he wanted, Davis bought his own movie theater, which could book the pictures he desired. The University Hills Cinema was only a short drive from his sumptuous home in posh Cherry Hills Village, a sprawling suburb south of downtown Denver, Colorado, where Davis lived with his wife Barbara and their five children. Davis and his kids would attend showings there regularly, and for fun his kids even worked occasionally behind the concession stand, selling hot buttered popcorn and iced soft drinks.

Oil might have made him rich, but owning a theater was fun. Increasingly, as the seventies rushed to their conclusion, fun was what interested six-foot-four-inch-tall, three-hundred-pound, fifty-four-year-old Marvin Davis. He wanted his life to be about fun as well as making money, and he saw no reason why he couldn't combine the two. Davis had developed a new theory of investing. He believed that "fun" businesses were often good businesses to own. If *he* thought they were fun, his reasoning went, so would

1

others, which would make them easier to sell once he wanted out. He observed that fun businesses also tended to sell at a premium price, because people would pay extra to be associated with things like movie theaters, professional sports, or the media.

The other corollary of Davis's investing formula was that a fun business must also be some kind of exclusive franchise. That insured value. It might be a sports franchise or a newspaper or a major movie studio, but it had to be an asset that would be almost impossible to replace.

This improbable mix of fun and business was a reflection of Davis's personality. As warm and loving as he could be with family and friends, he could be cold and ruthless in business. As tender as he could be with a sick child, he could say and do whatever it took to make a deal succeed. Although he made millions, his companies often made suppliers and contractors wait unusually long periods of time before outstanding bills were paid. Davis was a man of great charity and very shrewd business practices.

As he grew wealthier and more successful, Davis's confidence in his own abilities grew. He yearned to reach beyond the confines of the comfortable environment he had created in Denver. He was getting increasingly restless with the oil and real estate businesses that had made him wildly wealthy. He felt they were near their peak but believed that he himself had a long way to go. He began to look beyond the next horizon . . . for *fun*.

Paying attention to whether his investment was also fun was a luxury Marvin Davis hadn't always enjoyed. Although his father, Jack Davis, was moderately wealthy and successful, Marvin had struggled for many years to make it in the oil business. After graduating from New York University in 1948, it was almost twenty years before he really came into his own. At one point he had drilled eighty dry holes in a row and come close to giving up the fight. It finally turned around for him in the late 1960s, when his wildcatting paid off with a series of gushers along the Powder River Basin in Wyoming. By the end of the 1970s, Davis was the leading independent oilman in the United States.

From 1975 to 1981, according to records kept by the Petroleum Information Corporation, Davis drilled almost twelve hundred wells, of which slightly more than half produced at least some oil or gas. While at least one company drilled more wells than Davis, no one else drilled in as many unproven, untested areas. Davis really built much of his fortune by bringing in small wells rather than huge gushers. The difference was that he drilled so many that his total output of crude oil added up to a significant position in the energy industry.

Davis was the beneficiary of a massive shift in the international energy markets. In the early 1970s the primary oil-producing nations banded together into an organization called the Organization of Petroleum Exporting Countries (OPEC). Twice in the seventies, in 1973 and 1979, OPEC triggered boycotts of the major Western industrial nations, rapidly pushing up the price of oil. The value of existing stockpiles of oil and oil reserves still in the ground skyrocketed. Marvin Davis suddenly became richer than he had ever imagined possible.

In 1977 Davis moved into real estate when he purchased a 22,000-acre ranch just outside Denver for $13.7 million. He sold it a month later for about $26 million to a subsidiary of Phillip Morris that built residential homes. Davis then formed a partnership that began buying and building hundreds of millions of dollars in commercial real estate in downtown Denver, including many of the city's landmark office buildings and hotels, just in time to cash in on the boom in business brought about by rising oil prices. Exhibiting an uncanny sense of timing, Davis sold almost all of his Denver property a few years later, just before the oil prices fell and the Denver commercial real estate market crashed.

As the 1970s neared their end, Davis also was being pushed in new directions by concern over his own mortality. Having grown up in affluence, Davis was well aware that no amount of money could guarantee health or happiness. He had suffered through years of his father's heart disease and his daughter Dana's lifelong battle with diabetes. During the late 1970s, he also had a health scare of his own—a mild case of melanoma, or skin cancer, according to Davis (who prefers not to discuss it because he fears that stories about his health might cause potential business partners to be wary about getting involved with him). His bout with cancer, however insignificant, appears to have made Davis consider his life and his place in history. In 1981, at age fifty-five, Davis was determined to be remembered as more than a rich, obscure Denver oil wildcatter.

As his wealth grew, so did Davis's social contacts. Rubbing elbows with the truly rich and famous in the nation's most posh resorts only added to his restlessness. Davis had bought homes in Vail, Colorado, and Palm Springs, California, where he and his family and friends would vacation. Soon the Davises were enjoying the company of such neighbors as former president Gerald Ford, Henry Kissinger, and Lucille Ball and her husband Gary Morton, whose home was not far from the Davis's home in Palm Springs. Lucy was, of course, for many years one of television's premiere comediennes, while Gary was full of the kind of old show business stories Davis could listen to for hours.

The Davises soon added other friends in Palm Springs, including Frank Sinatra and his attorney Marvin "Mickey" Rudin, who soon began doing legal work for Davis as well.

Beginning in 1974 the Davises were inviting all of their celebrity friends to Denver each winter to participate in a giant formal charity event to benefit medical research. Dubbed the "Carousel Ball," it quickly became Denver's most-publicized, star-studded event of the year, raising millions of dollars to speed up the search for a cure for diabetes. As it grew, Davis also found that many of his new friends, including corporate leaders, movie stars, and top politicians, were also good business contacts and, in many cases, potential investors in his deals.

Davis's search for a fun business seemed to take him in ever-wider circles. He bought and sold a radio station. He invested in a Los Angeles–based movie-production company run by his friend Mace Neufeld. He came close to acquiring two different major-league baseball teams, with the idea of moving the franchise to Denver. A $12 million deal for the Oakland Athletics fell through at the last minute when the A's couldn't shake loose from a long-term lease with the Oakland Coliseum. He came even closer to buying the ailing *Denver Post* for about $75 million. He backed out at the last minute after an analysis by his aides indicated that the newspaper would require a huge additional capital expenditure for new presses, a sum that he felt would be unreasonable when coupled with high-cost union contracts that were difficult to work around. He felt the union contracts which the newspaper was locked into would prevent him from realizing a satisfactory return on his large investment. The *Post* was later acquired by the Times-Mirror Corporation, which ran into all of the problems Davis had anticipated and eventually sold out.

Davis also looked toward Hollywood. He first became interested when he found that he could buy Columbia Pictures for a good price. The stock market value of Columbia's parent, Columbia Pictures Industries, had been depressed by a series of management changes and failed films, making it a likely candidate for a takeover. Davis was intrigued, but ultimately he was put off by Columbia's relatively small film library, a wildly uneven earnings record, and a lack of outside assets to exploit.

Despite his reputation as a wildcatter, Davis wasn't really looking to take risks. What he wanted to find was undervalued assets that would cover his downside risk while also providing the potential for significant profits if the business actually could be made to work.

In the oil business, where he faithfully followed the adage "he who drills the most holes has the best chance of success," Davis never used his own money. He was the master of "the hedge," or what oil men called "free exposure." Davis called it "a third for a quarter." That meant that the cost to explore each well was put up by three partners, each of whom received 25 percent of the ownership in that well. The other quarter went to Davis, without any cash investment, as manager of the property. In other words, they paid and he drilled. And as the price of oil rose and rose, they all got rich—especially Marvin Davis.

Early in 1981, two things happened that changed Davis's business direction once again, making him more determined than ever to diversify away from oil. First, he was confronted with a messy government lawsuit. Federal investigators (in a 1979 lawsuit) charged that Summit Transportation Company, an oil wholesaling firm Davis headed, had violated oil pricing guidelines created after the OPEC crisis. It had violated the rules by selling oil from recently discovered wells, which were regulated by federal law, as oil from old wells, which were not government regulated. Davis resigned as chairman of the firm and in early 1981 agreed to pay a $20,000 civil penalty. Summit was forced to pay a $3 million fine as well as $17 million in refunds, plus interest, to certain customers.

The other big event in the winter of 1980–81 was a decision by Davis to cash in some of his accumulated profits. He sold about 850 producing wells to Hiram Walker Resources, the Canadian distilling and energy company, for $630 million.

This left Davis flush with cash, disillusioned with having all of his eggs in the single oil basket, and more ready than ever for *fun*.

As long as it was profitable.

2

FOX CHASES ITS TAIL

IN 1969, AT the urging of its investment bankers, the board of directors of Twentieth Century–Fox decided that Richard Zanuck, who had been brought in as president by his father, Fox chairman Darryl F. Zanuck, needed an experienced manager to handle financial and administrative duties. Dennis C. Stanfill was recruited from his position as vice president of finance at Times-Mirror, operator of the *Los Angeles Times* and many other media properties, to back up the Zanucks.

Two years later Darryl F. Zanuck was forced out, only months after firing his own son Richard. Stanfill was elected chairman.

In late 1978, again at the urging of its bankers, the board of directors of Twentieth Century–Fox decided that Stanfill needed at least two additional executives to assist him. One would be experienced in theatrical motion-picture production, while the other would administer the nontheatrical side of the company, including a growing list of outside businesses acquired with the profits from the biggest hit movie of all time, the hugely successful *Star Wars* (1977).

The pressure on Stanfill had begun after he forced out Alan Ladd, Jr., the popular head of production who had fought to get *Star Wars* made and properly distributed. Stanfill was constantly pressuring Ladd to be more conservative financially. Ladd felt that Stanfill's restrictions were just the kind of nickel-and-dime pettiness that interfered with his relationships with Hollywood's top creators, who were the key to making millions. The studio finally became too small to hold both of them, and Ladd moved on to independent production in association with Warner Bros. Almost immediately, most of the production staff that Ladd had brought with him to Fox also left.

Almost simultaneously in 1979, to satisfy his board of directors, Stanfill, the CEO, hired Alan J. Hirschfield as chief operating officer to handle the movie business and C. Joseph La Bonte as president to take charge of nontheatrical business. Little did Stanfill know that history would soon repeat itself. The backup would once again push aside the boss.

In 1979, however, flush with cash, Stanfill and his new executive team saw few dark clouds on the horizon. There was concern over the failure of the studio to produce hit movies since *Star Wars,* but its sequel, *The Empire Strikes Back,* was one of the biggest successes of the year and created another bounty of cash. Hirschfield was expected to step up production. The real concern was about the future ownership of the studio. There were a number of outsiders who had indicated an interest in buying Fox, including Chris-Craft Industries chairman Herbert J. Siegel, who owned about 10 percent of Fox's stock. Stanfill remained confident that he could fend off such advances as long as the company was doing well. La Bonte later recalled his first impression of the company as rich in assets and potential.

How rich? A year later, in 1980, as part of the annual budgeting process, Stanfill and his managers decided to find out. They determined to do a thorough examination of the entire company and then use the information to create a five-year strategy. They mobilized department heads at every level of the organization and had each come up with a report and plan for presentation, all in one day, to the studio's board of directors. Most of the executives involved in creative areas complained, but Stanfill insisted on a complete inventory of the growing empire he ruled.

While he wasn't always comfortable with the colorful characters in the movie industry, Stanfill was right at home when it came to running a tight, efficient organization. Born and raised near Nashville, Tennessee, Stanfill graduated from the U.S. Naval Academy at Annapolis, Maryland, with a strong background in economics. In

1959, after a stint in the navy, he moved to Wall Street as a corporate finance specialist, joining Lehman Brothers, one of the best-connected firms in the investment world. It was also Twentieth Century–Fox's investment banker.

In 1965 Stanfill moved to Los Angeles as vice president of finance at Times-Mirror, which was in the midst of a program of rapid expansion and upgrading of its media properties. Stanfill's job was to restructure the company's finances as it evolved into a much larger corporation.

Four years after arriving on the West Coast, Stanfill was contacted by some of his former associates at Lehman Brothers, who were working on behalf of Twentieth Century–Fox. That led to his 1969 appointment as executive vice president (under the Zanucks) as well as to membership on the executive committee of the board of directors.

Stanfill didn't know much about making movies or TV shows, but he cut a dashing figure as an executive. He was a tall, elegant man with patrician stature. From his earliest days, his operating style was to be reserved and low-key but firm. He had an intellectual air but could be extremely charming. He was invariably polite but tended to keep associates at arm's length. He was willing to listen to all opinions but in the end liked to keep all key decision-making power to himself.

Stanfill, who owned (or held options to buy) less than 1 percent of Fox's stock, was always aware, however, that his position was dependent on the goodwill of his board. He usually spoke with board members at least once a week, sometimes as often as once a day. After all, the threat of an outside takeover was growing. Siegel's Chris-Craft, by the time of the board meeting in autumn 1980, owned about 20 percent of Fox. Herb Siegel had long wanted to own a movie studio, and he was particularly interested in Fox because it owned three lucrative television stations and had an option to buy a fourth, which Siegel hoped to merge with two TV stations Chris-Craft already owned.

Another 5 percent of Fox was held by Tandem Productions, a highly successful, privately held production company owned by A. Jerrold Perrenchio and producers Norman Lear and Bud Yorkin ("All in the Family," "Maude," and others). Discussions about merging Fox with Tandem had produced nothing but rumors, and Stanfill had been unsuccessful in his attempts to buy out Siegel. Fox had then sued Chris-Craft to block an attempted takeover (leading to a countersuit by Chris-Craft).

Even worse, earnings for 1980 were off sharply from the previous year, when the smash hit *The Empire Strikes Back* had been released. Despite his promises to Stanfill, Hirschfield had not been able to boost movie production to at least a dozen films a year.

Earlier in the year, Hirschfield had brought Sherry Lansing to Fox from Columbia Pictures as head of production. And he had hired Norman Levy, also from Columbia, to head distribution and marketing. However, there had not been enough time yet for them to pump up production and distribution. Hirschfield also had hired Harris Katleman, a producer based at Columbia, who previously had headed TV operations at MGM, to run the TV division of Fox.

So there was a range of pressures on Fox as its board assembled in the fall of 1980 to hear twenty- to forty-minute presentations from the head of each division. Among the directors were Donald N. Frey, chairman of Bell and Howell; Princess Grace of Monaco, once a famous Hollywood actress; F. Warren Hellman, a San Francisco–based partner with Lehman Bros.; John H. Johnson, a hugely successful black publishing executive from Chicago; Paul H. Nitze, a high-level Defense Department consultant who had also served in the State Department; William P. Rogers, former secretary of state in the Nixon administration; Gerald H. Trautman, chairman of Greyhound; and John L. Vogelstein, a director of E. M. Warburg, Pincus and Company, a high-powered Wall Street investment firm.

There was no question that Fox had become an impressive mountain of assets. Aside from its basic movie and TV businesses and the sixty-three-acre studio lot in west Los Angeles, Fox included a film-processing lab; a record- and music-publishing division; sizable soft-drink-bottling operations; movie theaters in Australia and New Zealand; the Aspen Ski Corporation; a luxury resort and other real estate in Pebble Beach, California; and a fledgling home-video company based in Farmington, Michigan.

The division heads' presentations took the entire day, and everyone on the board seemed surprised by the size and scope of what now constituted Twentieth Century–Fox. To help put it in perspective near the conclusion of the long meeting, La Bonte scrawled out a set of figures and put it on the overhead projector so that everyone could read it together. It compared the value of the assets with Fox's current stock market value, then about $35 a share. It was immediately obvious that the company's stock was probably worth at least three or four times what it was selling for.

There was a moment of dead silence as they all studied the slide in the dark. Then, from the back, one board member gasped, "Holy shit!" That brought a round of embarrassed laughter. As the meeting broke up, there was a sense that something had happened. A seed had been planted.

After the full board meeting, Stanfill met with Hirschfield, La Bonte, Hellman, and Vogelstein. It was obvious to each of them that Fox had become hugely undervalued by the market. This financially wise group realized that conditions were ripe for a leveraged buyout, where insiders buy out the public shareholders with borrowed money, which is then repaid over a period of years out of company profits. While the leveraged buyout (LBO) would become quite common a few years later, in 1980 it was a bold and unusual step.

It didn't take long for their plan to evolve. Financing for an LBO would be provided by a number of sources, most prominently E. M. Warburg, Pincus and Company, through Vogelstein, and the First National Bank of Boston, represented by William Thompson. The principals would be Stanfill, Hirschfield, La Bonte, Vogelstein, and Hellman, but small pieces of ownership would also be offered to about fifteen of Fox's top executives. The public was told that the purpose of making Fox private was to insulate it from outside raiders whose presence was interfering with the studio's ability to attract top film and TV talent.

A month after it was first announced, Stanfill made a few more details public. The new entity would take over the film- and TV-production divisions, all land holdings, the soft-drink-bottling operations, the international theaters, and the resort and recreation assets in return for an unspecified amount of cash. Separately, Fox would spin off to existing shareholders ownership of the TV stations, the film library, and an interest in certain future movie productions. It was a deal later estimated to be worth about $45 for each of the 10.5 million Fox shares outstanding.

It would make Stanfill, Hirschfield, and La Bonte very, very rich. As they celebrated the new year of 1981, the deal looked very possible. The management was in control, the financing was in place, and it seemed unlikely that anyone else was going to rush in and offer so much more money that the deal could be spoiled.

As the bankers studied the plan, however, they became concerned about how the new company would be managed. There were signals from Hirschfield that he might not stay if he was not assured control over day-to-day affairs. Hellman, Vogelstein, and Thompson decided they wanted Stanfill to retain his position as chairman and to take an overview role but pass his title and power as CEO to Hirschfield, thus assuring that he would continue.

Stanfill, however, wouldn't hear of it. He and Hirschfield already were beginning to crowd each other in the executive suite, and he was determined to remain firmly in control. Stanfill complained bitterly that Hirschfield had reneged on a promise to move his primary residence from New York to Los Angeles and that he was away from the studio too often.

During the third week of January, the deal came unraveled. Stanfill, in a terse announcement, said that the plan to go private had been ended. He declined to give any reasons, leaving the press to speculate that the executives involved in the attempted buyout lacked financing.

Inside Fox, the truth was obvious. Executives were being forced to choose between Stanfill and Hirschfield, who now barely spoke to each other. There was constant gossip and backbiting. There was also considerable paranoia, fed in part by an efficiency expert hired by Stanfill who was asking various executives personal questions. There were also rumors that Stanfill had hired private detectives to check on the private lives of some executives, including Hirschfield. Stanfill angrily denied it, but two sources close to Marvin Davis insist that they saw the records and bills from the detective agency after Stanfill left the studio.

Outside Fox, the investment community also was buzzing. The failure of the leveraged buyout and internal turmoil made the studio appear vulnerable. Wall Street believed that Fox had been put "in play," which meant that whatever Stanfill might say, Fox was for sale to the highest bidder. It was no longer a question of whether it would be sold, but of when and for how much.

Almost immediately, Stanfill began looking for new financing for another attempt to take Fox private, this time without Hirschfield. His plan was to make Herb Siegel, who still held a large block of Fox stock, his partner in the deal, with the new board to be divided between his team and Siegel's representatives.

Hirschfield, meanwhile, according to two sources, was so angry at Stanfill that he, too, decided to find an outside buyer for the company who would favor his position. Among those he approached were Sir James Goldsmith, a British corporate raider. And with rumors already in the air that Saul P. Steinberg, the unpredictable, multimillionaire chairman and president of Reliance Group, a large insurance and management services group, was interested in Fox, Hirschfield flew to New York to meet with him.

Hirschfield laid out for Steinberg the same information that had been presented to the board a few months before. He showed him the huge hidden asset value of Fox and suggested ways they would share in the bounty.

Steinberg didn't say much, but he did promise to let Hirschfield know if he was interested. In reality, he was very interested, but he didn't think that buying Fox was necessarily the way to get his share of the deal. Instead, within a day after the Hirschfield meeting, Steinberg began buying thousands of shares of Chris-Craft Industries stock. When he had nearly 5 percent, Steinberg called Siegel and broke the news to him. "You and I," said Steinberg, "are going to buy Twentieth Century–Fox together." The implication was that Steinberg would be the partner in control and Siegel the junior partner.

That didn't sit well with Siegel, who now felt that his control of Chris-Craft also might be threatened. He began to think that the situation was getting out of hand. He either wanted to buy Fox or get out of it, but he no longer was willing to wait around for new developments.

One who was more than willing to buy Siegel's interest in Fox was Kirk Kerkorian, the millionaire owner of 49 percent of the once-proud Metro-Goldwyn-Mayer, a film and TV studio that competed with Fox. Kerkorian, raised in California by Armenian immigrants, had first become wealthy by buying up surplus airplanes after World War II. He bought and sold used airplanes, and also used some as the foundation of a charter airline, which he ran. He built and sold the International Hotel in Las Vegas, and then in 1968 purchased MGM when this legendary studio that had produced *Gone with the Wind* was down on its luck. He later built the MGM Grand Hotel in Las Vegas, nearly shuttering the movie studio while he concentrated on his new hotel. Then, in the late 1970s, Kerkorian decided that the movie business made sense again. He split MGM in two—one company just for movie holdings and the other, MGM Grand, for operating hotels.

When Kerkorian revived his interest in movies, he realized that he needed to rebuild the studio's distribution system. He had shut it down, and MGM was releasing whatever movies it made through another studio, United Artists.

To get back into distribution, Kerkorian started looking for a second movie studio to buy. He felt, according to his advisors, that tremendous efficiency in the operations of movie studios could be attained by combining several production units into a single administrative and distribution system. He already was actively involved in trying to acquire Columbia Pictures when he approached Herb Siegel about buying his stake in Fox. Siegel stalled him. He didn't really take Kerkorian very seriously because he knew that Kerkorian had most of his money tied up in Columbia. Siegel didn't know that Kerkorian was in the process of making a secret deal to sell his Columbia stock to the company's management at a sizable premium, providing him with millions of dollars for acquisitions.

As Dennis Stanfill considered his options in late January 1981, he had no way of knowing that powerful forces had been put in motion that would quickly swirl beyond his control.

3

MARVIN BAGS A FOX

J. IRA HARRIS had earned a reputation as the top corporate deal maker in Chicago by carefully collecting information from a wide variety of sources and then following his instinct as to when it was time to act. By the middle of February 1981, Harris was convinced the time to act on Twentieth Century–Fox was at hand, and he was determined to play a role.

Harris already was consulting with Chris-Craft chairman Herb Siegel on what to do with his interest in Fox, but it had become clear to him that Siegel was more likely to play a supporting role than a leading role in whatever deal came along.

Harris also was acquainted with Marvin Davis, through several deals they had both been involved in over the years. He had read about Davis's recent sale of a large portion of his oil wells and knew that the Denver millionaire would be looking for somewhere to invest his cash.

Davis was in the downtown Denver offices of the Davis Company when the call came in. He exchanged friendly greetings with Harris, whom he had always liked. After all, they had a lot in common. Both still spoke with the strong Bronx accent acquired in their youth, although by now they lived elsewhere, and both had made

14

their fortunes while operating slightly outside the mainstream of American capitalism.

Harris, forty-three, had attended the University of Michigan and then returned to New York to sell mutual funds door-to-door. That led to a job in institutional sales of stocks and bonds with a company that in 1964 dispatched Harris to its Chicago office. In 1969 he joined the Windy City office of the investment banking firm of Salomon Brothers, quickly becoming its leading corporate marriage broker.

A tall, dark-haired, stocky man with an impressive presence, Harris could be a teddy bear one minute and gruff and demanding the next. Whatever his mood, Harris churned out deals at a rate far exceeding most of his peers. Whether on the golf course, at home, or at the office, he was usually in the middle of a number of complicated transactions. He developed a wide circle of influential friends nationwide, creating a network of information and contacts that paid off again and again.

Harris began his phone conversation with Davis that February by congratulating him on the sale of his oil wells to Hiram Walker. "You made a great sale," boomed Harris. "Now I've got a great buy for you."

"What?" asked Davis.

"Twentieth Century–Fox," said Harris.

Davis chuckled. "I love it," he shouted back. "I love it."

Over the next few days, both Davis and Harris worked actively to put together a deal. Davis studied the financial documents and put his staff to work analyzing every aspect of the company. Harris kept talking about the value of the film library, while Davis increasingly became excited about the value of the studio's Los Angeles real estate.

Not all of Davis's advisors thought that buying Fox was a good idea. In particular, Gerald Gray, chief financial officer of the Davis Company, had questions. He wasn't sure the studio was worth as much as others claimed, and he doubted it would be easy to sell and exploit all of the assets. He cautioned Davis to reconsider, or to at least reduce some of the risk by bringing in partners.

As he always had done in the oil business, Davis's instinct was to find a way to use OPM—other people's money—in the Fox deal. He made a few calls and quickly found a silent partner. For some years, Davis had been doing business with a New York–based commodities trader named Marc Rich. They had remained friends even after some bad advice from Rich had led to the government's action against Davis and the Summit Transportation Company the year before. Davis knew Rich had made a fortune trading in oil and natural gas, just as Davis had, and was looking for ways to diversify his investment portfolio. Rich indicated that he was interested in taking half of the investment in Fox and would be willing to let Davis keep all of the voting control. Davis promised to keep Rich informed. They both agreed that it would be best to keep their plans confidential.

Next stop for Davis was the Continental Illinois Bank in Chicago, where he had been doing business for years. He explained what he needed and how he wanted to go about acquiring Fox. No problem, Davis was assured. The bank then issued him a letter promising unlimited credit.

Davis now had the financial muscle he felt would be needed to impress Siegel.

On a Wednesday in early March 1981, Ira Harris set up a meeting with Siegel at the Chris-Craft offices in New York. Harris was already there waiting when Davis arrived with his attorney, Edward Bennett Williams. It quickly became clear that Siegel was willing to sell, but only if the price and terms were right. One thing Siegel insisted on was finding a way for him to gain control of the Fox television stations. Davis didn't mind the condition; he was eyeing the other lucrative Fox assets.

By the end of that week, the terms were agreed on. Williams drew up a letter, which Siegel signed. Chris-Craft would sell its Fox stock to Davis; and in return, Davis would do his best to work out a spin-off (a separate sale to current Fox stockholders) of the Fox television properties. Chris-Craft agreed not to be part of any other offer for Fox that might be made by others, and Davis promised to raise his offer to match any other bidders. Siegel also released Harris from his legal and ethical responsibility as an advisor to Chris-Craft, so that he could work solely for Davis.

For Siegel it was another frustrating but lucrative experience. A former talent agent whose client list once included Jackie Gleason and Perry Como, Siegel had long dreamed of running a major movie studio. He had tried to acquire Paramount Pictures in the 1960s but lost out to a higher bid by Charles Bludhorn's Gulf + Western Industries, which left Siegel to walk away with a sizable profit. He had been in another long struggle to acquire Piper Aircraft, which he eventually lost but made millions of dollars as the value of his stock increased. And he had acquired Chris-Craft, diversifying it out of its original business of making boats and turning it into a media company.

Davis next met with MGM's Kirk Kerkorian to make sure there would be no last-minute bidding war for Fox by his most likely competitor. He told Kerkorian that his main interest was to take over Fox and then sell off its many lucrative assets. He was only mildly interested in running its movie studio, which he felt could operate without the valuable Century City studio real estate.

Kerkorian said he, too, wanted Fox, but not for its assets. He wanted it for its movie and TV production and its worldwide film-distribution network.

The men made a verbal agreement that after Davis acquired the studio, he would sell Kerkorian the movie- and TV-production divisions. They also agreed that it would be best to keep the deal a secret until the appropriate time, so no papers were drawn up. However, they did shake hands. They had a deal.

Davis was now ready to move in on his prey.

On Friday morning, February 20, 1981, Dennis Stanfill was at home in San Marino, a ritzy suburb east of downtown Los Angeles, with a bad case of the flu. He had instructed his secretaries not to bother him unless it was very important, so he was surprised when a call came from his office. His secretary was apologetic, but the caller, attorney Edward Bennett Williams, insisted that it was absolutely urgent.

Williams told Stanfill that he was representing Marvin Davis of Denver and that they were in Los Angeles to see him. He said it was imperative that they see him as quickly as possible. Stanfill agreed to meet at his office that afternoon. As soon as he hung up, Stanfill ordered a limosine to pick him up. He then called La Bonte and asked him if he had ever heard of Marvin Davis. Stanfill had only a vague notion of who he was. Stanfill asked La Bonte to quickly see what he could learn about Davis.

Hirschfield, in the meantime, was away on vacation and couldn't be reached.

By the time Stanfill got to the studio, Williams and Davis were already there. On Stanfill's desk was a magazine article, the only information about Davis that could be found quickly.

Williams presented Stanfill with a one-and-a-half-page letter offering to buy the studio for $60 a share in cash plus one share of a new company, which would own the TV stations, that would be spun off to existing shareholders. As the largest single shareholder,

Davis knew that Herb Siegel would end up with most of the new TV-company stock. In all, the offer by Davis for Fox was worth about $70 a share, or a total of about $703 million. Williams also presented Stanfill with a copy of the letter signed by Siegel and a copy of the commitment letter from Continental Illinois Bank. La Bonte was stunned, he later recalled. He had never seen a bank document that basically promised cash in any amount to back up whatever Davis promised.

Stanfill remained cool and noncommital. He understood that this was a serious offer and promised to give it all possible consideration.

When Davis and Williams left, Stanfill discussed the offer with La Bonte. They both knew that the offer Davis presented was far higher than the $45 a share they contemplated paying to make Fox private. They had considered that amount a stretch in terms of the financing that was available to them, despite the studio's rich hidden assets.

The next day Stanfill conducted a board meeting by telephone from his home. Among those on the line were Princess Grace in Monaco; William P. Rogers in Bethesda, Maryland; Gerald Trautman in Phoenix; and Warren Hellman, just off the ski slopes in Vermont. Attempts to reach Hirschfield remained unsuccessful.

The board agreed to meet and discuss the offer at a previously scheduled meeting on February 27 in Los Angeles, a meeting that had been called to consider the Stanfill bid to go private. That idea was now put on the back burner.

By Monday, February 23, the offer had leaked to the newspapers, causing a wave of publicity. Stanfill already was having mixed feelings. On the one hand, he feared losing control of the company to anyone. On the other hand, he thought Davis might be the white knight he had been seeking to buy out the public shareholders while remaining an absentee landlord who would leave Stanfill alone to run the show. Stanfill also realized that this deal would make him very rich. Between the stock he owned and the stock options he held, he would be entitled to a little over $7 million when the deal closed.

To check out Davis, Stanfill hired the Washington, D.C., law firm of Troy, Malin and Pottinger, the same firm he had used a year earlier to check out Siegel when filing a lawsuit against Chris-Craft.

On February 27, with all of the directors present, Stanfill laid out Davis's offer but made no recommendation. Davis, accompanied by Williams, was then ushered in before the board. Davis was aggressive and enthusiastic in his comments. He called Fox a well-run company and said it was his intention to make few changes. One board member later recalled Davis saying, "I am not a looter."

The board agreed to further consider the bid and to allow Davis's people to inspect the studio's books. Over the next month, each side studied the other. A team of about a dozen lawyers and auditors, under Williams's guidance, scoured the Fox books, while two New York–based investment banking firms, Kidder, Peabody and Company, and Dillon, Reed and Company, evaluated the Davis offer.

Everything seemed to be falling into place. The board was to meet next on March 27, with the expectation that it quickly would agree to accept the Davis bid. Instead, on the day before the meeting, the entire deal collapsed.

There was a lot of confusion at the time about what was really happening. The rumor in Hollywood was that Herb Siegel had changed his mind about selling his stock and was now demanding that Davis pay a higher price. In retrospect that seems unlikely, because the Chris-Craft agreement to sell the Fox stock to Davis had already been signed. A more likely scenario, put forth by several sources but denied by Stanfill, is that Stanfill, feeling ambivalent about the deal and cocky knowing that Davis badly wanted the studio, tried to force Davis to increase the amount he would pay for the Fox shares. Davis then became angry and decided to show Stanfill that he could just as well walk away from the deal.

Stanfill was left with shareholders who had counted on getting the Davis money and were now upset, and a resumption of the internal warfare at the studio. Also, it was obvious that no one was going to rush forward with as good an offer, let alone a better one.

Meanwhile, Davis cooled off and met with Ira Harris for breakfast a few days later in Palm Beach, Florida. Harris soothed Davis and got him to agree to renew his bid on the same terms. Davis then returned to Los Angeles and attended the Academy Awards ceremony, which had been delayed for a day because of an assassination attempt on President Ronald Reagan. Davis sat in seats issued to Dennis Stanfill, who was in London for the premiere of the Fox movie *9 to 5*.

On April 1 Stanfill flew home to meet with Davis again. The next day they announced that the deal for Fox was back on. The board met on April 6 and gave final approval. The definitive merger agreement was signed on April 7, and a stockholders' meeting was called to give its final approval on June 8, 1981.

This time it was Davis who had some surprises to deliver, however. In early May he notified Stanfill that some changes would have to be made in the proxy statement before it was sent to the Securities and Exchange Commission. Stanfill called another board meeting by telephone and put lawyer Williams on the line to explain what Davis was doing.

Davis, said Williams, would not be buying the studio alone. He had two partners. One was the Aetna Life and Casualty Company, which would invest almost $200 million in return for half of the Fox real estate and half of its nontheatrical holdings, including Pebble Beach and Aspen.

Williams also told them that Davis had a silent partner, Richco of the Netherland Antilles, a secretive commodities brokerage firm that traded oil and gas around the globe. It was headed by Marc Rich, Pincus Green, and Alex Hackel. It would end up with fifty percent of the Fox stock, while Davis would maintain 100 percent of the voting control.

Williams then revealed that to finance the purchase Davis would be borrowing up to $550 million from a syndicate of banks headed by Continental Illinois. In the end, Davis would put up only about $50 million of his own money to pull off a $724,681,000 purchase (plus the spin-off of the TV stations and assumption of Fox's long-term debt of $426 million). In addition, his family put up loans of $61 million and Rich provided loans for another $61 million.

The board was shocked by the last-minute changes, but there seemed little choice except to go forward. They sang "Auld Lang Syne" at the last public stockholders' meeting. And at midnight on June 12, 1981, Twentieth Century–Fox, which had been public since William Fox first sold stock in 1925, became a privately owned company. And Marvin Davis became the first individual to control a major movie studio since Howard Hughes sold RKO in 1953.

At a party in New York, at exactly midnight on the twelfth, Dennis Stanfill was toasted by his thin, pretty wife Terry and a group of their friends. He had gained $7,541,102 and a new boss.

Marvin Davis had bagged his Fox.

FOX FIRES

MARVIN DAVIS WAS an unlikely movie mogul. Yet, as he began a ritual of flying in his private plane from Denver to Los Angeles every Thursday afternoon for the weekend, he relished the excitement and energy of the studio. In his heart, those first weeks, he knew it probably wasn't going to last long. Still, he enjoyed the constant whirl of deal-making, the show-biz talk, the way everybody seemed to know his name when he walked through the lobby of the Beverly Hills Hotel, and his newfound status, which guaranteed him the best seating in the most chic restaurants as well as invitations to parties with Hollywood's movers and shakers.

He was even amused by the stacks of scripts that arrived unsolicited at his Denver office, only to be returned unopened. And the calls from friends who wanted to know if he could help them out with reservations at Pebble Beach or the Aspen Ski Resort.

"I loved the action," Davis recalled later.

It was heady stuff for an upper-middle-class kid from the streets of New York City, even one who had become a multimillionaire.

Marvin Harold Davis was born in Newark, New Jersey, on August 28, 1925. His father, Jack Davis, had come to the United States from England a little more than a decade before, at the age

of fifteen. A promising student who had been offered a scholarship
to a prestigious London school, Jack Davis had run away from home
at age fifteen because his strong-willed mother was pressuring him
to become a rabbi. Instead he became an amateur boxer and, by
lying about his age, enlisted in the British navy.

By the time he was nineteen, Jack Davis had arrived in New
York City with less than a dollar in his pocket. He cleaned toilets
and took other menial jobs until finding his way into the garment
industry. He soon started his own enterprise. Working long hours,
he built the J. Davis Dress Company (later called Jay-Day Dresses)
into a thriving manufacturer of inexpensive women's dresses.

Jack Davis, who died in 1979, became a millionaire, although he
never achieved the kind of affluence his son would enjoy. It did
allow him to buy a comfortable home on the Upper West Side of
Manhattan, take cruises to Europe, winter in Florida, and lunch at
the 21 Club. A natural salesman, he had a knack for remembering
names and faces, and he was very bright. He loved to talk politics,
which led him to become active in the Democratic party. He contributed to state and national candidates. He met presidents Frank-
lin D. Roosevelt and Harry Truman and was invited to the White
House by John F. Kennedy, whom he vigorously supported. He
listed among his close friends the late Senator Jacob Javits of New
York. During World War II he served on the War Resources
Board, which gave him a lifelong appreciation of the value of
having access to a steady supply of natural resources.

That was one reason why Jack Davis was receptive when he
became friendly with an oilman from Evansville, Indiana, named
Ray Ryan during one of the family's annual winter visits to Florida.
Ryan soon convinced Jack Davis to invest in his oil exploration
activities in the Illinois Basin, which covered parts of Illinois, Ken-
tucky, and Indiana. Eventually Davis also became active in recruit-
ing his friends as investors as well. By the mid-1950s Davis and
Ryan were no longer in business together, but by then a seed had
been planted in Jack's son Marvin, who was drawn to the life of the
oil wildcatter like iron filings to a magnet. (Ryan was killed in 1977
when a bomb blew up his car in Indiana. The murderer was never
found, but police suspected that the underworld had paid Ryan
back for testifying against two men who had attempted to extort
money from him in 1964.)

Marvin Davis enjoyed the fruits of his father's success. He attended high school at the upscale Horace Mann School for Boys in
Riverside, New York. Even then he was known for being aggres-

sive and street smart—and having a huge appetite. He was over-weight as a child; he did slim down when he attended college, only to fill out again later.

Davis first attended Syracuse University, but after six months he transferred to New York University. During the summers, he worked for Ryan in the oil fields of Indiana. In 1947 he graduated with a business degree. After college Marvin Davis felt he still had a lot to learn, so he went off to Texas to work in the oil business with H. L. Hunt. He moved to Denver in 1952 to set up Davis Oil and ended up making the Mile-High City his home. He did return to New York long enough to marry at age twenty-eight, bringing his wife Barbara back to Denver, where she gracefully fell into a background role as wife and mother.

After the Arab oil crisis made him rich, in the 1970s Davis became quite charitable, although always on his own terms. He didn't really join the mainstream of polite Denver society; rather, he created his own alternatives. He gave generously to certain Jewish charities and other causes he supported, such as diabetes research, but donated almost nothing to most other local charities.

One grand Davis plan went sour rather fast. After a doctor saved his father's life, he donated $5 million to create an institute for geriatric patients. Plagued by administrative problems and financial squabbles, the institute closed its doors permanently within five years.

Marvin Davis arrived at Fox looking at the company as a rich trove of assets waiting to be unbundled, but he also found that he loved the glitz and warmth of show business. It fit right in with his personal style. He would greet visitors to his big office on the ground floor of the executive office building at Twentieth Century–Fox with a big bear hug, often accompanied by a gift, such as a pen with the Fox logo, or even a wristwatch if he wanted to say thank you for some worthy deed. Davis also brought along his strong sense of family values and a demand for a businesslike atmosphere. That occasionally clashed with the free-wheeling style of Holly-wood, but it was the studio that changed, not Davis. And although he never instituted a dress code, it was obvious that after his arrival, most Fox executives suddenly took to wearing a jacket and tie to the office.

Davis was also unaccustomed to working closely with women who weren't either his wife, his daughter, or his secretary. He told a story at a charity dinner one night about his first meeting with Sherry Lansing, then head of production at Fox. When he first came to the studio, Davis said he asked who actually made the movies. He was told by a group of his executives—that is, he *thought* he heard—"Jerry Lansing." So he said, "I want to meet him." A few minutes later a very pretty, lithe brunette strolled into his office and smiled at him. "No, no honey," he said. "I don't want any coffee right now."

The brunette answered, "I'm Sherry Lansing."

"No," insisted Davis, "I want *Jerry* Lansing, the guy who runs the studio."

"No, it's *Sherry* Lansing," she said, "and I run the studio."

His aides gasped, waiting for a reaction. Marvin seemed confused. "In the oil business we only work with guys." Davis recalled at the dinner when he spoke about the incident that he felt confused. "I never worked with a broad. So I thought she was supposed to get the coffee."

Lansing would lament later that getting coffee was one of the few things she would be allowed to do without the approval of several other executives during her frustrating three years at Fox. But at least for a while, she was able to get along with Davis.

The person who most quickly bumped heads with Davis was Dennis Stanfill. In retrospect, it seemed inevitable. Davis was a down-to-earth, meat-and-potatoes, slap-on-the-back kind of guy. Stanfill was reserved, formal, and more likely to select gourmet French cuisine than a corned beef sandwich. Together they were like oil and water.

Stanfill had insisted that Davis make it clear in the purchase proxy that he contemplated no change in management. Davis had stated in a letter inserted into the proxy that he wasn't buying Fox to break it up, even though he actually had an unwritten deal with Kerkorian at the time to do exactly that, by selling off the movie and TV operations.

Stanfill chose to listen to those outside the studio who assumed that Davis, busy with his oil business, would need Stanfill to run Fox. To secure his position after the sale, in light of all of the power struggles he had been facing with Alan Hirschfield, Stanfill began lobbying Davis to give him total authority to run things. Instead Davis began attending meetings and frequently would interrupt Stanfill. Davis also would meet with lower-level executives to find out what was going on instead of going through channels—meaning Stanfill.

In any case, Davis didn't really see any great need for Stanfill.

Davis was his own financial wizard and had a team of Davis Company advisors who kept him wired into the financial markets. That made Stanfill, who had no line function at the studio, somewhat redundant. It was Hirschfield, Levy, Lansing, La Bonte, and Katleman who appeared to be doing all of the work. Even so, Stanfill might have lived out the nearly three years left on his lucrative contract if he hadn't challenged Davis to fire Harris Katleman over some relatively minor expense-account abuses.

It came less than three weeks after Davis officially took ownership of Fox, but it was a situation that had been brewing for more than a year.

Harris Katleman had been brought to Fox by Alan Hirschfield in March 1980 to rejuvenate the sleepy television division. A native of Omaha, Nebraska, who had grown up in Los Angeles and attended UCLA, Katleman began his entertainment-industry career as an office boy and then an agent at MCA under the direction of Lew Wasserman. He moved in the late 1950s to New York to work for Goodson-Todman, the producer of such popular game shows as "What's My Line?" Katleman became very rich working for Goodson-Todman, which gave him a percentage of each show he produced. Still, he yearned to get back to the action in Hollywood. So in 1970 Katleman returned to Los Angeles to run the TV division of MGM, which recently had been taken over by Kirk Kerkorian. After five highly successful years, he moved to Columbia Pictures Television as an independent producer. That's where he met Hirschfield, then Columbia's chairman.

Hirschfield was forced out of Columbia Pictures in the wake of a scandal over check forgery by David Begelman, who had been head of movie production. Hirschfield had hired, fired, rehired, and once again fired Begelman before being ousted by the Columbia board, which sided with Begelman. Hirschfield then took a make-work job at Warner Brothers for a year before joining Fox in 1979.

Now Stanfill had taken the position that Katleman's expense-account abuse was a moral issue on which he could not yield. Inside the studio, it was widely assumed that Stanfill actually was using the expense-account–abuse issue to try to cast a shadow on Hirschfield. This was especially damaging at the time, because galley proofs of a book detailing what had happened at Columbia, *Indecent Exposure: A True Story of Hollywood and Wall Street,* by David McClintick, a former *Wall Street Journal* reporter, were feverishly making the rounds in Hollywood. The book made the Columbia executives who had moved to Fox extremely sensitive about any hint of scandal.

When Katleman first arrived at Fox, he found a demoralized TV operation with little on the air except for the long-running hit comedy series "M*A*S*H." And he quickly discovered that "M*A*S*H" was being sold into the TV syndication rerun market for a smaller price than it should have commanded.

Katleman was a thin, silver-haired executive with the easy charm of a top salesman. He prided himself on his outstanding relationships with the top talent in Hollywood, which he fostered with generous contracts and a management style that was part hype but mostly gentle persuasion.

From June 18 to June 28, 1980, Katleman had gone on a trip to Europe to attend the International Television Festival in Monte Carlo, and he had stopped over in Paris. On his return, he dumped his expense slips onto his secretary's desk and told her to make out his expense-account voucher, which he quickly signed and submitted.

It turned out that there were at least $2,500 worth of questionable charges among those expenses. In one case there appeared to be two meal charges made at different places at the same time. In another case, the bill from a women's clothing store had been charged as a restaurant tab. When challenged, Katleman offered to write a check for any discrepancies, but that didn't satisfy Stanfill.

Stanfill took the matter to the board, but he was brushed aside. They said it was too small to bother with and told him to handle it himself. If Stanfill had fired Katleman immediately, it would have ended there. But instead, he demanded—and received—a letter of resignation from Katleman dated January 16, 1981, which Stanfill then put into his desk drawer. That led to cynical speculation that Stanfill was waiting to see how Katleman did in the spring, when TV shows are sold to the networks for inclusion in the fall schedule. If Katleman failed, Stanfill already had his letter of resignation. Stanfill later said he held off dismissing Katleman on the strong recommendation of Hirschfield. As it turned out, Katleman had a spectacular selling season, getting five shows on the air.

From the moment Davis arrived at the studio, it was obvious that he felt most at home with Hirschfield and Levy, both fellow ex–New Yorkers. It was equally obvious that he was least at ease around Stanfill, the cool, formal, analytical midwesterner. Stanfill, who really hadn't trusted Hirschfield since the leveraged buyout fell apart, appeared to feel the need to put Hirschfield in his place in order to define his own position. The most public way to accomplish this was to finally use Katleman's letter of resignation, which Stanfill suddenly took out of his drawer shortly after Davis's purchase of Fox was official. Stanfill announced that he was accepting Katleman's resignation as of June 29, 1981.

However, when June 29 passed, Stanfill learned that Katleman was still on the job. His orders had been countermanded by an aide to Marvin Davis who was acting for the new owner. Stanfill called Davis for confirmation and then flew to Denver for a face-to-face meeting to demand that Katleman be fired immediately.

Stanfill must have had a premonition about what might happen. He removed most of his personal effects from his office before he left and typed out the letter of resignation he was prepared to present if Davis balked. As it turned out, Stanfill never did return to his office.

In Denver Stanfill went directly to the Davis Company offices. He later recalled having been cool and calm and not at all emotional. Stanfill said he told Davis that by intervening in his decision, Davis had totally undercut his authority as CEO. Stanfill suggested that this was not a good precedent if Davis wished him to manage the studio on his behalf.

Davis seemed unmoved. Stanfill added that it was his duty to uphold the standards of the company, and that by reversing his decision, Davis had, in effect, breached his employment contract as chairman.

Stanfill didn't realize that Davis had done his homework. The oil man had phoned the presidents of all three major TV networks and learned that Katleman was one of the few Fox executives doing a good job. He knew it would be foolish to lose such an employee just as he was trying to get the studio into high gear. Also, Davis liked what he had learned about the television business, which offered more predictable returns than the volatile movie division, and he realized that if Katleman left, it would take months for someone new to get up to speed.

To Davis, TV was very much like his oil business: you get someone else to put up most of the cost of production (the network license fee), and you do as many new shows as possible in search of a gusher that will pay for all your mistakes and then some.

Davis not only refused to fire Katleman, he also eyed Stanfill carefully and replied, "We're [Davis and his associates] going to be calling the shots from now on."

On the flight back to Los Angeles, Stanfill thought about ways to heal the breach. He believed that Davis would reconsider and beg him to return. Instead, when he got off the airplane, reporters and TV cameras already were waiting for his statement. Sources close to Davis had quickly leaked the news that Stanfill was out.

Less than a month later, Alan Hirschfield was elevated to the positions of chairman and CEO.

The publicity surrounding Stanfill's forced exit led to an investigation of Katleman by the Los Angeles County District Attorney's Task Force on White Collar Crime in the Entertainment Industry, which reported the following February that while there were discrepancies in the Katleman expense account, they were not material enough to warrant prosecution or other action. Katleman was to go on to a long, generally successful, tenure at Fox.

Stanfill, rich but bitter, filed a lawsuit against Fox and Davis demanding about $22 million in general and punitive damages for breach of contract, for "sanctioning a fraud" (Katleman's expense account), and for comments made about him in a newspaper article. Five years later, after endless depositions and pretrial motions, just as the case was about to go to trial, Stanfill accepted an out-of-court settlement of $4 million from an insurance company representing Fox.

Half a dozen years after his ouster, Stanfill was quietly running an investment firm in Los Angeles and insisting that he wouldn't want another studio job. However, he obviously was still hurt by the way he had been treated by Davis. "He acted in direct contradiction of what he said he was going to do," says Stanfill. "Rather than building the company and retaining it, he proceeded to dismantle it and strip it of assets. And he executed an almost total change in management."

With Hirschfield set by the end of July 1981 to run the movie- and TV-production side of the studio, Davis could once again focus on how best to exploit the Fox assets to begin paying off the huge debt taken on at the time of the purchase. Davis began to realize that it was going to take more time than he had thought to get top dollar, especially for the real estate. He had no intention of acting hastily. After all, he was enjoying being a movie mogul, and his son John, who had just graduated from the Harvard Business School, was excited about coming to work at the studio.

Davis also was discovering an additional side benefit. His new position as a mogul provided increased status and unlimited access to many of the richest, most powerful people in the world, many of whom were just dying to invest with Davis in oil exploration on the usual third-for-a-quarter terms. Some who invested worked at Fox, such as Hirschfield and Katleman. Some of the rich and famous people Davis knew also became Twentieth Century–Fox board members—replacing all the Stanfill board appointees such as Princess Grace. The new board added a touch of prestige to bolster Davis's image while he systematically sold off almost everything Stanfill had acquired. Among those Davis appointed to the Fox board, often in return for substantial director's fees, were former secretary of state Henry Kissinger, former president Gerald Ford, Cleveland Browns owner Arthur Modell and Shearson/American Express chairman Sanford I. Weill.

What about his handshake deal to sell the movie- and TV-production and distribution divisions to Kirk Kerkorian? Davis had stalled Kerkorian until the problem sorted itself out. On July 28, 1981, Kerkorian acquired United Artists Corporation and its worldwide movie distribution network from Transamerica Corporation for $380 million. Kerkorian no longer had any interest in, or need for, Twentieth Century–Fox or its worldwide movie-distribution network.

Davis notified the Beverly Hills Hotel that he would be taking a bungalow for his weekly visits on a yearly basis from then on, for an annual rent of $365,000.

Marvin Davis was having fun.

5

NEAR-FATAL ATTRACTION

MARVIN DAVIS WAS too busy to spend much time at Twentieth Century–Fox during the first six months of his ownership because the oil business was booming. Each time he came to the studio in those first weeks, however, he relentlessly pushed his favorite idea for a movie.

"Dollface," he would say to Sherry Lansing, using his pet name for Fox's head of production, "why don't we do a sequel to *The Sound of Music.*"

It had been one of Fox's biggest hits, agreed Lansing, but times had changed. An old-fashioned, big-budget musical would be enormously expensive to mount, even if you could clear all of the rights. There was also no way to replace Rogers and Hammerstein, the original composers, who had passed away. Even if you could, she would add, the last few attempts at similar projects had all been flops. Fox's 1969 production of *Hello Dolly,* with Barbra Streisand and songs already proven on Broadway, was such a flop that it almost threw the studio into bankruptcy.

"But Dollface . . ."

Lansing felt an affection for Davis, but it quickly became obvious to her that he wasn't the answer to the problems hounding her at Fox. In truth, she felt she had lost an important ally when Dennis Stanfill left, even though she had been hired by Alan Hirschfield and was widely perceived to be in his circle. At least Stanfill had always treated her fairly and listened to what she had to say. She felt that Davis patronized her and wouldn't take her seriously.

Even worse, Lansing saw Davis becoming ever closer to her chief tormentor and nemesis, Norman Levy, who headed Fox's movie marketing and distribution. Davis had taken an instant liking to Levy, even more than he had to Hirschfield. When Davis came to town, Levy was his frequent lunch or dinner companion (they even liked similar foods) and a sounding board for all of his ideas. They were both from New York, close in age, and clearly drew their attitudes from the same post–World War II generation.

To Lansing it was as if the executive suite was becoming a kind of boy's locker room, from which she was excluded.

Lansing constantly thought about quitting. She had held a series of executive posts, and in the back of her mind her goal was to establish credentials that would allow her to become an independent producer, making only the movies she could proudly put her personal stamp on. She also was tortured by thoughts of her biological clock running down before she had the opportunity to have children and a family life.

Two things kept Lansing at Fox. First, she had become a symbol of what a woman could accomplish, a role model for other young female executives, and there was constant pressure on her to live up to that image—even when that image did not reflect reality.

Second, and more important, Lansing felt an obligation toward the movies she had put into development and the producers, directors, and writers she had lured to the studio with promises that she would protect their films from the vagaries of the system. She thought of them as her children and her life at Fox as a bad marriage that had her trapped. She yearned for the day her children would be grown and she could escape.

Shortly after first meeting Davis, Lansing met with two of the key producers then associated with Fox, Richard Zanuck (partnered with David Brown) and Daniel Melnick, who had been her employer, mentor, friend, and occasional social companion. "This is not going to work," Lansing complained.

"You can get along with him," insisted Melnick.

"You don't understand," said Lansing. "This is not about working hard or being smarter or being more passionate or convincing someone of my point of view. This is about a man who doesn't trust women in this capacity. I don't know how to overcome it. This is a nice man, but he is always going to think of me as 'Dollface.' "

It wasn't just because she was a woman, either, Lansing firmly believed. It was because she didn't *think* like Marvin Davis and Norman Levy, about anything. "Being a woman," Lansing told Melnick and Zanuck, "just makes it harder."

As Lansing pondered what to do about Davis, she realized that she had spent much of her life trying to prove that she was more than just another pretty face. Born in Chicago on July 31, 1944, Lansing had earned a degree in theater from Northwestern University with honors. She moved to Los Angeles and taught math at a high school in Watts, a predominantly black area, while working to begin a show-business career. Her first success came as a model for Max Factor cosmetics and other products, which led to a few small movie roles, including *Rio Lobo,* with John Wayne, in 1970. Lansing also was reading and evaluating scripts for a producer, and she soon decided that what was going on behind the camera was a lot more interesting than being an actress.

After jobs with a couple of independent movie companies reading scripts and developing movies and TV shows, Lansing worked as executive story editor at MGM, where she got to know Dan Melnick, then head of production at MGM. When Melnick moved to Columbia Pictures in 1977, she followed, rising to senior vice president of production.

Lansing arrived at Columbia just as it was achieving great box office success, but the studio was thrown into internal turmoil by a scandal. David Begelman, a former talent agent, was caught forging several checks. At first his boss, Alan Hirschfield, tried to be supportive of Begelman, but when the scandal became public, Hirschfield took the position that Begelman had to go. This pitted Hirschfield against many of the most powerful people in Hollywood, longtime friends of Begelman who supported him because of his success in making movies, as well as the very men who had gotten Hirschfield his job, Wall Street investment bankers Charles and Herbert Allen, Jr.

After graduating from the Harvard Business School in 1959, Hirschfield had worked for the rich, private family behind Allen and Company, who were long-time friends of his father. When they moved into entertainment, Hirschfield was sent west to represent their interests, first at Warner Bros. and then at Columbia. When the crunch came, however, the Allens sided with Begelman, who was credited with picking the movies that turned Columbia from an also-ran into a profitable powerhouse. Hirschfield was forced to leave Columbia (as was Begelman not long afterward). He moved to Warner Bros. for a year and then on to Fox.

Ironically, at Columbia Hirschfield had been shunned by some old Hollywood hands as a Wall Street outsider who was forced on the studio. Now he joined Fox because of the perception that he was a movie-industry insider.

When Begelman finally was ousted from Columbia, it started a chain reaction of other changes in the executive suite. Melnick and others had been forced out, but Lansing had remained and appeared to be in line for the position as head of movie production under the regime of Frank Price, who had been elevated to president of Columbia Pictures. At the last minute, however, Lansing was passed over for the job. She claimed she was told it was because she was a woman, although Price denied it. He said she wasn't ready for the responsibility.

The contract settlement that Hirschfield had agreed to when he left Columbia Pictures severely limited his right to recruit Columbia employees to Fox, but it was only natural that he should look to his old friends. He knew who he could work well with, and that was important because Fox had to move quickly to raise its level of production.

One of the people Hirschfield wanted was Norman Levy, then head of distribution at Columbia. After Begelman's departure, Columbia briefly had been run by a trio of Levy, former Universal Studios head of television Frank Price, and Patrick Williamson, who headed Columbia's international sales. Price had quickly become first among equals in the eyes of the board, which named him president. Levy's contract said that if Price left, he would be next in line. This was widely seen as a threat to Price, although he denied that it concerned him. In any case, Levy felt he had to get out from under Price.

In November 1979, shortly after he joined Fox, Hirschfield asked Levy to have lunch with him at the Shezan Restaurant in New York City. Levy brought along his attorney, Burton I. "Buddy" Monash, a well-known New York divorce lawyer who also had an active corporate-entertainment practice. Monash, with a slight build and dark, intense eyes, had a reputation as a tough litigator and hard-nosed negotiator.

It wasn't a tough negotiation for Levy, however. Hirschfield wanted him and was willing to pay the price. Hirschfield admired Levy because of his reputation for picking up commercial independent films to augment the movies produced within the studio, and doing a good job of selling them. Hirschfield felt that "pickups," as they are called in the movie industry, were a way to rapidly increase the number of movies Fox had to distribute while production was increased on the studio's own movies, a process that would take at least eighteen months. Levy, he believed, could give him immediate results.

Levy had a reputation in Hollywood as an innovator in the integration of movie advertising, publicity, sales, and distribution. He had spent much of his career at small and often troubled companies, where he was credited with creating strong distribution strategies against tremendous odds. The one criticism that dogged Levy was that he was a loner. He particularly didn't like to discuss his plans with the makers of the movies he sold. He felt that each of them thought his or her movie was special and thus couldn't see the overview that was his operating perspective.

A native New Yorker, Levy was a burly man with black hair that was rapidly turning gray. He started in the movie industry in 1957 in the publicity and marketing departments of Universal Pictures. After a decade he moved to National General Pictures, a much smaller movie company (that was also in several other businesses), which was trying to carve out a major position in show business. Instead, National General sold its entertainment operations. Levy moved to Columbia Pictures in 1974 to run the movie-distribution division. This was shortly after the arrival at Columbia of Alan Hirschfield. The company was then in deep financial difficulty and on the edge of bankruptcy. That's when Hirschfield brought in Begelman to head production. Hirschfield, Levy, and Begelman subsequently had half a dozen outstanding years together at Columbia and the trio was widely credited with turning around a bad situation.

Levy had played a central role in this turnaround. When he arrived, the studio was short of cash. It was able to rebound because Levy picked up some nonstudio movies that became hits, including *Lords of Flatbush,* the movie that introduced Sylvester Stallone to the silver screen.

Now, over lunch in New York City, Hirschfield was promising Levy the moon if he would work the same magic at Fox. The first problem was that Hirschfield had a contract that said he couldn't hire Levy, and the second problem was that Levy had a contract with Columbia that had about two years to go. Monash, an authoritative man with a confident demeanor, assured them both that the problem of Columbia's contract could be handled. And Hirschfield told them he wasn't going to worry about his noninterference contract with Columbia.

That left only the terms on which to settle. A salary of $300,000 a year to start was agreed on, along with a generous bonus based on performance. Levy would be chief operating officer of the entire motion-picture operation with the exception of production, which would begin reporting to him eighteen months after his arrival. This was to allow Levy time to rebuild the domestic- and foreign-distribution and marketing arms of Fox, all of which they agreed were in trouble.

Next the three men discussed a short list of candidates for head of production. One name that came up was Herbert Ross, a highly regarded film director *(Turning Point)*. The person they finally settled on was Sherry Lansing, who they all knew from Columbia, where she had played a key role in such films as *The China Syndrome* and Oscar Award–winner *Kramer vs. Kramer*. The consensus was that Lansing had good relations with talent and would work well with the new team, and that bringing in a woman would help create a fresh, distinctive image for a reawakened Twentieth Century–Fox.

By the time they toasted one another at the end of lunch, it had been determined that Levy would come to Fox as soon as Monash could get him out of his contract, and that Lansing would be hired in the meantime to gear up production.

Afterward, Monash drew up a deal memo outlining the terms, which Hirschfield then signed. That agreement was to become the subject of considerable controversy.

Monash next went to Columbia and declared them in breach of Levy's contract because his client's authority had been usurped by Frank Price. Columbia was represented in the negotiation by Victor Kaufman, a fast-rising young attorney who nearly a decade later would become chairman of restructured Columbia Pictures Entertainment. An exit settlement was reached, although Levy later had to sue Columbia to get a bonus payment he felt was due him.

While Levy was struggling to get out of his contract at Columbia, a process that took the next three months, Hirschfield began to woo

Lansing. Despite her subservient position at Columbia, she was hesitant. She was already close to an agreement to enter independent production in association with Melnick, she wasn't sure she wanted to work closely with Levy again, and she was skeptical about whether she would have real creative freedom at Fox.

If Hirschfield was anything, he was a brilliant salesman. A tall man with silver-gray hair, full of charm and wit, he painted a picture for Lansing of a team injecting renewed energy into a great studio. He promised again and again that she would have freedom and would report only to him. He promised to be there whenever she needed him and to make sure Lansing had all necessary resources.

Lansing had a hard time making up her mind. Finally she decided she would always regret it if she said no and didn't take her shot as head of production. After all, she reasoned, she could always go into independent production later. In fact, in her contract she was given that option after eighteen months—or immediately, if Alan Hirschfield were to leave Fox.

Shortly after New Year's 1980, at age thirty-five, Lansing became the first woman to head production at a major movie studio. Almost immediately her new status, coupled with her movie-star looks, seemed to capture the imagination of the nation. Lansing was inundated with interview requests from newspapers, magazines, and the electronic media. At first Hirschfield encouraged her to talk, in order to bolster the studio's image. There were stories in *Time, Newsweek,* and most of the major women's magazines. She was the subject of flattering profiles in major newspapers and was deluged with offers to speak, appear at seminars, write books, and do endorsements. Most of it she shunted aside as she faced the reality of her situation.

To Lansing it was like a cruel joke. She was suddenly admired and envied by people all over the globe, but at Fox, nothing was going as planned. She arrived to find that the entire production team had departed, leaving empty halls and offices. When she tried to discuss who she could hire with Hirschfield, he was either too busy or unavailable or wanted to put off the decision. She discovered that she didn't have the power to put significant projects into development, which meant spending money to hire producers, directors, and writers, without Hirschfield, and he was frequently away in New York. She joked about getting to know his wife as she left phone messages at their Westchester County, New York, home, most of which Hirschfield never returned.

This was the great tragedy of Alan Hirschfield. Despite his charm and intelligence, he hated details and couldn't make decisions. Often his decision turned out to be a refusal to make a decision, which forced Lansing and others to either abandon projects or take the initiative. When they did push ahead without Hirschfield's approval, he would second-guess them, often pouring out a tirade of sarcastic complaints.

Hirschfield did make a handful of deals with producers to take up residence on the Fox lot and make their films for the studio. Among them were Zanuck-Brown; former Columbia executive Stanley Jaffe; former Columbia producer Frank Yablans; and Dan Melnick, former head of production at MGM and Columbia, who was given an almost unbelievable deal, even by the wildly generous standards of Hollywood.

During Hirschfield's long, difficult battle over Begelman, Melnick had remained his unflinching supporter. Shortly after Hirschfield left, Columbia hit it big with one of Melnick's films, *All That Jazz.* Thus, shortly after Hirschfield got to Fox, Melnick was offered the presidency of the studio. He refused, and eventually the job went to his close friend Lansing. Later, Melnick accepted a deal as an independent producer based at Twentieth Century–Fox. That meant that Fox would have first opportunity to option films created by his company, IndieProd. In return Melnick was given a ten-year contract. For the first five years he would produce and for the next five he would be a studio consultant. He was guaranteed a retainer of about $500,000 a year plus a producer's fee of at least $200,000 for each picture. In addition, IndieProd could draw on a million-dollar-a-year fund for operating expenses.

When he actually made a movie, Melnick was to get ten percent of every dollar the studio received in rentals—not a share of profits, but a share of the gross amount. He also had the right, within certain generous budget limits, to force Fox to finance and produce three movies over the life of the contract without any additional approvals.

With tongues wagging all over town that Melnick was really at Fox to back up Lansing, an additional stipulation was added. She had no power over Melnick's projects or any authority to decide if the studio would make them. No one would ever accuse her of favoring her mentor.

A month after Lansing, Levy arrived and things really turned sour. Levy didn't know that Lansing had been promised that she would always report directly to Hirschfield or that she had never been told that Levy's contract said she would begin reporting to

him in eighteen months. Lansing found out the truth when a mutual
acquaintance told her that Levy said he would soon be in charge of
movie production. When she confronted Hirschfield, he admitted
to having made conflicting contractual obligations and promised to
find a way to work it out.

Stanfill, in the meantime, noted the conflicting clauses and refused to sign Levy's contract. Levy already was being paid under the
deal memo written by Monash, and that, in essence, became his
contract.

Lansing also learned that there were some filmmakers who
wouldn't work with Levy. While highly competent in distribution
and marketing, Levy had a reputation for not returning phone calls
and for refusing to discuss his distribution plans with the filmmakers. Levy would create the best possible sales campaigns for their
movies, but he wouldn't play the game of making famous directors
and producers feel they had a say in the process.

Lansing soon learned that this meant that directors Steven Spiel-
berg and Sydney Pollack and actors Robert Redford and Paul
Newman, along with many others, simply wouldn't work with Fox
as long as Levy was going to be handling the distribution of their
films. They would tell Lansing they loved her and then go elsewhere to make their movies.

Lansing, while becoming one of the most famous woman in the
country, thus found that she couldn't attract the best talent, didn't
have real authority to green light the production of movies, and was
in the middle of a back-stabbing political battle between Stanfill and
Hirschfield every day at the office. "The world thinks I'm this big
powerful mogul," recalls Lansing, "and I can't get a pencil sharp-
ened."

Meanwhile, Levy was rapidly making deals to fill the Fox distribution pipeline with movies from Time Incorporated, the movie
unit of the ABC network, producer Melvin Simon, and others. Fox
would distribute the movies they made in return for a percentage
of the rental income generated. It appeared to Lansing and others
that Levy placed these pickups in prime playing periods like summer and Christmas while relegating the films the studio made under
Lansing to less-desirable windows of distribution. Levy adamantly
denied that was the case. All Lansing knew was that many filmmakers she approached simply wouldn't come to Fox because of the
perception that in-house movies were being given second-hand
treatment. She felt that Levy was making it more difficult for her
to succeed.

This was the unfortunate situation in which Lansing operated when Marvin Davis arrived and Stanfill departed. Hirschfield kept telling her that she was a symbol to all women and that she had to stick it out. And the producers and other creators she worked with on movie projects constantly made her promise not to desert them. Lansing felt stuck.

Davis tried to boost Lansing by making her feel she was part of a family at Fox. He would tell her that he wanted her to see him as a kind of surrogate father to whom she could come with any problem. He said he thought of her as a daughter, Levy as a brother, and Hirschfield as a son. He wanted them all to get along.

Instead, they were stalemated by the conflicting contracts. Both Levy and Lansing had been promised in writing that they would control movie production and report only to Alan Hirschfield. Since it was impossible for them both to do the same job, with the same authority, the stage appeared to be set for an internal civil war that could end only with one of them leaving the studio.

In mid-summer 1981, shortly after Davis took over, Levy was contacted by David Begelman, the new head of production at Kirk Kerkorian's MGM. He wanted Levy to come there as head of movie distribution at a higher salary, with even stronger job guarantees.

Davis, who had become fast friends with Levy, heard that he was thinking of leaving and insisted that there was a solution to the contract conflict with Sherry Lansing. He offered Levy a compromise. He would give Levy a promotion in return for dropping the guarantee in his contract that movie production eventually report to him. Instead, said Davis, he would make Levy vice chairman and a member of the board. Levy would receive a raise to $350,000 base salary for the first year of his new contract, $375,000 for the second year, and $400,000 for the third year. The world would see him being elevated, and as a member of the board, Sherry Lansing would, in a sense, be reporting to Levy.

Levy accepted, and in August 1981 he was named vice chairman.

When Levy's lawyer, Buddy Monash, was called in to negotiate the contract, Davis realized that they were acquaintances from the days when both attended New York University. Shortly after that meeting, Davis invited Monash to move to Los Angeles and take charge of business and administrative affairs at the studio. Monash soon arrived and engendered strong loyalty in some and dislike in others. He was perceived as Davis's extra set of eyes and ears at the studio. When there was a tough, nasty job to do, Davis gave it to the former divorce lawyer, Buddy Monash.

In the fall of 1981 the first two films for which Lansing had been solely responsible were ready for release. One was Melnick's first Fox movie, *Making Love,* an $8 million production about a love triangle involving two gay men and a woman. The other was *Taps,* a $15 million Stanley Jaffe production about an insurrection in a military school. It would introduce a crop of promising young actors, including Sean Penn, Timothy Hutton, and Tom Cruise.

Taps was screened for Levy. As Lansing remembers it, Levy felt it was too dark and would not be commercial. Lansing says Levy called it a "downer," and asked her to reshoot the ending in which the kids in the school are killed by the National Guard. She adamantly refused. Levy told her that if they had to release *Taps* as presented, to protect the studio he would sell off at least a half interest before its opening at Christmas.

Levy's recollection of the incident is different. He maintains that he never asked that the ending be changed, but that he was upset over the proposed marketing campaign and any reservations stemmed from that.

Regardless, Lansing loved the movie. She felt it made an important antiwar statement and called it a "masterpiece."

Davis finally said he would see it and decide for himself. He came out of the screening full of praise. He compared the film to drilling an oil well and hitting a gusher. He wouldn't sell any of it.

Taps was set for a big premiere in New York City, which would be attended by Davis and many of his friends as well as all of the key Fox executives. During the week before it opened, the reviews started coming in, and most were negative. Some critics absolutely hated it. Davis called Lansing into his office. He wanted to know why she had changed the ending of the movie since the time he had seen it a few weeks before. According to Lansing, as Davis remembered it, the kids lived at the end. Now the reviews all said they die. "Why," he demanded, "did you change the ending?"

Lansing protested that she hadn't changed anything. "The kids were dead six weeks ago, four weeks ago, and now," she told Davis. "Dead is dead." Later, Davis, in an interview, denied he ever changed his mind about the film.

Lansing recalled that as she left his office after he had accused her of changing the ending, she felt sick to her stomach. What bothered her wasn't that her first showcase movie might fail, Lansing recalled, but rather that she worked for a man who couldn't face the harsh truth without reshaping reality to fit his concerns of the moment. She thought for an instant about storming back in and resigning but bit her lip and waited instead for the opening.

On the night of the premiere, the Manhattan audience was unusually quiet. At the party afterward, there was a sense of doom. They seemed sure, en masse, that *Taps* was a bomb. Lansing danced the night away with Stanley Jaffe in a bright red dress, sure she was about to be fired.

But instead, *Taps* became one of the top-grossing hits of the Christmas season. Lansing's job was safe, although her faith in Davis was badly shaken.

At least for a little longer, the uneasy truce continued at Fox.

6

STUDIO ZERO, MARVIN PLENTY

ON A THURSDAY afternoon in June 1982, Marvin Davis swung his three-hundred-pound girth out of his company-owned Gulfstream jet aircraft, which had just landed at the Santa Monica Airport, and climbed directly into a waiting limousine. With one car in front and one car behind the limo, both carrying members of Davis's personal security force (led by a former FBI agent), the three-vehicle caravan sped through West Los Angeles and along Pico Boulevard to the studio. As it swung around the gatehouse at the entrance, past a line of cars and trucks waiting for permission to enter, Davis glanced out his window at the studio's authentic-looking replica of a New York street, which had been built in 1969 for the movie *Hello Dolly.* He couldn't help but think about growing up on the mean streets of the real New York City, where even as a kid he had known he was going to be something special.

Davis thought about his friend and associate Norman Levy, who also had grown up in New York, and wondered if he had ever imagined running one of Hollywood's most famous movie studios. He decided that the first thing he would do would be to call in Levy, whose company he enjoyed more than any of his other employees. While Alan Hirschfield made him crazy by rarely delivering on his promises and "Dollface" Sherry Lansing, in the year since he had taken on the studio, had annoyed him by making movies that didn't make money, Levy had become his confidant. Besides, he was the one executive whose division continued to rake in a healthy cash flow. Thank God for Norman, Davis thought.

The limo swung to a stop in Davis's personal parking space directly in front of the long, low-slung Twentieth Century–Fox executive office building. One of the security guards jumped out of the trailing car, swept his eyes around for any signs of trouble, and then quickly opened the door for Davis. Dressed in a dark pin-striped suit, starched white shirt, and red striped tie, Davis bounced along the short sidewalk to the rear entrance, the one closest to his office, and then up the few stairs. Within a minute he was seated behind the broad mahogany desk in his big ground-floor office, the same office that only a year earlier had been occu-pied by Dennis Stanfill. Waiting for him on the desk, beside a large electronic calculator, were the Hollywood trade papers, a folder with some mail, and another folder with papers and memos that needed immediate attention. Davis pushed it all aside and hit a button on his telephone. A few minutes later, in answer to Davis's summons, Norman Levy arrived. Davis greeted him with a bear hug. It was obvious that there was a genuine affection be-tween the two men.

They chatted about the prospects for the new crop of summer movies and the recently reported financial results for the first half of the year. Davis grumbled about the failure of Fox's in-house movies created under Sherry Lansing including *Author! Author!* with Al Pacino and Neil Simon's *I Ought to Be in Pictures,* which starred Walter Matthau. Then Davis complimented Levy on the success of his pickups. In the past year, Levy's acquisitions had included several huge hits, especially *The Cannonball Run,* with Burt Reynolds and an all-star cast in a crazed cross-country race, and *Porky's,* a raunchy teen comedy that had become one of the biggest hits of the year. Fox had also just opened *The Man from Snowy River,* an old-fashioned Western Levy had picked up from Australia.

"I don't think we're paying you enough," Davis declared, which shocked Levy. "We're going to tear up your old contract. I think we can do better."

Davis then outlined the new terms he had in mind. Levy was to be given a new three-year contract that immediately increased his annual salary from $375,000 to $500,000. The contract also gave Levy the right at the end of the term to become an independent producer or a consultant to the studio at his full pay for several additional years.

Davis also told Levy that his internal struggle with Sherry Lansing, which had continued even after Levy was named as vice chairman, would be coming to an end. Davis had decided that Lansing could stay on, but only if she took a lesser role as a production executive reporting to both Hirschfield and Levy. Davis said that he hadn't told Lansing yet.

Levy later said that he also had been given a verbal promise of 5 percent of the equity ownership of Fox, which Davis said he couldn't put in writing until he bought out his silent partner, Marc Rich, who had gotten into hot water with the government over the illegal sale of oil to Iran and other matters. Rich had fled to Europe and the U.S. government had put a freeze on all of his assets, including his half interest in Fox.

Davis said that he would instruct Buddy Monash to draw up the papers and that he would see Levy again for dinner to discuss any other details.

It was a curious irony that Davis could be so generous to Levy while cracking down, often ruthlessly, on costs and expenses in every other area at Fox. Among Monash's cost-cutting targets were several of the producers Hirschfield had brought in with generous contracts. Despite the promise of their new movie, *The Verdict,* with Paul Newman, which Fox would release around Christmas 1982, Richard Zanuck and David Brown were being put under pressure because Davis aides believed that their contract paid so much that there was no way the studio could ever make a profit from their work.

The number-one target was Melnick, whose film *Making Love* had opened a few months before and flopped. Davis and Monash considered the contract Melnick had gotten from Hirschfield unconscionable, and they set about to find a way to break it and rid themselves of Melnick.

Not surprisingly, Sherry Lansing was deeply unhappy about what was happening. She not only saw her friends—whom she considered talented filmmakers—being driven out, but she also saw other producers whom she didn't feel were as talented coming in. She had to listen as they announced that they would be making movies for Fox at Davis's or Levy's request, without her agreement.

Lansing's authority was constantly being eroded. It seemed to her that even minor decisions now required approval, not only from Hirschfield but often from Levy and Davis as well. When she did get a movie made, she felt that Levy did not distribute it properly.

If all of that didn't tell Lansing that her position was tenuous, she could have read it in the show-business trade papers. There were persistent rumors that she would be forced out soon. Finally she went to Davis and confronted him about it.

Davis told Lansing that when her contract was up on January 1, 1983 he would be happy to give her an "indefinite" extension—a phrase she instantly recognized was the kiss of death.

She could stay, Davis assured her, but there would have to be some changes. Davis expected her to become a production vice president reporting to Levy. She knew in her heart that she would rather starve first. Her real wish was to become an independent producer as she had long intended.

Before Lansing could figure out just what to do, another tragedy struck. Norman Garey was a prominent show-business attorney who, with several partners, had recently formed a new law firm that wasn't doing well enough to cover its considerable start-up expenses and overhead. Garey represented both Lansing and Dan Melnick.

When Davis instructed Buddy Monash to either renegotiate Melnick's contract or find a way to get rid of him, it was Garey whose phone rang. Melnick's reaction to the request to rewrite the terms, transmitted back to Monash by Garey, was a total refusal to even consider it.

Monash then started an exhaustive review of every contract, expense report, and document that in any way involved Melnick. He finally came up with a screenwriter who appeared to have kicked back part of his fee to Melnick. In his own defense, Melnick said he had kept Sherry Lansing and others at Fox informed about the deal. It just wasn't in writing anywhere.

Melnick was wary of Lansing for another reason. Several years before, Monash had represented Melnick's wife in a long, drawn-out, very ugly divorce proceeding. Now Monash was to force Melnick to divorce Fox.

At one point, Melnick's staff charged that someone was wiretapping the phones at his company, IndieProd, which was located on the Fox lot. Despite an extensive investigation, including scrutiny by the FBI, it remained unproven.

Monash finally found his wedge. A little-noticed, rarely used clause in Melnick's contract allowed Fox to add interest charges against the funds in IndieProd's million-dollar annual administration fund. Monash tallied it up and announced that by autumn,

IndieProd had used up all of its funds for the year and would now have to pay its own expenses.

Melnick, disgusted, wanted to get back to making movies. He instructed Garey to settle the contract—but to exact a sizable payoff.

Fox finally agreed to pay Melnick $2.5 million to go away, but Garey was concerned about tax consequences. He told Melnick he thought he could get Fox to pick up the IRS tab. Melnick considered the point settled. Monash, however, refused to concede on the tax question. Garey's inability to accomplish what he had all but promised upset Melnick—a reasonable response considering that this little detail would cost him about $750,000 in taxes.

Garey wrote to his malpractice insurance carrier that he was afraid his client, Melnick, might sue him. He also became depressed, in part because he was taking medication and because he had a lot of other financial problems. Apparently, the tax question was the final straw. Garey went home, put a gun to his head, and killed himself.

Melnick, devastated by the loss of his long-time friend, insisted that he never would have sued Garey. In the end, Melnick took Fox's $2.5 million and paid the taxes himself. He also took a number of projects with him that would have gone to Fox, including *Footloose,* which became a hit for Paramount.

Lansing, too, was shocked by Garey's suicide. She took it as another powerful sign that she had to get out of Fox. Lansing went to her old friend Stanley Jaffe, one of the few producers still in favor at Fox, and made a secret deal to go into partnership with him at another studio.

Lansing's contract expired on January 1, but technically Jaffe was tied to Fox for several more years. The out in his contract was a "key-man" clause tied to Lansing. If she left, he had the right to get out of his contract within sixty days. The problem was that he had just completed the movie *Without a Trace,* which was due for release by Fox. Both Jaffe and Lansing felt that if Jaffe told Fox he was leaving, Fox would sabotage distribution of his movie, even though Levy had promised strong support for its release in early 1983.

So Jaffe flew to New York in secrecy and quietly negotiated a new independent-production deal at Paramount Pictures with that studio's chairman, Barry Diller, and its president, Michael Eisner. Jaffe-Lansing would be housed and supported at Paramount and given the right to make a certain number of films within set budget limits. In return, all of Jaffe-Lansing's movie projects would be offered first to Paramount.

Now timing was everything. Lansing had to delay her departure long enough to allow *Without a Trace* to be properly distributed and still leave time for Jaffe to opt out of his contract.

Sources close to Davis said that Lansing was to have been fired, whatever she decided to do, and that the ax fell in December, right before Christmas. According to Lansing, that is when she resigned, much to Hirschfield's and Davis's surprise.

Lansing remembered Marvin Davis being angry when she quit. He didn't like the idea that she was going to work for someone else. She would only say at the time that she had something lined up but couldn't talk about it.

According to Lansing, when Davis later learned that she was going to Paramount not as an executive but to produce, Davis told her that all was forgiven. When he ran into her at a party he gave her an affectionate bear hug. In a way, Davis was getting what he had wanted all along. For months he had been itching to shake things up in the executive suite. What few knew, however, was that he didn't intend to stop with Sherry Lansing.

In autumn of 1982, during the annual Carousel Ball in Denver, Davis had another surprise for Levy. He wanted him to take Hirschfield's job as chairman. Levy spent the rest of his trip to Denver convincing Davis to give Hirschfield more time. Davis later told associates that Levy didn't have the guts to take on such a big job, whereas Levy claimed he was being loyal to Hirschfield, the man who had lured him away from Columbia Pictures.

It was an argument that eventually would explode, with unforeseen consequences for both Levy and Hirschfield.

For Davis, seeing the studio become a success wasn't just about money. It also had become important because it enhanced his position in Hollywood, where he was spending more and more of his time. Davis may have bought Fox to get at its lucrative real estate, but along the way he had become enamored of show business. He loved the characters, the color, the parties, even the cliquishness. Now he needed a few hit movies to prove he really belonged.

His newfound love of show business, however, would not stand in the way of business. Almost from the day he arrived, Davis had begun looking at what he could sell and how he could maximize profits.

Before the leveraged buyout became common, Davis was practicing the art of buying a company with borrowed money and then using that company's profits to pay off the cost of the purchase. That is essentially what he did at Twentieth Century–Fox, which resulted in enormous profits for Davis and his silent partner Marc Rich, even as the studio's core businesses floundered.

With the purchase of the studio in June 1981, Davis and Rich owned a studio burdened with over $1 billion in debt. Part of that was eliminated in the deal with the Aetna, which became a partner in most of the Fox real estate and other assets. By December 1981, Davis, Rich, and Aetna began selling off some of those assets. The Coca-Cola bottling franchise in the Midwest went for about $102 million. The following July, Davis and Rich sold the Fox record company and the music-publishing division for just over $50 million.

As quickly as the cash came in, Davis and Rich took it out. Some was used to repay bank debts, but most went into their pockets. Over the first two years of the Davis-Rich ownership, most of the debt was refinanced and shifted onto the studio—and off of Davis and Rich.

In December 1983, in a complicated transaction, Davis and three partners bought out Aetna's stake in the jointly owned properties. It was done with money borrowed from banks in excess of what was actually needed, which allowed Davis and Rich to also declare dividends for themselves.

Eventually, all of the outside businesses and valuable real estate Dennis Stanfill had acquired for Fox with the profits from *Star Wars* was stipped away and sold off, with the proceeds going to Davis and Rich. That included the movie theaters in Australia and New Zealand, the Pebble Beach resort, and the Aspen, Colorado, resort (although the Davis partnership group ended up as buyer of some of those assets).

Davis also engineered a deal with CBS Inc., which became Fox's partner in a joint venture to produce, manufacture, and distribute prerecorded video cassettes. Fox (meaning Davis) didn't put up any cash, but it did provide certain guarantees that Fox movies—past and present—would be distributed to the home video market through the new venture, called CBS/Fox Video. CBS handed Fox about $45 million in cash and a half interest in a valuable studio lot it owned in the eastern part of the San Fernando Valley.

By the end of 1984, the studio was deeply in debt, but Davis and Rich had made out very nicely. They had gotten all of their purchase money out of Fox, eliminated their personal debts, and pocketed millions in profits.

The studio was losing large sums of money on the books, but much of that was a write-off of the original purchase price. That meant taxes were reduced even while there was a positive flow of cash from operations.

Two things were on the horizon, however, that were to shake things up once again. First, under pressure from the U.S. government, Rich wanted to sell his half of Fox, preferably to Davis. Second, after Sherry Lansing left, things went from bad to worse. Fox under Alan Hirschfield was making one movie after another that bombed at the box office, costing far more than the occasional success. Davis, who had brought his son John and daughter Patty in as production executives, was spending a lot more time at the studio and was even reading scripts, and yet nothing he or Hirschfield or Levy did seemed to turn things around. As 1984 rushed toward a close, Davis knew that even with the best advice from tax lawyers and accountants, he would soon have to inject new money to keep Fox afloat, something he dreaded doing.

Meanwhile, Stanley Jaffe's *Without a Trace* opened that March, with full support from Levy's marketing and distribution team, only to become another box office disappointment for Fox. Jaffe quickly announced that he was leaving Fox because his contract had been voided when Sherry Lansing left. Soon after, Jaffe-Lansing, their new company, was formed at Paramount. After several modest successes there they produced *Fatal Attraction,* which was released in the fall of 1988 and became one of the biggest hits in the history of the motion-picture industry.

7

MOVIE MARTIAL ARTS

IN THE SPRING of 1984, Twentieth Century–Fox's movie division was in a tailspin. Paramount Pictures, on the other hand, had been at the top of the heap in Hollywood for most of the last ten years. Its movie successes included such hit pictures as *Raiders of the Lost Ark,* the second and third *Star Trek* sequels, *Flashdance, Trading Places, Terms of Endearment,* and *Footloose.* Paramount was winning a larger share of the moviegoing audience—about 21 percent, according to the trade paper *Variety*—than any other studio.

Yet Paramount wasn't a happy place. For a decade it had enjoyed the most stable management in the movie industry under the leadership of Chairman Barry Diller and President Michael Eisner, but it operated with a system that wore people down. To get a movie made, a production executive had to be totally passionate about the script and confident that it would be a huge success. If the studio executive pushing the project wasn't willing to stand up for his (or her) movie deal and defend it again and again, then the project was as good as dead. Diller would play the tough cynic and Eisner the enthusiastic optimist, as both pounded away until they had exactly the deal they wanted, just the script they expected, and precisely the casting they thought best.

While other studios were becoming banks that financed projects brought to them by powerful talent agencies fully packaged—that is, they arrived on the studio production chief's desk completely assembled, including a script, a director, and stars—Paramount wouldn't pay the agents' price. Its executives preferred to assemble each movie piece by piece in their own fashion. While others thought that for a movie to be successful it needed only the right stars, Paramount also demanded the right story. Sometimes it cost them such subtle films as *The Big Chill,* which involved complex relationships (although Diller did occasionally push through a sophisticated project, such as *Reds* or *Ragtime*). But more often it resulted in movies with a simple, melodramatic motif, such as the underdog who makes good (*Bad News Bears, Flashdance, Staying Alive,* and others).

In the decade that Diller presided over Paramount, profits from the studio increased nearly tenfold as the company came to represent the cutting edge in movies, network television, TV syndication, home video, and more.

The Paramount system of passionate advocacy drove some people away. Those who stayed often became smarter and tougher for it. Five years after the Paramount team was broken up in 1984, more than half of the major Hollywood studios were run by "graduates" of the Diller-Eisner academy of movie martial arts. And for the most part, they were the most successful studios. *Manhattan Inc.,* a New York City business magazine, dubbed them "the Killer Dillers." The cover headline copy read: "Barry Diller taught his protégés to bite, kick, yell—and return phone calls. Now they're running Hollywood."

There have been endless arguments over who really was responsible for Paramount's extraordinary success between 1974 and 1984, but there is no question that the studio reflected the personality of Barry Diller more than any other individual. A complex, brilliant man with a penetrating intellect and an intimidating style, it was Diller's nature to constantly test people to see how far he could push them, for better or for worse. When a project caught his fancy, he wanted to be in on every last detail. He could argue for hours over the tag line for a one-sheet, the movie poster displayed in theater lobbies.

Diller's taste in movies generally was considered elitist, while Eisner was seen as champion of the popular mass-audience projects. Behind their backs producers referred to them as "the Chic and the Shit."

Diller, balding and broad shouldered with thick features and penetrating blue eyes, was the bachelor with trendy friends like record mogul David Geffen, designer Calvin Klein, actor Warren Beatty, actress Debra Winger, and director Mike Nichols. Eisner, tall, with curly light-brown hair, was the down-to-earth family man who would gladly give up a flashy Hollywood party to spend some quality time with his wife Jane and their three children. Together they covered the broad spectrum of the marketplace, putting a unique imprint on the films made by their regime. Not all film-makers liked the studio's hands-on approach, but they learned to either accept it or go elsewhere.

One who learned that lesson well was a savvy southerner named Lawrence Gordon, who produced the Paramount hit *48 Hrs,* which introduced Eddie Murphy to the big screen, and other films. Gordon was a close friend of Eisner, who had brought him to the studio. Still, when *48 Hrs* director Walter Hill complained about the way he had been treated at Paramount, Gordon offered their next movie project to another studio. Eisner, believing that Gordon and Hill had an obligation to give Paramount first look, felt betrayed. To retaliate, he locked Gordon out of his offices and had his furniture removed. Gordon went to court and won a temporary injunction to stop him, but that was the end of his days at Paramount. Gordon and Eisner later got back together as friends, but Gordon continued to harbor a grudge against Diller, who he felt had treated him shoddily at the time.

Without question, Diller could be ruthless once he made a decision. Yet at times he also could be surprisingly shy, a trait often mistaken for coldness. Frequently, Diller was tough, abrupt, difficult, and bullying. He had no patience for the foolish, the unprepared, or those who thought they could get by with flattery. He constantly tested his associates, sometimes just to get a reaction. If they stood up to him, he usually would back off. If not, he would just as quickly lose respect for them. And once an underling lost Diller's respect, he or she was done.

At his best Diller had the ability to push people and movie projects several steps beyond what anyone else would have thought possible. What few knew was that by the spring of 1984, Diller himself was being pushed to the breaking point. Despite record profits, Martin Davis (no relation to Marvin Davis), the newly installed chairman of Gulf + Western Industries, which had owned Paramount Pictures since the late 1960s, was treating Diller as if he were a truant schoolboy who needed to be taught a lesson. What really galled Diller was that he felt that he had been the one who helped Davis get the job following the sudden death of Charles Bluhdorn, the man who had first brought Diller to Paramount. Now Davis adamantly denied that Diller had helped him up the ladder.

Diller had always been a doer, not a dreamer. As his dislike for Martin Davis grew, however, he began to long for his old friend Charlie Bluhdorn. They had fought, bitterly at times, but they had always kept it on a business level and remained friends. They might have disagreed, but there had always been a mutual respect buried beneath the harsh words.

There was nothing simple about Bluhdorn, yet Diller always felt that he knew where he stood with the founding chairman of Gulf + Western Industries. With Martin Davis, Diller felt as though he stood on the outside looking in—and he wasn't really sure why.

During the Bluhdorn years, both Diller and Davis had played important roles, reporting directly to the chairman. Diller and Davis had little contact, however, because the Bluhdorn style was to hold on to all final authority while dealing with each of his key executives in a very personal and direct way. A complex man of great vision in business matters, Bluhdorn could be generous with rewards, but he also was capable of punishing those who crossed him in any way. It wasn't easy to anticipate how he would react to a given situation. Even to those who worked closely with him, Bluhdorn was rarely predictable.

Charles Bluhdorn, born in Vienna, Austria, in 1926, was a strong-willed, self-made millionaire. He acquired a small Michigan auto parts company in the late 1950s and then parlayed it into one of the first multinational conglomerates, with wide-ranging interests in precious metals, sugar in the Dominican Republic, and a constantly shifting portfolio of investments. He was a master at using borrowed money to make even more acquisitions, which then increased his net worth, giving him even greater buying power. He was among the first to use what Wall Street in the 1960s called "Chinese paper"—long-term commercial debt instruments that offered a high rate of interest and were backed by little more than faith in the issuer. Two decades later, slightly altered, they would be called junk bonds.

In 1966, Paramount, having fallen on hard times along with most other Hollywood studios, was fending off a takeover attempt by two Broadway producers, Cy Feuer and Ernest Martin. Both men were in partnership with Herb Siegel, the former talent agent who later would take over Chris-Craft Industries and attempt to acquire Twentieth Century–Fox. Paramount's president, George Weltner, sent aide Martin Davis off to find a "white knight" who would block the takeover. Davis came up with Charles Bluhdorn, who suddenly appeared on the scene in 1966 and made a preemptive bid of $83 a share, far above the stock's price at the time.

Bluhdorn wasted no time in putting his stamp on Paramount. He often was assisted by Martin Davis, who soon earned a reputation as the new chairman's "henchman," ready to carry out any tough task. Davis had started in show business in 1947 as an office boy at the Samuel Goldwyn Company in New York. He soon became a press agent and in 1955 moved into advertising and publicity at Allied Artists. He joined Paramount in 1958 and was named head of sales and marketing in 1960. By the time Bluhdorn arrived, Davis was chief operating officer and executive assistant to the president of Paramount Pictures Corporation. Shortly after Bluhdorn took over, Davis was named to the Gulf + Western board, and in 1969 he moved to Gulf + Western on a full-time basis.

In the late 1970s Bluhdorn assigned Davis to represent the company during a Securities and Exchange Commission investigation of some improper financial dealings by another executive. When the SEC abandoned the investigation in 1981, Davis's status rose even higher with Bluhdorn.

Paramount, meanwhile, had stumbled through the late 1960s and early 1970s with a few hits but little consistency. Bluhdorn had given himself the title of chairman of the studio, but actually it was being run by several different executives, most prominently no-nonsense producer Frank Yablans and Robert Evans, a stylish young man with a knack for handling temperamental talent.

While maintaining a position in movies, Bluhdorn strongly moved Paramount into television, which he felt would provide a more consistent source of revenues. Often he took a personal hand in trying to interest the three major TV networks in Paramount's shows and old movies. One deal he made shortly after buying Paramount was the sale of a package of old movies to ABC, the television network that perennially came in third behind CBS and NBC. Bluhdorn worked out the broad strokes of the deal with ABC chairman Leonard Goldenson, but it was left to others to work out the details. On the ABC side it was dropped into the lap of a twenty-four-year-old vice president in the programming department named Barry Diller.

Diller was sitting at the pool at the Bel Air Hotel one Saturday afternoon when he was called to the phone and told about the deal. When he heard the titles involved and what Goldenson had agreed to pay, Diller screamed into the phone, "Over my dead body!"

By early the following week, Diller had killed the deal and begun his long relationship with Charles Bluhdorn. At the time, the head of West Coast programming for ABC was Leonard Goldberg, who recalls that Bluhdorn was one of many movie tycoons who used to come in and do verbal battle with Diller. "Barry was from Beverly Hills but had the instincts of a street kid," says Goldberg, who twenty years after first hiring him would go to work for Diller at Twentieth Century–Fox as head of movie and TV production. "Barry was the first creative type to be put in charge of buying old movies. Before that it was considered a business affairs job. . . . Barry was tough and smart, a classy guy, and in a world where people made a lot of excuses, he got the job done."

Diller went on to distinguish himself by helping invent the made-for-television movie of the week and the long-form miniseries drawn from best-selling books. Rising to the position of head of programming, he was also one of the architects of a plan by ABC to concentrate on younger viewers in major urban areas. This strategy later propelled the network into first place in audience ratings.

By 1974 Bluhdorn was so impressed by Diller, then thirty-two years old, that he recruited him to be head of Paramount. Diller agreed to take the job only after Bluhdorn offered him the title of chairman of the studio. Frank Yablans left almost immediately and Robert Evans a short time later. At the time, Diller's appointment was a shock in Hollywood, where they said Diller was too young and lacked experience in movies. As it turned out, he was the first of a new generation of studio executives trained in television, where story, speed, and cost control are more important than personal connections. Diller understood the new business methods movie studios had to use if they were to thrive.

In 1976 Diller recruited another bright young ABC executive named Michael Eisner, who had shown an extraordinary instinct for popular programming. Diller, the only person to respond to two hundred resumes Eisner had sent out, had first hired Eisner in 1966 from CBS. Eisner rapidly made his mark in daytime and children's programming. His idea for an animated series featuring the singing group Jackson 5 moved ABC from number three to number one on Saturday mornings. After Diller left ABC, Eisner took charge of prime-time evening programming. For the first time, ABC became number one in its ability to attract audiences during the lucrative evening hours.

Beginning with *Saturday Night Fever* in 1978, the Diller-Eisner team became the most successful in Hollywood. And Diller and Eisner became two of the best-known and best-paid executives in the entertainment industry.

Bluhdorn would scream and fight with Diller, but he also provided an important executive role model. "The sheer force of the man [Bluhdorn] was just remarkable to watch," recalls Diller. "He was so many things, and you could see he had a brain that was better than yours. Charlie had a brain that could multiply boxcars of numbers, like those people who go on stage and do tricks like what's nine billion divided by 468 and out comes the answer. . . . Yet he was also the only businessman I would describe as a true romantic. He had the soul of a romantic. When he saw something special, he could be moved. There are thousands of examples. Take *The Godfather, Part 2,* Charlie personally convinced [director] Francis Coppola to do it, not for the money, but on the romance, because he believed in it."

In February 1983 Bluhdorn had a sudden heart attack and died on an airplane returning from the Dominican Republic. Diller was stunned. He was also immediately drawn into the selection of a replacement by the Bluhdorn family.

Press accounts at the time speculated that the choice was between Martin Davis, then an executive vice president, and David N. Judelson, Gulf + Western's president, who handled the non–show business side of the complex company. Diller said that he was asked if he wanted the job himself, and he declined. It was then that Diller was approached by Bluhdorn's widow, Yvette, about selecting Judelson or Davis or looking for someone else. Although there was considerable opposition inside the company to Davis—who had been Bluhdorn's in-house "hatchet man" for years—Diller supported his selection. Diller said that he and Davis talked and Davis promised that he would carry on Bluhdorn's tradition and not make any major changes, especially at Paramount.

Davis strongly denies ever having made such promises.

Barely a year later, Diller felt betrayed by Davis, who had begun reshaping the company he had inherited. Davis had sold off Bluhdorn's portfolio of stocks and investments and had used the money to reduce the large Gulf + Western debt. Davis also had begun to pare the company down to a few core businesses.

As part of the reorganization, Davis had promoted Diller to be head of Gulf + Western's leisure-time group, which, in addition to Paramount, included the large publishing house Simon and Schuster, Madison Square Garden and its resident sports teams, and money-losing Sega Enterprises, which made coin-operated amusement and video games. At first Diller had been flattered by the additional responsibilities, but as time wore on he found that he had little interest in the New York City politics that entangled Madison Square Garden, the shifting fortunes of the New York Knicks basketball team, and the alien world of Simon and Schuster, whose strong-willed executives had never made Diller feel comfortable. He yearned to get back to making and selling movies and TV shows, the things he knew best.

For a decade Diller had split his time between offices and residences in New York City and Los Angeles. While most of the major movie studios had long before consolidated operations in Los Angeles to save money and to keep the business and creative operations in close contact, Paramount remained split in half. Bluhdorn had enjoyed being able to stroll out of his office over to the Paramount suites, where he would look over the advertising posters being made up and discuss upcoming releases with the distribution executives. It had remained split after Bluhdorn's death, but it was becoming harder for Diller to look forward to trips to New York. Each time, he knew he would see Davis, whom he no longer liked or trusted.

Diller was in a dark mood one morning in the spring of 1984 as he stopped by his office in the Gulf + Western building in Manhattan to attend to some last-minute business. In the back of his mind he hoped to avoid Davis before rushing off to the airport, where the Paramount plane was already warming up on a runway to carry him to California.

Diller stuffed a few papers into his carrying case and dashed down the hall toward the elevator. As he waited impatiently, Diller felt his body tense. Martin Davis was calling to him. Davis said he needed to see Diller "just for a minute."

There was a knot tightening in Diller's stomach. He automatically assumed that Davis was about to criticize him again for not spending sufficient time at Simon and Schuster or worrying about Madison Square Garden. As they talked, however, Diller noticed an edge to Davis's voice. Davis was talking about Michael Eisner.

He told Diller that he didn't think Eisner was a team player and that under his regime, he wanted Paramount to be run more as a team. "I can't live with Eisner any longer," Davis finally blurted out, according to Diller, "Fire him."

Diller was taken aback. He'd had his battles with Eisner, it was true, and recently their relationship had become strained, but he didn't see any reason to break up a winning team.

"Why?" demanded Diller. "Leave him alone!"

"I can't," said Davis, reminding Diller that he himself had complained about Eisner many times in the past. Besides, most of his information about Eisner had come from Diller. The fact of the matter was that Eisner and Davis barely knew each other. Since Davis had become chairman, they had spoken only briefly, partly because both Davis and Diller wanted a clear chain of command. This meant that Eisner had to communicate with the parent company's chairman exclusively through his immediate superior, Diller.

Through a spokesman, Davis later denied trying to fire Eisner at the time, although he was unhappy with the way things were being run.

Eisner, who had no idea that any of this was going on, had certainly been much closer to Charles Bluhdorn than he was to his successor. Quite often over the years, Bluhdorn had called Eisner directly to discuss something that was happening at Paramount. Diller had not complained about this because he knew that it was the way Bluhdorn worked. Gulf + Western's organizational chart was just a bunch of lines on paper. Bluhdorn made up the rules as he went along.

Martin Davis's demand to fire Eisner, as Diller remembers it, struck him as the last straw. In his opinion, the order was in direct conflict with the promises Davis had made the year before. Just thinking about what the demand represented ate at him.

"This is insane," Diller told Davis that spring day in 1984. "And I can't figure out why you're doing this."

Once again Davis claimed that Eisner wasn't a team player, recalled Diller. One example he cited was the way Diller and Eisner split the annual bonus pool of profits. Davis thought they took too much for themselves and didn't share fairly with other Paramount executives (in 1983 Diller got 31 percent, Eisner 26 percent, and all others 43 percent). Diller later learned that Davis had forced another division head to fire his number-two deputy, the purpose being to put the division head in his place. Now, apparently, Davis felt that he could do the same thing with the Paramount team.

Diller later asserted that Davis did not expect him to quit. However, Davis said that Diller's contract was running out later that year and noted that Gulf + Western had made no move to negotiate a new deal. Davis intended to just let it run out.

Diller, who was supposed to be in Los Angeles that night, stood his ground. That "one-minute" meeting lasted eight hours. Diller wouldn't leave until he had convinced Davis not to fire Eisner. By the end of the day, Davis had agreed to put off the decision.

Diller never told Eisner what had happened, but it began to put a considerable strain on their relationship. Eisner took Diller's new coolness to be a signal that there might be problems, but the chill Eisner felt was really just Diller withdrawing into an emotional shell so that he could figure out what to do.

Diller finally got onto the airplane, which had been warming up for more than eight hours for his flight to Los Angeles. He remembers thinking that despite all of the difficulties he had had with Michael Eisner over twenty years, this was not the way it was going to end. Yet in his heart, Diller realized that a fuse had been lit that day and that eventually it would lead to an explosion. What Diller couldn't foresee was that that explosion would rearrange most of the top executive chairs in Hollywood.

"I thought, What am I doing in this company now?" Diller recalled three years after the fact. "I don't have a relationship [with Martin Davis]. I can't function this way. He just threatened me. This is the end for me."

Actually, the end wasn't to arrive for almost six months, but from that day forward both Diller and Davis began making their preparations for it. Even though Eisner had a contract that said that he would be chairman if Diller left, Davis soon would decide that he wanted his close friends Frank Mancuso, Paramount's head of marketing, and Arthur Barron, who oversaw Paramount for Gulf + Western, to run the studio. Both men lived in New York and operated in the more quiet, corporate style Davis admired.

For his part, Diller looked at the entertainment-industry landscape for other opportunities. He quickly zeroed in on the most vulnerable of the studios, Twentieth Century–Fox. A short time later he put in a call to Marvin Davis in Denver and made an offer.

"Marvin," said Diller. "How about selling me half of Twentieth Century–Fox?"

"It's not for sale," replied Davis. "But I might give you 25 percent to run it for me."

"That was not, in effect, my first choice," recalls Diller. "But it began a discussion."

8

WHO OUTFOXED WHOM?

BARRY DILLER AND Marvin Davis approached each other with the finesse of luxury car salesmen trying to bag a hot prospect. Each had something to sell, but neither wanted to appear too anxious. Each had something to hide, at least until after an agreement was reached. Each needed the other, but neither wanted to admit just how badly. And both wanted all negotiations conducted in absolute secrecy, just in case there wasn't a meeting of the minds.

Davis normally would have done extensive background checks and consulted with all of his aides knowledgeable about movies, but this wasn't a normal situation, for two reasons. First, he was dealing with Barry Diller. You don't question living legends as you would a mere mortal, thought Davis. Second, many of the aides Davis would have asked for advice might lose their jobs to make way for Diller, so there would have been a built-in bias.

Davis and Diller couldn't have been more different. Later it would seem obvious that there was no way they could get along. During their courtship, however, both were on their best behavior.

Davis assured Diller that Fox would break even for the year. The truth was that the studio was going to lose money on an operating basis in 1984—aside from any tax write-offs—and that the long-term debt had almost doubled during the previous year. Fox's banks were putting tremendous pressure on Davis to bring in new management capable of turning a bad situation around. Davis had long before realized that for all of his glib charm and easy manners, Alan Hirschfield couldn't do the job. Neither could Norman Levy.

Davis also was tired of being embarrassed by the repeated failure of Fox's movies. Recently, both *Rhinestone,* with Dolly Parton and Sylvester Stallone "singing," and *Two of a Kind,* with John Travolta and Olivia Newton-John, had not only flopped but had made Fox and Davis into laughing stocks. Now Davis, whose youngest daughter had just completed high school in Denver, was getting ready to move his primary residence to Los Angeles. He had just purchased a $21 million mansion from singer Kenny Rogers. Davis wanted to arrive a successful mogul, not just another rich schmuck from out of town.

Davis had no idea that Diller was being edged out of Paramount. Diller's stance throughout the negotiation was that he was loaded with options and was doing Davis a favor. It was a bluff, but then Diller had always been a poker player. In fact, one of his regular poker buddies was Dan Melnick, whose situation at Fox Diller had followed with interest. One reason Diller insisted that his Fox contract contain very strict language stating his power and duties, and his rights in regard to Marvin Davis, was because of what he had learned from Melnick's situation. Diller also was determined to avoid a repeat of his authority problems with Martin Davis.

Out of this emerged a five-year contract, dated October 1, 1984. It was breathtaking, even by Hollywood standards. Diller was to receive a base salary of $3 million, plus 25 percent of any increase in the equity value of the studio during his stewardship—a clause potentially worth millions more. Diller and Davis, said the contract, "will be in frequent and regular contact," but actually were required to meet only twice each year. Davis also was restricted from having contact with Fox employees "in such manner as shall derogate, limit or interfere with Diller." Fox agreed to lend Diller $1.5 million interest-free to pay off a similar loan at Paramount, and guaranteed Diller a generous expense account, insurance, and other executive perks. Diller could walk away at almost any time, but Fox could only get out of the contract if Diller died, breached a specific clause, or was found guilty of a felony. Diller would profit even if he left after five years. He was to get a 17.5 percent share of any appreciation in Fox assets for three years after his contract.

There was also a key-man clause that allowed Diller to leave if Davis sold more than 20 percent of the studio.

Hollywood wags quickly dubbed them "the Odd Couple" and the contract "the Stalin-Hitler pact."

Davis knew that Hirschfield had to go, but he got Diller to promise to give some of the other Fox executives a chance, in particular his friend Norman Levy.

Davis met with Levy and also asked *him* to give *Diller* a chance. Davis genuinely felt that Diller and Levy could work together, just as he secretly felt that Diller wouldn't really hold him to all of the restrictive covenants in his contract about the extent of Davis's influence and about not talking to Fox employees without Diller's permission.

As it turned out, Davis was to be proven wrong on all counts.

With the ink not yet dry on Diller's contact, Davis turned to his next task. He asked Hirschfield to fly to Denver for a chat. Davis really liked Hirschfield but had concluded long ago that he couldn't run the company, control the employees, or pick scripts that would become successful movies.

Davis told Hirschfield that the bankers were forcing him into it. Together they created a scenario in which Hirschfield would be moving to New York to open a new investment firm in partnership with Davis. The story turned out to be a total fabrication. The only thing that was real was that Hirschfield's status would change to consultant, and he would go on collecting his full $500,000 annual salary for two more years of his contract.

After Sherry Lansing left Fox, Hirschfield and Levy had picked a personable producer named Joe Wizan to run production. Although he put the hits *Bachelor Party* and *Revenge of the Nerds* into production, the losers continued to outnumber the winners and Wizan seemed to have difficulty controlling costs. He was out after a year, and Davis stepped in to choose the next head of production. He hired producer Larry Gordon. During negotiations Davis said to Gordon, "Let me ask you a question. These guys are always getting pregnant and before I know it, I'm in for millions of dollars in these pictures and then we don't make the movies. What makes you think the same thing won't happen with you?"

"Marvin," responded Gordon. "I've spent twenty years knocking guys like you up. When I go on the other side of the desk, I'll be on the pill."

Gordon, a lean, personable man with sandy hair and a long, oval face, quickly became a popular figure at the studio, where Hirschfield and Levy pretty much left him alone to do his job. The studio was desperately short of pictures, and Gordon's mandate was to make as many good commercial films as quickly as possible. He still was handicapped, though, because many top creative talents wouldn't come to Fox because of Levy, but he had enough friends in the industry and projects he had initiated before taking over to at least get the machinery moving again.

Now, less than three months after his arrival, Gordon had a bitter pill to swallow indeed. He faced the prospect of working for Barry Diller, whom he had never forgiven for throwing him out when he was at Paramount and who, he was firmly convinced, didn't like him or the movies he made.

Larry Gordon had grown up as part of the only Jewish family in a small city in Mississippi. He spent much of his childhood frightened of redneck bullies who would beat him up, not because he was Jewish but because he was a skinny kid with a big mouth. Later Gordon would say that nobody in the movie business frightened him because all they could do was throw him off the lot.

Gordon started his career at the ABC network and then moved to Columbia Pictures. He was head of production at American International Pictures for three years when it was churning out low-budget B movies for teenagers. As an independent producer, his most successful picture before coming to Fox had been *48 Hrs,* which he followed with *Brewster's Millions* and *Streets of Fire* for Universal, neither of which was well received. Hirschfield had brought him to Fox, where he was in preproduction on *Commando* and *Predator* when tapped for the top production post.

Gordon's successes had already made him a very wealthy man, rich enough, in fact, to do pretty much whatever he wanted. In Hollywood lingo, Gordon had "fuck-you money," meaning that he could tell off anybody he didn't like. He had taken the executive job at Fox because he relished the challenge, but he wasn't willing to stay in an unhappy situation.

With Diller's arrival, Gordon was ready to exercise a clause in his contract that allowed him to return to independent production. Before his first meeting with Diller, Gordon called his old friend Michael Eisner to see what was going on. He learned that Eisner was involved in complicated negotiations to move to the Walt Disney Company as chairman, replacing the late Walt Disney's son-in-law, Ron Miller, who had just been fired. He also learned that Diller had already offered the job of president of Fox, the number two position, to Eisner.

Diller said later that Eisner at first agreed to come to Fox, but later changed his mind when the opportunity arose to take the top job at Disney.

On Diller's first day at Fox, he met with Gordon and several others in the conference room on the ground floor of the executive office building. Diller was in shirt sleeves, but he still had on a starched white shirt and pale blue tie. The slacks of his suit were neatly pressed and his black shoes were highly polished.

Gordon, however, was in jeans and an old shirt open at the neck, with no tie. He didn't see any need for formality, particularly since he didn't even want to keep his job. Gordon certainly wasn't going to bow and scrape to Barry Diller.

Diller was cool and calm. In a voice so soft that everyone in the room had to strain to hear him, Diller said that he really wanted Gordon to stay on. He acknowledged that they had bumped heads in the past but felt they could work together.

Gordon pointed out that he had no obligation to stay once Hirschfield was gone, and said that he had decided to trigger the clause in his contract permitting him to become an independent producer at the studio. He didn't even want to consider staying on; only the terms of his divorce were open to discussion.

Diller again told Gordon he wanted him to remain. He denied that he was trying to bring in Eisner.

"If I knew you were coming here, Barry," said Gordon, "I would never have come. I don't think I can work with you."

From Diller's point of view, if Eisner wouldn't take the job, Gordon was the next best choice—at least until someone better came along.

Gordon finally said that he might stay if certain conditions were met. The primary one was that he had to be named president of the entire studio, not just head of movie and TV production. He wanted the same job that had been offered to Eisner.

The meeting broke up without either man making a final decision.

By the end of Diller's first week, Eisner had been hired as chairman of Disney and Frank Mancuso had been named by Martin Davis as the new chairman of Paramount. With considerable reservations, Gordon then accepted the position of president and chief operating officer at Fox.

Next Diller met with Norman Levy. Fully aware of the problems encountered by Sherry Lansing as well as Levy's reputation at Columbia, Diller knew it was highly unlikely that he would want Levy to remain at Fox. Diller wanted a shift of emphasis from films simply picked up from outside for distribution by Fox, which was Levy's strength, to movies actually made at the studio. Besides, Diller liked being involved in marketing and distribution strategy, which he felt would be impossible with Levy around. Diller also knew through Sherry Lansing and others that there were some important filmmakers who didn't like Levy. Since there were other filmmakers who didn't like Diller because of his tough style at Paramount, the new chairman of Fox felt that he had to reduce his handicaps. Getting rid of Levy was just a matter of timing.

Levy, meanwhile, was disgusted by the turn of events. During the previous two years, Marvin Davis had offered him the top job at least three times, and each time he had refused out of loyalty to Alan Hirschfield. Davis had made his final offer in May 1984 while he and Levy were having dinner one night. According to Levy, Davis had said that Hirschfield's days were numbered. He then said he wanted to know, once and for all, if Levy would take the job. Levy responded that although he supported Hirschfield, he would take the job as chairman. That was the last Levy heard about the job offer until Hirschfield called him from Denver in August to announce that he had just been fired and that Barry Diller was replacing him.

On Diller's first day, he told Levy that he had heard good things about him from Marvin Davis and others. He also said that he was going to take his time making decisions about who to keep. Levy wanted to believe him, but almost immediately he heard that Diller was asking others a lot of questions about marketing and distribution. "It seemed the likely person he would ask about these things would be me," recalls Levy. "When he didn't, I began to feel this thing wouldn't work out."

A week later, late in the day, Diller came into Levy's office, located at the far end of the hallway on the ground floor of the Fox executive office building. Levy was rushing to finish up his work so he could get home. It was the eve of Rosh Hashanah, the Jewish New Year, and Levy was anxious to be with his family. Diller, also Jewish, was aware of the holiday and knew that Levy was leaving for a long weekend. Diller told Levy that it simply wasn't going to work out, that he wished Levy well but he wanted his own team in place.

Levy felt betrayed. Diller had not given him the chance that both he and Davis had promised him. And to cut him down on the eve of the Jewish holidays struck him as a sacrilege.

According to his contract, Levy had until the end of 1984 to decide if he wanted to be an independent producer or a consultant to Fox at his full salary of $750,000 a year. By the time he decided he wanted to consult, however, Diller had decided that Levy was in breach of his contract and refused to give Levy anything.

Levy protested and threatened to sue. Diller and his executives then produced a laundry list of things they said Levy had done to breach his agreement. Some were petty, but others appeared to involve alleged unethical behavior and possibly even illegal activities. There were two key complaints about Levy. The first was that he had improperly manipulated the allocation of certain revenues to selected movies in order to cheat HBO, the largest pay-TV service. The other was that Levy had taken kickbacks, disguised as legal payments, in return for distributing certain movies made by outside producers.

The first charge turned out to be untrue in regard to Levy. Fox's deal with HBO said that how much the pay-TV service paid for a movie was based on how well the picture had done in theaters. There were levels of revenue that triggered higher payments. This was easy to manipulate because movie distributors and the theaters that show their films do a lot of negotiating on final payments. If a film hasn't performed as well as expected, the studio generally will give the exhibitor a break on the "settlement," as it is known as. On other popular films, the exhibitor might pay a bit more. It appears that someone in a Fox sales branch had been manipulating these settlements to make sure that certain films would meet the minimums in the HBO contract. Ultimately, the charges were unproven. The studio said Fox did pay around $1 million back to HBO.

The other charge remained unproven as well. The studio said in court documents that it believed that Levy had made improper deals involving movie pickups. It named several producers that it thought Levy was in cahoots with, including New Century Productions, Cineplex Corporation of Toronto, and a company controlled by producer Arnon Milchan. All involved actively denied any wrongdoing. Levy's attorney called it a "witch hunt" and said Fox was actually just looking for leverage to force his client to renegotiate about $2.5 million in termination payments. None of the allegations were ever proven.

Levy sued Fox for about $21 million, charging that Davis had breached his promise to give him 5 percent of the ownership of the studio and that Fox had failed to live up to the terms of his contract. Eventually it was settled out of court, with Levy receiving approximately $1.5 million. Both his career at Fox and his friendship with Davis were over.

Diller's honeymoon with Marvin Davis, in the meantime, was surprisingly short. Davis soon saw that Diller was not going to attract the top executive talent leaving Paramount. With a few exceptions, these people were following Eisner to Disney. There was more than a little competition involved. Eisner was angry with Diller, who he felt had left him in the lurch at Paramount. Diller had not bothered to warn Eisner in advance when he quit. Later they would rekindle their friendship, but at the end of their long Paramount run, there were clearly a lot of bad feelings.

When executive after executive, beginning with production superstar Jeffrey Katzenberg, opted to join Eisner at Disney rather than Diller at Paramount, it reflected a sense that Diller's management style had alienated a lot of people. Eisner was more the father figure, the protector, while Diller was seen as a challenging, distant figure. Once the executive exodus was over, some of the creative talent—producers, directors, writers, and actors—who had been associated with Paramount under Diller and Eisner also went mainly to Disney. The one notable exception was James L. Brooks, who was drawn to Fox as much by Larry Gordon as by Diller.

From the start the media constantly compared Diller, Eisner, and Mancuso (at Paramount), and Diller was not coming out very well in the analysis. Marvin Davis quickly began to wonder if he had made the right choice.

Davis also discovered that Diller had meant it when he said the Denver oilman was no longer going to meddle. Anybody Davis talked to had to report the conversation back to Diller, which put quite a chill on relationships. Davis also was shocked that Diller had canned Levy and several others so quickly.

Marvin Davis also received a gloating phone call from Martin Davis, who told him that Diller couldn't be trusted and predicted that Diller would not be successful in running Fox. Martin Davis says he only called to congratulate Marvin Davis on hiring Diller.

Davis was beginning to realize just how different he and Diller were. Diller was cool, smart, and careful about what he said. Davis was earthy and emotional and would sometimes blurt out whatever was on his mind.

The relationship also was strained because Diller was shocked by what he found waiting for him at Fox. His first early warning came when he paid a courtesy call on Alan Hirschfield, who was still moving out of his Fox office. He told Hirschfield that Davis had said that Fox would break even for fiscal 1984. Hirschfield laughed and predicted that Fox would lose $70 million.

Diller immediately called Davis and said, "I've just had the most astounding conversation." Davis responded that Hirschfield didn't know what he was talking about. (In fact, Fox ended up doing even worse than Hirschfield had estimated.)

Three weeks after his arrival, Diller met with the Fox bankers, who painted a bleak picture. For the first time, Diller realized that by coming to Fox he had bought time for Davis, who would now be able to extend certain loan agreements. Even so, Diller learned, without some major financial moves, there was no way that Fox would have enough money to continue its operations. Says Diller:

> The overpowering need when I first arrived was to pay the bills. The truth of the matter is that I found out . . . that the company was not only technically bankrupt, but that on the following February 11 the company literally would run out of its last resource, its last penny. Literally, the projection was—and this was endlessly investigated— that the company would be bankrupt and unable to meet its obligations.

During his first few months, Diller added about $40 million to the company's losses by writing off many of the movie and TV projects that had been in development when he arrived—a standard practice in the industry to ensure that a new regime was not saddled with someone else's mistakes. Davis noted that it also had the effect of making things look as bad as possible at the studio. As for Diller, the procedure would allow him to make even more money later on, when things got better, since the agreement was that he would receive 25 percent of the appreciation of Fox's assets.

Diller ruthlessly began to cut costs and look for new sources of revenue. He instituted an across-the-board 15 percent cut in employees in every department and dismissed many of the resident producers, especially those involved in developing movies. Some of them were there because of their friendship with Marvin Davis. Once Diller arrived with his iron-clad contract, however, Davis couldn't save them.

Diller also pushed Davis to dump his high-profile board of directors, which did little but cost a great deal of money. Even worse for

Davis's reputation, most of them had lost money on his oil deals at what turned out to be the top of the market (former president Gerald Ford later said he had broke even). Oil prices had been declining throughout the 1980s. In some cases, including a deal with producer George Lucas *(Star Wars),* Davis dipped into his own pocket and repaid their investments to maintain goodwill.

Diller also confronted Harris Katleman and told him to make massive cuts in budget and personnel in the TV division. In essence, Diller instructed him to fire the entire staff that worked on developing TV movies and miniseries. Fox, Diller said, would no longer fund those kinds of low-profit-margin projects. He also told Katleman to concentrate on getting series on the networks, especially half-hour comedies, which have the highest payoff in the used program aftermarket. Diller, who at ABC had helped invent the TV movie and the miniseries, was now refusing to make them anymore.

At first Katleman was outraged. He didn't think he could do it. Within a year, however, he found not only that the cuts could be made, but that the streamlining actually led to new successes. Katleman also came to appreciate Diller's in-depth knowledge of the TV business and his appreciation of real talent. Katleman was to be one of the few holdovers to survive and prosper under Diller.

Considering what had happened to Katleman under Stanfill, then Hirschfield, and now Diller, a joke made the rounds in Hollywood. They said if there's an earthquake, rush over and stand next to Harris Katleman. He can survive anything.

Diller and Gordon, now Twentieth Century–Fox's chairman and president, respectively, next brought in a new executive to handle finances and administration and to replace Buddy Monash, who was considered too close to Davis. Their choice was Jon Dolgen, a native New Yorker and Cornell University graduate. Dolgen had been a Wall Street lawyer before joining Columbia Pictures, where he rapidly worked his way up the executive ladder. He decided to leave Columbia because they insisted he moved back to New York to work at corporate headquarters. Dolgen and his family wanted to remain in Los Angeles.

Sharp, confident, and aggressive, Dolgen arrived at Fox with a reputation as a tough guy with a thorough understanding of the emerging markets for pay TV and home video. He was a tough negotiator and fit right in with Diller's management style of pushing people to their breaking point.

Dolgen, with dark hair and haunting eyes that seemed full of mischief, was a solidly built man of medium height. If he had played baseball, he probably would have been the fireplug of a catcher who blocked the path to home plate, no matter who was sliding toward him. There was a sense about him of power and the determination to get whatever he wanted. He could be a screamer when angry, but he also quickly showed that he knew how to organize and run a movie studio to get maximum efficiency and profits.

Dolgen began looking for ways to raise money for production. He engineered a new pay-TV deal, arranged for some limited partnership financing for movies, sold some assets, forced CBS/Fox Video to advance the studio money against future movies, and explored going to the stock market for additional financing. "When I got here in January '85 the place was a mess," says Dolgen. "The entire infrastructure appeared to have broken down. The way they thought about lawyering, about finances, about information flow, [about] control of their library—all of it was outdated by a decade at least. No one had gotten down and gotten the job done."

Fox also was burdened by a very large debt of around $430 million, which required a continuous flow of cash just to pay off interest charges of around $70 million a year. Diller realized that there simply wasn't adequate capital to bring down the debt and produce new movies and TV shows.

Diller also knew that under his contract with Davis, the oilman was required to put money into Fox to insure sufficient resources to make new products. When he pressed Davis for additional funding, however, Davis kept putting him off, forcing Diller to keep finding other ways to raise money. The relationship between Davis and Diller was deteriorating rapidly. Diller was terse with Davis on the phone and usually avoided contact when the oilman made his occasional visits to Fox. Both men sensed that they were headed for a showdown.

Davis, unwilling to invest additional money in Fox, suggested that Diller see Michael Milken at Drexel Burnham Lambert in Beverly Hills and arrange for the studio to borrow $250 million. Milken had become famous as the "King of Junk Bonds," securities carrying an unusually high interest rate that are used to finance companies that are not huge or well known or considered blue chip. Brilliant but low-key, Milken operated like a "godfather," with a strict code of loyalty, doling out favors to some and collecting favors from others. Later he would be caught up in a huge scandal involving insider trading and other violations of securities laws and would be forced out of Drexel Burnham Lambert. But in 1984, when Diller met him, Milken was still on top.

Diller was forced to learn a whole new vocabulary. At Paramount he had never had to deal with finance or stock market issues. Now he had to learn many financial terms. As he had throughout his life, he educated himself. He read books and talked to people who understood Wall Street and finance. Milken was concerned about the weakened financial condition of Fox but agreed to sell $250 million in high-interest commercial paper. Diller became caught up in the process and worked on the prospectus.

Diller, however, had second thoughts shortly before the $250 million offering was made to investors. "Until then I wasn't morally responsible for the money owed to the banks," says Diller. "I learned [that] if I raised this new money, and went out with the road show [to meet investors around the United States] to sell it, it would be on my head."

Diller made the two-hour drive from Los Angeles to Palm Springs one Saturday to meet with Davis. The oilman's large, modern desert resort home was in one of the most posh areas of the city and was surrounded by a well-guarded wall. Diller made his way in from the bright sunshine to the dark interior hall, and after a short wait he was ushered into the library, Davis's office. Davis was on the phone.

Diller was in no mood for small talk. He quickly told Davis that he had decided it would be impossible for him to go forward with the Drexel bond offering. "I'll only do it if you will sell me actual equity in this company," Diller said. "I don't mean 25 percent of X to Y. I mean I want to own assets. My equity contribution in return will be the $250 million I'm raising."

Davis said no.

"Then why should I raise it?" asked Diller.

Davis's eyes narrowed. "You have no choice," said Davis. "You've left your other job. You're here. It is your mess now."

Diller couldn't believe his ears. Suddenly Diller remembered a friend who had warned him about Davis just before he took the Fox job. The friend had said that everybody who got into business deals with Davis got burned, while Davis always walked away richer. Davis was unbeatable.

Diller left, angry and dejected. The Diller-Davis relationship would never recover.

Diller returned to Los Angeles and told Milken that the deal would not go through. Feeling defrauded by Davis, Diller called his attorney, who wrote the first in a series of letters warning Davis that, in Diller's opinion, his contract was being breached as long as Davis refused to inject new equity into Fox. One early letter from Diller's lawyer to Davis's attorney warned:

Mr. Diller is going out of his mind over this mess. He must spend all of his time straightening out the company. We write because we can't deal with Mr. Davis in any other way. . . . We are only deferring action on this breach for now because the first priority is to get the company out of trouble.

Davis, in the meantime, found an unexpected benefit in the huge losses Fox suffered during 1984 and 1985. For months he had been negotiating with the U.S. Justice Department to acquire the half interest in Fox held by his silent partner Marc Rich, who had by then become a fugitive from American justice. Thanks to the losses piled up by the studio, Davis was able to place an extremely low valuation on the company when working out how much he would pay.

Rich had never taken an active role at Fox. He had visited the studio a few times and chatted with the various executives he met at Davis's annual Carousel Ball. In late 1981, Rich had told Davis that he wanted to get more involved. He wanted to switch his shares to voting stock, which would give him an equal say with Davis. His intention was stated in an SEC filing made public in January 1982. Before it could be carried out, however, Rich's world began to collapse.

Legally the Fox shares were held by Richco, a subsidiary of Marc Rich and Company, of New York, which for tax purposes was based in Netherland Antilles. A shady, secretive character, Rich was known as a highly aggressive commodities trader who made millions buying and reselling crude oil, natural gas, and other products. The government began an investigation of Rich and his partner Pincus Green, which led to a series of charges in September 1983. The U.S. attorney in New York charged that Rich and others were involved in the biggest tax evasion case in U.S. history, amounting to about $48 million. They also were charged with racketeering and with illegally trading oil with Iran during the official U.S. boycott imposed during the Iran hostage crisis of 1979 and 1980. When Rich and company refused to turn over certain records to a grand jury, they were fined about $20 million in penalties. Rich and Green fled to Switzerland and became fugitives. The U.S. government then froze all of their assets, including the Fox stake.

Davis wasn't the only one interested in Rich's half of Fox. Although he still owned MGM and United Artists, Kirk Kerkorian saw the library and other assets of Fox as valuable property. Through attorney Gregson Bautzer, Kerkorian made active representations to Rich in Switzerland and had discussions with Davis.

As it turned out, the Justice Department wanted to keep things relatively simple. It just wanted the money from selling Rich's half of Fox so it could be applied against what Marc Rich owed in fines and penalties. The feds saw Davis as the logical buyer, since he owned the other half and, under his contract with Rich, had right of first refusal on any sale of the Fox shares. Shortly after Diller arrived, the Justice Department agreed to sell Rich's half to Davis for the bargain-basement price of $116 million plus assumption of Rich's half of the debt.

There were some who said the price was too low. Davis suggested that they look at the Fox balance sheet, which was bleeding red ink.

Marvin Davis had once again paid a fire-sale price for stock he knew he eventually would resell at a tremendous premium over what it had cost him.

9

LIFE ON THE EDGE

ON A COOL, CLEAR southern California morning in early 1985, Barry Diller gazed out of the window of his office in the Fox executive office building and thought about how far he had come and how much farther he had to go. He had not let the small minds at William Morris, ABC, Paramount, or anywhere else stop him in the past. And now he had no intention of playing dead to please Marvin Davis.

The more he thought about it, the more angry Diller became. He remembered how bitter he had felt when he called off the $250 million Drexel offering. He knew that without additional capital, he couldn't make the movies and TV shows that would place Fox—and Diller—at the top of Hollywood once again. He became determined to find a way to convince Davis to inject additional funds. It wasn't as if he was asking Davis to throw money away. He would build the value of the studio over time, and in the short term, Davis's return on whatever he invested would be greater than he could realize on almost any other investment.

Diller decided that would be his approach. He wouldn't make demands. He would create a business plan that was fully reasoned and well thought out. He would show Davis why it made sense to invest $150 million. He would make his case and Davis would listen and they would both benefit.

Although born and bred in affluence, Barry Diller had always operated like someone with something to prove. He had always pushed a little harder than normal, whether it was to have fun, to move his career forward, or to accomplish a corporate goal. Now he would draw on everything he had ever learned or thought or believed to convince Marvin Davis that it was in both of their interests to provide the resources to make Fox great again.

Barry Diller was born in San Francisco on February 2, 1942, but by age seven he had moved with his mother, father, and older brother Donald to Beverly Hills. His mother, who passed away in 1986, was a charming, strong-willed woman who had been a powerful influence in his life. However, it appears his father, who constantly challenged him, was the one who shaped Diller into someone who could never be satisfied with simple answers.

His father and uncle ran Diller Housing, which built thousands of tract homes in the years immediately following World War II in the San Fernando Valley, West Covina, and other parts of southern California. Most were modest dwellings sold to war veterans with government-backed mortgages. When the housing market cooled, Diller Housing moved into office buildings and other commercial real estate.

Barry and Donald, who was killed in the 1960s in a motorcycle accident, attended public school in Beverly Hills. Many of his schoolmates came from show-business families, including the children of Dean Martin, Oscar Levant, and Lana Turner, although Diller doesn't remember being enthralled by "the biz."

When he was about sixteen, Diller's friend Terri Thomas, daughter of entertainer Danny Thomas, introduced him to a recent transfer from Connecticut, Terry Melcher, the son of actress Doris Day. They became best friends and a frequent foursome with Terri Thomas and Judy Lovejoy, daughter of actor Frank Lovejoy.

As a child, Diller had no hobbies that he can remember, and he claims to have been a terrible student who frequently skipped school. Melcher remembers Diller as one of the most popular kids at Beverly Hills High and one of the few who was at home both with the rowdy crowd and the preppy clique. "He was more grown up than the rest of us," recalls Melcher, now a successful record producer ("Kokomo" by the Beach Boys, among many others). "He had crazy friends, but he also had the kind of friends who ran student government, although Barry himself was never involved."

Diller and Melcher would carpool to school most mornings. Melcher automatically would dial the radio to a rock and roll station, while Diller preferred either classical, Frank Sinatra, or his favorite, Judy Garland.

It was the end of the Eisenhower era, before drugs and the Beatles, and Beverly Hills was still a kind of small town where everybody knew one another. Diller and his pals would go to concerts to see such pop stars as Bobby Darin, or to clubs like the Coconut Grove, Ciros, and the Cloisters.

Although he wasn't much of a student, Diller's family used their influence to get him into Stanford University in Palo Alto, south of San Francisco. First, however, he was required to successfully complete a course in Stanford's summer prep school. He lasted only a few weeks before deciding Stanford was not for him.

Back in Los Angeles, Diller enrolled at UCLA but dropped out in less than four months. After that he just laid around for about half a year, much to his father's displeasure. It was then that Diller decided he wanted to be in show business. He had heard that a good place to start was the mailroom at William Morris, the largest and best-known talent agency in the world. He applied but wasn't hired. So Diller repeatedly phoned family friend Danny Thomas, then one of William Morris's biggest clients. He finally reached Thomas in his dressing room at the Las Vegas hotel where he was working and asked for help. Diller gave Thomas the name to call at William Morris and wouldn't hang up until Thomas promised to do it the very next day. Diller was hired in the William Morris mailroom within a week.

Diller soon learned to get his mailroom chores out of the way quickly, leaving him the rest of the day to read memos, telexes, contracts, letters, and anything else that passed through. He would go to the big file room and pull out everything the agency had on a certain star. He would read the contracts, deal memos, letters, biographies, receipts. "They encouraged everybody to share information and I read everything," recalls Diller. "I stayed in the mailroom longer than almost anybody because I didn't want to leave. I was learning so much. It was like going to school."

He moved on to become secretary to a top television agent and then became an assistant (or junior agent) and was sent around with the senior staff to observe and learn. "I was monstrously curious about the whole thing," says Diller, "but I had no idea how I would put this to work, since I didn't want to be an agent."

When Diller was twenty-three, Terri Thomas's sister Marlo introduced him to the man she was dating. Leonard Goldberg, then in his early thirties, had just taken over as head of programming for the ABC network on the West Coast. He was impressed by Diller and offered him a job as his assistant. "I told Sam Weisbord [then president of William Morris] that I was leaving," Diller remembers. "He looked up from his fruit salad and said, 'Well, we sure wasted a lot of money on you.'"

Shortly after joining ABC in 1967, the head of the network's programming in New York quit, and Goldberg was tapped to replace him. "Leonard called me," says Diller, "and told me we were going to New York."

As the 1960s came to a close, Diller left his family home for the first time and began his new life as a TV executive living in a tiny garden apartment on Seventy-sixth Street in Manhattan. He arrived an assistant, but Diller was soon running the department. "I was a monster of such proportions you couldn't even calculate it," Diller laughs. "I had an immense amount of power much too early and an immense amount of enthusiasm and a sense of what was right and wrong."

Diller is credited with having invented the made-for-television movie. Until then, when a TV network wanted to run a movie, it bought one that already had been shown in theaters, typically for about $800,000 per title. What Diller and others at ABC came up with was a two-hour movie that was made to be shown on TV and that cost only about $400,000. So the network got original programming at half the cost.

Diller claims to have gotten more credit than he deserved for development of the TV movie. He calls it a team effort.

Diller played a more definite role in the development of the multi-part TV miniseries. Universal Studios had produced a show for ABC that, when completed, was designed to run for four hours on TV. Diller hated the Universal project, but he liked the idea of a longer program form. He realized that while many novels were too complex to be made into movies, they were perfect for multi-part television. As an experiment, he took an option on the rights to a powerful book about World War II called *QB VII,* by Leon Uris.

By that time, Len Goldberg had left ABC and was a producer at Screen Gems, a large production company. Diller asked Goldberg to make *QB VII* into a series of interrelated TV movies that would be run together. "Screen Gems didn't want to do it," said Diller. "They asked me what we would do with it. Spend $250,000 for rights to a TV show?! Nobody had ever paid $2."

But Diller finally convinced Screen Gems, and *QB VII* was a smash hit, drawing a larger audience on its second night than it had on the first. The miniseries format was launched.

Jack Valenti, the longtime president of the Motion Picture Association of America, who has observed Diller closely since he first moved to Paramount in 1974, noted that Diller seemed to change to meet the challenges of each new job. "He's grown sizably," says Valenti. "When he took over Fox a lot of people there called me and said, 'What kind of man is Barry Diller?' I said, 'You'll think he's remote, sometimes glacial, sometimes he seems to put a shield in front of him. He's a hard man to know, tough, thick-skinned. But he's also a man capable of unwavering loyalty, support, [and] affection, and if he's with you, he will not cut and run. He will stand with you. He's a guy who cares. He just doesn't wear it on his sleeve.'"

One of Diller's closest friends, superstar manager and producer Sandy Gallin, whose clients include Dolly Parton, believes that Diller went to Fox in search of a challenge. "He worked hard at Paramount and got it totally organized," says Gallin. "It became enormously successful, and he started to enjoy life. He had a gigantic amount of time to do things, for recreation. I think he became bored and wanted a major challenge again."

Gallin explains that Diller lives his life for the calculated risk. "Fun for Barry is going on motorcycles, doing things others might call dangerous," says Gallin. "He loves to play in the ocean: boats, water-skiing, jet ski. He loves to snow ski and he likes to be a daredevil. . . . He has a sense of adventure. He has enormous energy, the same energy in his personal life that he has in business."

Valenti describes Diller as someone who operates with a unique vision and supreme confidence: "He is a man who is not afraid to buckle on armor and go into the field to do battle."

So in early 1985, Diller prepared for his financial battle with Marvin Davis. He was determined not to be stopped from making Fox a success.

Diller carefully formulated his presentation to Marvin Davis to convince him to inject new capital into Twentieth Century–Fox and get the company moving again. Diller told Jon Dolgen what they would need. Over the next couple of weeks, Diller, Dolgen, and others at the studio worked many, many hours shaping logical arguments, and developing materials to support their request.

The presentation was made to Davis in the main conference room at the studio. Davis had just arrived for a visit and had left his jacket behind in his office. Diller, also in shirt sleeves, with a silk off-white tie, pushed his distaste for Davis aside and put his heart into selling his plan. He told Davis that with additional equity, they could turn the studio around and Fox's value would soar. Davis would then have many more options. He could borrow money against the enhanced value of the studio, he could sell part of it to the public at a premium, or he could borrow money from private sources at a more reasonable rate of interest.

"If you believe in these businesses at all," added Dolgen, "then you have to believe that this is a better investment than anything else you will find."

There were charts, projections, analyses, all covered with figures that supported Diller's request. After more than two hours, Diller felt he had spilled his guts on the table.

Davis, recalls Dolgen, was "nonresponsive." He just sat passively and listened. And then he said no.

When Diller alluded to possible legal action to force Davis to live up to his contractual promises, Davis just shrugged. He had lots of lawyers and wasn't about to be pushed into anything he didn't want to do.

Later, faced with Diller's lawyer's threats of a messy public lawsuit, Davis offered a compromise: rather than taking a dividend of $50 million from money about to be paid to the studio as an advance from the CBS/Fox Video venture, as he had originally planned, Davis would leave it in the studio as new working capital. He also engineered a new $400 million line of credit from a group of banks led by Continental Illinois. But that was as far as he would go.

Diller, who expected Davis to put up at least two or three times that amount in new equity, was enraged. He instructed his attorney to proceed putting Davis on notice that he was breaching the contract. Diller was determined to force him to either put in more— much more—or else move aside and make room for somebody who would. "I said [to Marvin Davis] 'It's very simple,' " Diller recalls. " 'You either make an agreement to sell the company, or I sue you for fraud. Because I have no choice. I'm in this company hook, line, and sinker.' "

From then on, Diller and Davis were engaged in open warfare. Any pretense of friendship between the two men was now dropped, and each began to use derogatory pet names when referring to the other.

Davis's view was that he was still in charge and that he had no obligation to sell out or bring in a partner. He said he wanted to pass Fox on to his children. Still, Davis wanted to avoid a public lawsuit. Davis briefly considered simply firing Diller and paying off his contract. But he knew that would get him into hot water with his bankers. Besides it wouldn't be easy to replace Diller.

Faced with the imminent prospect of Diller's lawsuit, Davis decided it was time to lay off some of the risk. After all, he now owned 100 percent of the studio, and he had long ago taken enough cash out of the studio to cover his entire original purchase cost. Davis concluded that the time had come to sell at least part of his Fox holdings.

Davis began to explore his options with his bankers and advisors. What he quickly discovered was that there were lots of potential buyers for the studio, some who would pay a price Davis would consider. However, there was no one willing to buy half of Fox, which was what Davis wanted. Davis still liked owning a studio too much to simply walk away, and his family was even more strongly against a sale.

There was one buyer, the bankers said, who might be willing to buy just half. He already had inquired about the availability of Fox several times. His name: Rupert Murdoch.

Davis picked up the phone and called Murdoch, the Australian-born media mogul whose U.S. properties already included the *New York Post,* the *Chicago Sun–Times* and *New York* magazine.

Oddly, on the very day that Davis called, Murdoch was thinking about Twentieth Century–Fox. He had made a note to ask his key executives whether Fox might be for sale.

Murdoch had come close to buying a share of Fox once before. During the period when Dennis Stanfill was looking for someone to help him do a leveraged buyout, some bankers had approached Murdoch about taking 40 percent interest. Murdoch had been interested, but Stanfill had seemed hesitant to give up so much control. Murdoch had studied the situation in some detail and liked the prospects, but before he could act, Davis had arrived and made a preemptive bid.

Later, in 1984, Murdoch had invested in Warner Communications, whose stock was depressed because of the huge losses suffered by its Atari video game division. Murdoch's initial intent had not been to take over Warner, according to Stanley Shulman, an investment banker at Allen and Company in New York, a member of the News Corp, board, and one of Murdoch's closest advisors on financial matters. "[Warner chairman] Steve Ross misread Rupert's intentions," insists Shulman.

Murdoch and Ross had both gone to Shulman's country home for a day of recreation and to discuss a possible purchase of all or part of Warner's interest in Showtime, the pay-TV network, by News Corp. Warner had announced that it was selling its share of Showtime because of its Atari-induced difficulties. "At the end of the day Murdoch said to Ross, 'Do you mind if I buy some Warner shares?' " Shulman recalls. "Then as we bought, we kept Steve informed."

Still, he says, Ross became alarmed as Murdoch raised his stake to 5.6 percent of Warner Communications, then worth about $140 million. Says Shulman, "Steve called a meeting with Rupert and myself and said, 'Look, this is disruptive. Please stop.' We said, 'We're a public company and we have a right to make an investment, but we have no intention of doing anything more [to take over Warner]. We're here and prepared to be your friend.' "

Instead, Ross reacted to Murdoch like a rooster seeing a fox enter the henhouse. Ross called Shulman in late December and said that in twenty minutes, Warner would be announcing a deal in which Chris-Craft—the company controlled by Herb Siegel—was to buy a large block of Warner stock. This would make it impossible for Murdoch to take control of Warner and, in effect, would isolate his block of stock, whose value would now fall. "The litigation between News Corp. and Warner by then had taken on a life of its own," says Shulman. "It had gotten quite nasty."

Despite his reputation as a tough corporate predator, Murdoch hated the negative publicity he was getting from the Warner investment. He felt it was exactly the wrong image for him to build in America. "I'm about building a company. I'm not about making money in the stock market. I thought I was getting quite the wrong reputation," recalls Murdoch.

Murdoch agreed to let Warner buy him out for about $180 million, a profit of $41.5 million on his initial investment. Warner also reimbursed Murdoch $8 million for his legal and administrative expenses.

Murdoch, who already owned a TV network in Australia, believed that communications, media, and entertainment would be the most important businesses in the future and that they would be driven by quality programming. If a show was good enough, Murdoch reasoned, it always would attract advertising revenue. After his skirmish with Warner Communications, Murdoch's desire to own a company that could produce that kind of high-quality programming with worldwide appeal remained unrequited.

When Davis called Murdoch and offered to discuss the sale of half of his interest in Fox, Davis admitted that the studio was pretty close to being broke and needed more cash. Davis said that he wasn't prepared to put in more cash, so he was looking for a partner who would inject new equity.

Murdoch wanted to buy all of Twentieth Century–Fox. But he quickly decided that half was better than nothing. He felt that the problems at the studio were primarily a hangover from the previous regime. "We put our faith in [Barry Diller]," says Murdoch. "Certainly I never intended to be the silent partner that Marc Rich had been."

Murdoch's News Corp. agreed to pay a total of $250 million for 50 percent of Fox. Of that, $162 million went to Davis for the half ownership Davis bought from Rich six months before for $116 million. In addition, Murdoch agreed to advance Fox an additional $88 million to get the studio going again. Davis also agreed to use most of the money that he would receive in the deal to retire the Fox bank debt and reduce its long-term debt.

Diller, who knew Murdoch only slightly, immediately became concerned about his own position. The change in ownership gave him the right to cancel his Fox contract. Instead, Diller insisted on drawing up a new agreement that kept all of the previous contract in force, but also gave him the right, without stating any reason, to just walk away from Fox any time within one year.

Davis pleaded with Diller not to make such a demand. He felt it would scare off Murdoch. Diller responded that he would tell Murdoch his reasons personally. When he did, Murdoch just said, "Fine, I'll take my chances."

Diller also used Murdoch's arrival to make things a lot less cozy at Fox for Davis. Diller told Davis he could no longer use studio services for free, since the partnership had to account to both partners for everything. Davis would now be billed for his office space, secretary, and all personal items, including any services provided each year for the Carousel Ball. "You will not bill me for those things," stormed back Davis. "I'm still a partner in this company. I still own 50 percent."

"Your 50 percent entitles you simply to attend joint-venture meetings about this partnership," Diller replied coolly. "It doesn't entitle you to another single thing."

At that moment, Davis knew there had been a subtle shift in power. It just wasn't going to be as much fun at Fox anymore. The studio was no longer his private reserve.

The press speculated that Murdoch never would be satisfied with only half ownership. The *Wall Street Journal,* shortly after the deal was announced, quoted an unnamed investment banker who said, "It won't be long before Rupert Murdoch owns or controls Fox outright. He's really a one-man band. He's not passive and not collaborative."

Barry Diller quickly found that he and Murdoch were in tune on most issues. Davis soon found that he was being outnumbered two to one on every issue. Davis wasn't going to be pushed around, but he was definitely the odd man out at the new Fox.

10

MISUNDERSTOOD MOGUL

RUPERT MURDOCH HAD been a shadowy player on the world stage for almost twenty years when he bought into Twentieth Century–Fox. Yet he remained one of the most misunderstood players. In the United States much of his image problem stemmed from his management of the *New York Post,* which he had acquired in 1976. It had turned into a gossipy, sensationalistic tabloid frequently featuring lurid headlines. Since the American media is concentrated in New York—where he was synonymous with the *Post*—Murdoch came to be seen as a sleazy journalist playing to the lowest human values.

In England, where Murdoch owned both the best newspaper (the *Times*) and the worst newspaper (the *Sun*), in addition to some TV interests, he was seen as a ruthless businessman and union buster.

In Australia, where he owned both a TV network and several of the major newspapers, the public generally viewed his accomplishments in a positive light, although some were embarrassed by his methods. "He's seen as a very powerful man who has become important all over the world, which makes many people here very proud," explains an Australian journalist who has observed Murdoch's career closely for many years. "However, there's also a large group of people who are very, very mad that he owns 60 percent to 70 percent of the Australian print media and a lot of his papers are just garbage."

No matter how radical his ideas or how sensational his publications, Murdoch himself had become increasingly conservative over the years in manner, dress, and politics. A tall, trim man of medium build, he took to wearing dark suits and white shirts with subdued neckties. His oval face grew in character with age, as a hint of gray crept up from his sideburns until it became a shock of off-white set against his black hair. His thick, bushy eyebrows sat over deep-set eyes. The prominent nose and thick lips that filled out his jowled face seemed in contrast to his Australian-accented voice, which was high-pitched and surprising soft.

As his reputation grew, Murdoch himself seemed to change little. What few people realized was that Murdoch saw himself simply as a businessman with a unique operating style, not as the outrageous media mogul others painted him as. Unlike other executives managing an enterprise the size and scope of Murdoch's News Corp. and its many subsidiaries, he made almost no long-range plans. He might carry in his head a list of twenty-five or so companies or media properties that he would like to acquire, but he had no timetable for adding them to his holdings. Murdoch was the ultimate opportunist. His style was to improvise to fit the moment, buying up whatever became available.

Murdoch's acquisitions were tied closely to his vision of where the world economy and society were headed. That vision provided him with a philosophical net that encompassed all of his diverse activities.

Murdoch's vision was of an integrated world economy. He believed that media and entertainment companies increasingly must think in global terms to maximize the value of the products they produce. He saw quality programming as the lure to sell advertising all over the world.

That didn't mean that the same sixty-second TV commercial would work in every country or that one newspaper would satisfy readers on every continent. Murdoch was smart enough to know that most media is essentially local and must fit its environment. At the same time, however, he realized that business was growing multinational, creating new opportunities on a global scale.

One of Murdoch's News Corp.'s landmark deals was with the Gillette Company, one of the world's largest makers of razors, razor blades, and related items. In a single transaction with Gillette's New York City advertising agency, Murdoch sold the right to run ads on News Corp. media properties via TV and in print in the United States, Europe, and Australia. In each place, the advertisements were different, to fit local tastes, but the idea that they could all be sold as one was revolutionary. It also turned out to be very difficult to repeat, although Murdoch clearly hoped to do more such multinational, cross-media sales in the future.

Throughout the 1970s and 1980s, Murdoch's moves were geared to take advantage of this emerging world economy. He envisioned creating the single best-positioned corporation in the world to take advantage of media expansion, increasing leisure time, multinational brand advertising, an increasing thirst for information, and an endless desire for entertainment.

He considered his acquisition of Fox a giant step in the realization of his vision. Said Murdoch during an interview in his office at Twentieth Century–Fox:

> A really integrated media company has to be in the production of entertainment. It also has to be in news reporting. For both the question is one of how do you present it? In magazine form? Or television form? For all those things you've got to have a foot in the creative processes. Making movies is part of that. I went to entertainment not to get into entertainment. It was part of a broad strategy to get into the media industry, the heart of the media industry. I know you really can't talk about one global economy, but there really is. There are certain things that are common. Hollywood is still the magnet for the most talent. Studios here still have the preeminent position. So if one owns a studio, it's a great opportunity.

To many it was mind-boggling that someone from Australia would be the world's leading media mogul as the twentieth century draws to a close. However, if one examines Murdoch's background, one would see that Murdoch had prepared himself step by step. He might not always have known where he was going, but he always used the last step as a way to reach the next.

Keith Rupert Murdoch was born at midnight on March 11, 1931 in Avonhurst Private Hospital in Melbourne, Australia. Almost immediately it was decided to call him Rupert, to avoid confusion with his father, Sir Keith Arthur Murdoch, a veteran journalist and political kingmaker who was the head of (but didn't own) the largest Australian newspaper chain. Rupert's grandfather had been a prominent Presbyterian minister in a suburb of Melbourne.

Young Rupert began his journalistic career as editor of his high school newspaper. He also edited a literary magazine and was a leading debater.

The summer after high school graduation, his father arranged for Rupert to become a junior reporter on the *Melbourne Herald,* covering police and the courts. He then moved to England for college, taking a job as a cub reporter on the *Birmingham Gazette* for a short time.

In October 1950 Murdoch enrolled in Worcester College, which was part of Oxford University. He was politically active in left-wing causes and showed an interest in socialism, but he wasn't universally popular. His most serious scrape came when he campaigned to be treasurer of the Labour Club, which would be comparable to the Young Democrats in the United States, and broke rules against campaigning openly. He was forced to drop out of the campaign.

His father died suddenly on October 3, 1952, while Rupert was still a student at Oxford. Rupert flew home for the funeral and then back to Oxford for another year while the estate was being settled. He was determined to operate his father's newspaper holdings, despite skepticism within the Australian establishment about whether he was old enough or seasoned enough for the task. To bolster his credentials he spent several months working on London's *Daily Express* before returning home.

After estate taxes, the only things left from his father's holdings were the *Adelaide News* and *Sunday Mail,* small papers in a small city. When Rupert took them over, circulation was stagnant and revenues were declining. Young Rupert threw himself into the administration, finances, and distribution of the papers. It was also there that Murdoch, generally shy around women, met his first wife, Pat Booker. They married in a Presbyterian church on March 1, 1956. She had been born in Sydney and raised in Melbourne, and for a time seemed to offer him a taste of the sophistication of those larger cities. Soon, however, his constant travel and intense concentration on business made her feel left out. She found it difficult to adjust to his aggressive plans to expand and his completely unpredictable schedule, particularly after the birth of their daughter Prudence.

The *Adelaide News* became the first of many media operations that Murdoch would take from poverty to prosperity. As soon as there were profits, he used them to buy more properties, beginning with a local magazine and a radio station.

While in Adelaide, Murdoch relied heavily on the editor of the *News,* an old family friend who became a mentor in the early days of Murdoch's publishing career. Later, when that editor got the publication embroiled in a heated controversy, Murdoch stood by him, even though he could see it was cutting into advertising revenues. Soon afterward, however, Murdoch forced his former mentor out and replaced him with an editor who would tow his line. It established a pattern. Murdoch wanted strong editors, but only as long as they followed his direction. It was also one of the very few times he seemed moved enough by the morality of an issue to risk the political and commercial success of his business. Subsequently, he evolved into a smart businessman who shaped his company to make as much money as possible, even if its methods—and sensational approach—offended many.

When the Australian government offered the first TV station license in Adelaide, Murdoch applied immediately. After much political infighting, he got a controlling interest in his first TV station. He took time off to travel around the world, studying television operations in preparation. Out of that trip came his idea to start an Australian *TV Guide* called *TV Week,* which became one of the most successful new publications in the history of Australia.

In 1959, shortly after Murdoch's first TV station went on the air in Adelaide, he bought a chain of weekly newspapers in Sydney. Over the next decade Murdoch, who moved to Sydney in 1960, continued to acquire newspapers and television properties all over Australia.

Not long after the move to Sydney, Murdoch's first marriage failed. It was a bitter, deeply unhappy parting, especially for his daughter Prudence. It ended with legal wrangling that led to a financial settlement.

Soon after his divorce, Murdoch was interviewed by a cub reporter for one of his own papers. Pretty eighteen-year-old Anna Torv became his second wife in 1967. A much stronger willed woman than his first wife, she had three children, then began her own career as a novelist.

In 1964, Murdoch launched the *Australian,* the first national newspaper of Australia. For once it was a serious, thoughtful publication that dealt with important political and social issues. It was also a money-loser; but Murdoch showed the kind of determination that was to mark his career. For twenty years, through numerous refinements and a string of editors, he supported and nurtured the *Australian,* until it finally became not only an important national voice but also a solid success commercially.

Murdoch was able to support the *Australian* only because he was making a great deal of money with papers like the *Mirror* (Sydney), which used sensational headlines and bold graphics to attract readers.

In 1968 Murdoch made his first major acquisition outside Australia, the *News of the World* in London. As was his pattern, he promised to keep the old management in place, but soon after taking ownership he installed his own people.

Murdoch was able to reenergize the *News of the World,* which published only on Sundays, and it began to make him a great deal of money. Soon he decided that it was wasteful for his presses to sit idle for most of the week. He bought another failing paper, the *Sun,* which he remade into the most outrageous newspaper in London, a city with some very racy tabloids. Along with bold headlines and often wild, improbable articles, the *Sun* was famous for running a picture of a topless woman each day on its third page.

Although Murdoch began to make a great deal of money in England, both he and his wife apparently felt they were being treated as social outcasts. No matter what he did, and no matter who he cultivated among the top political and social figures, the Murdochs weren't recognized for being the leading citizens they felt they had become.

Murdoch had found Australia too confining. Then he found England too stuffy. It didn't accommodate his expanding life-style and ambition. He began to think about the United States, where he had traveled frequently. The United States encouraged his free-wheeling style of opportunistic capitalism, and New York City welcomed the rich, handsome couple with the quaint Australian accents.

Murdoch wanted to own U.S. newspapers, but he wanted to start small, learn, and then grow. In 1973 he acquired the San Antonio, Texas, *Express* and the *News* for $19.7 million. He applied English-Australian style tabloid journalism, which bumped up circulation but which also established his reputation in American journalism for sensationalism.

In 1979 Murdoch had engineered the purchase of the Ten Network in Australia, one of the two major broadcasters. Murdoch had danced around some sticky rules requiring the owner to actually live in Australia by claiming a dual residence in Sydney and New

York City. Later he arranged to have the language of the law changed so that it required him only to be a citizen, a status that eventually would force him to make other changes.

Murdoch studied the U.S. market and was most impressed by the *National Enquirer,* a tabloid distributed primarily at supermarket checkout counters. When he couldn't buy the *Enquirer,* Murdoch in 1974 created a similar publication called the *National Star,* later renamed simply the *Star.* It used an established formula of big, splashy headlines that promised information on subjects like UFOs, new diets, ways to improve your love life and so on. By the early 1980s it was selling over four million copies a week. His biggest move into U.S. newspapers, however, was still to come.

In 1976 Murdoch acquired the money-losing *New York Post.* Although he had promised to leave it intact, Murdoch quickly changed the editorial policy from moderate liberal to screaming tabloid with a conservative political slant. Many U.S. journalists were outraged because Murdoch imported English and Australian journalists as well as their editorial policies. While in the United States there is a complete separation of the news and editorial or opinion sections, the opposite is true in Australia and England. Murdoch applied the Australian policy in New York, pushing his favorite politicians, such as New York City's mayor Ed Koch, not only on the editorial page but also in news stories in the front section. The *Post* also slammed his political favorite's opponents in numerous stories. Media-savvy politicians soon realized the value of a Murdoch endorsement, and it gave him power that was far out of proportion to the circulation of the *New York Post.*

Despite raising the circulation with his tabloid approach, Murdoch was never able to make the *Post* a financial success. His problem was that in the United States, the kind of readers the *Post* attracted were more efficiently reached by advertisers through television. As one department store owner told Murdoch in an oft-quoted remark, "Rupert, the reason we won't advertise in the *Post* is that your readers are our shoplifters."

Murdoch had been helped in his purchase of the *Post* by Clay Felker, a well-known journalist who then was editing *New York* magazine, the role model for slick city journalism. Felker complained to Murdoch that he was having money problems at the magazine and was under pressure from his partners, who controlled the majority interest. Murdoch used this information to buy *New York* magazine out from under Felker, who walked away with most of his staff and a lifelong grudge against Murdoch. *New York* magazine got new editors and Murdoch was soon raking in the profits.

Along with *New York* magazine, Murdoch picked up the *Village Voice,* a liberal "alternative" newspaper for the hippest of the hip in New York, and *New West,* a fairly new magazine in California that was losing money. He sold *New West* before long.

At times Murdoch's British-style advocacy journalism got him into trouble. One of those whom Murdoch had supported vocally was President Jimmy Carter. During the Carter administration, Murdoch was accused of using political favors to get loans for an Australian airline he controlled that wanted to buy American-made airplanes. However, after Congressional hearings into the matter, nothing was ever proven. Later his support of Carter would lead to a bitter battle with Senator Edward Kennedy, who challenged Carter for the presidency in 1980 during the Democratic primaries.

In 1981 Murdoch acquired the *Times* of London, the most famous and powerful paper in the English-speaking world. It had suffered from a long strike and continuing union troubles, but he got it back on track, proving that he was capable of putting out a quality paper.

In England Murdoch decided to build a new printing plant. He warned the tough English newspaper unions that they would have to give up featherbedding and other inefficient practices, but they refused to listen. After all, for years they had gotten their way by hanging tough against management. This time, however, two factors were different. First, Prime Minister Margaret Thatcher had pushed through a number of anti-union laws. Second, Murdoch was determined to stand up to the unions in order to make his British properties more profitable. At the time, he badly needed more money, and he felt it could come from England. There was certainly room for improvement. William A. O'Neill, an Australian who runs Murdoch's media operations in Great Britain, claimed that the work four men could do in San Antonio and six men could do in New York required eighteen men in England.

In January 1986 Murdoch suddenly moved all of his newspaper operations to a new plant in Wapping, on eleven acres of reclaimed area around the London docks. An in-house union ran new high-speed presses. The work that had been performed by 7,000 union employees was now handled by about 3,100 employees. The new plant allowed for a greater number of pages in each publication, color, and other mechanical improvements. It also led to a bitter thirteen-month strike, with picketing and violence around the plant. But in the end Murdoch won. From that moment on, his

English newspapers began producing enormous profits, which he used to make even more acquisitions around the world.

Murdoch also moved ahead with new television technologies. In the United States he began laying the groundwork for Skyband, a direct broadcast service (DBS) that allowed viewers who purchased a small receiving dish and leased a decoding device to receive cable TV–style services. It had to be put out of business even before it was officially launched when research showed that it would not perform as anticipated in the marketplace. But Murdoch learned a lot from that attempt. It made him even more aware of how important it was to control sources of programming, especially sources of American feature films. It also forced him to recognize his own limitations. "There were problems with the distribution of the [receiving] dishes and questions about whether people would buy them. There were also problems acquiring programming resources," recalls Sir James Carruthers, a former Australian journalist and TV executive who Murdoch recruited onto the News Corp. board in 1981. "It all added up to a conclusion that [Skyband] was an even riskier venture than we were used to. It lost about $20 million."

Carruthers recalls that as part of the Skyband research, Murdoch looked into a satellite-TV venture in England. Begun in 1982, Sky Channel was designed to provide cable-TV systems all over Europe with English-language programming. Within a year it had gone through about $10 million in capital and was out of money. Murdoch injected new capital in return for 60 percent ownership. By 1987 it had expanded its program offerings and was reaching over 13 million subscribers. It was on the verge of breaking even. Then, recalls Carruthers, a competing service was started by ITV of England and others called Super Channel. Soon both Sky and Super Channel were losing huge amounts of money. Eventually Super Channel went out of business. Murdoch was forced to shrink his ambitions and reorient Sky Channel as a service for the United Kingdom alone. Later, when faced with another competitor, he relaunched Sky Channel as a DBS in Britain, again absorbing millions of dollars in losses.

As the News Corp. empire grew, certain astonishing things became clear. First, Murdoch operated a sprawling worldwide empire with fewer executives than any company of comparable size or complexity. In effect, the corporate staff was only a handful of people. The operating executives at each division also took on group-management responsibilities. Each week Murdoch got a flash report from every property in his empire, followed the next day by more-detailed data. As long as the property was meeting projections and there were no obvious problems, it ran autonomously.

Each time there was an acquisition, Murdoch would spend time getting it in shape and establishing the management, which was expected to follow his lead. Once up and running, however, they had a large degree of freedom.

"Rupert has a knack for instilling in the people around him an intense loyalty," says Bill O'Neill, who has worked for Murdoch in various capacities since 1961. "It's more psychological than economic. It's because he provides such intelligent and vibrant leadership. God, you don't know what the hell he will do next."

Murdoch himself doesn't know what he will do next. What he does know, however, is how much leverage (borrowing power) he has and how to make the most of it. He has amazed American investors by paying record prices for his acquisitions, in some cases far more than anyone thought they were worth. What the U.S. market watchers couldn't know was that those properties were worth more to Murdoch's News Corp. than they ever could be to any American Company. That was Murdoch's edge. He used the accounting rules of four different nations, as well as his dozens of interlocking corporations, for tax minimization and profit maximization. If one company had huge profits and another losses related to developing its business, he found ways to combine them so that the tax losses of one offset the profits of the other. That way he got to keep more of the profits and pay fewer taxes. It also provided him a built-in system to fund acquisitions.

Murdoch's key financial executive, based in New York, is Richard Sarazen, whom Murdoch met in 1973 when he did some accounting work for News Corp. He joined Murdoch as chief financial officer in 1974, and except for one short period when he left to run another company, has been News Corp.'s primary number cruncher ever since. A shy, intense, down-to-earth man with a quick sense of humor, Sarazen shared with Murdoch an ability to remember complex sets of numbers and financial details that would burn out the brains of most mortals. Sarazen remarks on how incredible it was that Murdoch constantly found new ways to use the interrelationship of his companies to increase profits and spur growth. "It's one of the few companies," says Sarazen, "where the parts really are probably worth less than the whole."

There are many ways that News Corp. saves money on taxes—all of them legal. Here is a simple example to demonstrate one aspect:

start with the purchase of a media property for $10. In the United States the tax man says that about $3 is real property and $7 is goodwill (the intangible image of the property), which must be written off for tax purposes over a period of about forty years. Which means that although you paid $10, the U.S. bankers think you still have something worth only about $3.

In Australia and the Netherland Antilles, however, where News Corp. has subsidiaries, the tax rules are such that that same title is viewed as having an unlimited life. As a result, it doesn't have to be written down for tax purposes at all. Instead, News Corp. can immediately add $10 in assets to its books. It can then go out and borrow more money against that new ten-dollar asset.

News Corp. also traded currency when it appeared profitable. Murdoch and Sarazen personally handled all trading, explains Sarazen. They would move around British pounds, Australian dollars, U.S. dollars, and the currencies of Switzerland, Germany, France, and other countries to increase their values. In simple terms, it is done by switching them from countries where the currency values are falling to countries where the currency values are rising.

Stanley Shulman notes that one problem many multinational companies face is having to pay the bills in one country with profits made in the currency of another country. Changing exchange rates can make it a nightmare and a constant source of losses. Murdoch, says Shulman, solved the problem by having ongoing relationships with more banks, in more countries, than any other similar corporation. That way he could borrow as needed in each country to keep everything in balance. "He was able to make banking arrangements all over the world," Shulman says, "because he created a sense of confidence in each place that was earned over a long period of time."

Murdoch also used to great advantage his control of his empire. As the owner, with his family, of a controlling 46 percent interest in the parent News Corp. in Australia, he was insulated from hostile takeovers or complaints from shareholders who wanted higher short-term results. As such, he could buy things and wait years for them to turn a profit. And he could borrow, or leverage, his company to a degree impossible in the United States. That was one reason why he kept his holdings in Australia, even after becoming a U.S. citizen. At the end of 1988, for instance, News Corp. had a worldwide debt of about $6.8 billion and total stockholders equity of about $5.1 billion. Having more debt than stockholders' equity is practically unheard of in the United States. Yet Sarazen says blithely that it's no problem because there is plenty of cash flow to cover the debt service (interest payments). Nor is News Corp. despite the large debt, concerned that a period of economic difficulty might throw it into a tailspin, according to Sarazen:

> This business and company are more recession-proof than most companies. Historically, in hard times people continue reading periodicals and continue going to the movies. We also have more publications supported by readers' subscriptions than by advertisers than most companies, which is the best situation in hard times.

"Good programming [for movies and TV] certainly makes friends and it certainly makes money," says Murdoch. "I mean we saw immediately we could take the programs here [at Fox] and sell them to new television competitors all over."

Murdoch's acquisition of Twentieth Century–Fox provided him with additional assets to borrow against as well as a key building block to making his global vision a reality. Far from satiating his appetite for entertainment businesses, it gave him an even greater desire to find new ways to use the Fox products to expand his international empire of interrelated companies. Says Carruthers,

> Rupert Murdoch is all about seizing opportunities. He pushes ahead and does things and keeps his eyes open and takes opportunities as they arrive. There is no way that he has a master plan or paper that gives an indication of where he'll be in two or three or five years. Who could have guessed a person with no interest whatever in movies would end up owning Twentieth Century–Fox, or Triangle Publications [owner of *TV Guide*], or that he would start a network. It happened only because he takes advantage of opportunities as they arise.

Murdoch, the sensational journalist and union buster, made some powerful enemies; but among bankers, investors, and corporate leaders he came to be recognized as a brilliant and daring businessman who was not to be underestimated.

It was a lesson that Marvin Davis was about to learn.

11

COCKTAILS
WITH KLUGE

RUPERT MURDOCH'S PURCHASE of half of Twentieth Century–
Fox had not yet been finalized in late March 1985 when Barry
Diller played host to both Fox partners for the first time. The
occasion was a brief cocktail party in Diller's studio office conference room. It was in honor of a visit by John W. Kluge, chairman
and controlling stockholder of Metromedia, a diversified communications company. Metromedia's holdings included seven big-city
television stations, thirteen radio stations, an interest in an outdoor
billboard company, radio-paging companies, cellular telephone system operators, a TV production entity, the Harlem Globetrotters,
the Ice Capades, and other attractions.

Kluge was in town to participate in the sixth annual investors'
conference sponsored by Drexel Burnham Lambert and junk bond
king Michael Milken. Drexel's annual conference was already part
of the folklore of American business. It attracted many of the richest, best-known businessmen, including most of the so-called corporate raiders, who would use the money Milken helped them raise
to forcibly take over other companies. Attendees at the meetings
at the Beverly Hills Hotel and Beverly Hilton Hotel in 1985
included secretive Cincinnati multimillionaire Carl Lindner, corpo-

rate raider Saul Steinberg (who had bought into Chris-Craft when it was after Fox), tough Miami-based entrepreneur Victor Posner, Texas oilman T. Boone Pickens, and New York investor Ivan Boesky, who within two years would be sent to prison and fined $100 million for trading stock illegally, based on inside information not available to public stockholders. The Boesky case also would lead to Drexel paying a record fine and the downfall of Milken on similar charges.

From Wall Street's point of view, it was as if all of the biggest, meanest sharks in the ocean all gathered in one place once a year. Thus the annual gathering had been dubbed "the Predators' Ball."

One person who wasn't planning to attend was Rupert Murdoch. However, it happened that on the very day that Diller was hosting cocktails for Kluge, Murdoch was going to be in Los Angeles briefly on a stopover between Australia and his home in New York City. Diller invited him to join them for cocktails.

As a courtesy, Diller also invited Marvin Davis to his little gathering.

Diller, of course, had met Michael Milken a few months before, when he had almost agreed to a deal for Fox to sell $250 million in corporate bonds. When Milken called in early 1985 and asked Diller if they could hold one of the evening events of the annual conference on the Fox lot (for which they would pay fair market rent), Diller was happy to comply.

Diller had known John Kluge for many years and had long studied and followed Metromedia. He had sold syndicated (used) programming to Metromedia while at Paramount and had been involved in joint ventures for other shows.

Diller also had seriously contemplated having the company he ran buy the Metromedia TV stations, or merge with them, at least three times. In 1977, at Paramount, Diller had spearheaded a fourth network attempt called the Paramount Television Service. It planned to assemble an ad hoc network of independent TV stations offering one night of programming each week to start, including a new version of "Star Trek" (a former network series that continued in reruns) and the first TV exposure of a Paramount motion picture. Serious consideration also was given to buying some TV stations, possibly Metromedia. In the end, Charles Bluhdorn, scared off by a period of economic recession, had killed the venture. Instead, Paramount had made a "Star Trek" movie, which went on to great success and spawned a series of sequels.

In the early 1980s Diller (representing Paramount) had explored a joint venture with Marvin Josephson, whose holdings included ICM, one of the largest talent agencies. Diller and Josephson had met with Kluge about joining forces to launch a fourth U.S. network. They decided there weren't enough independent TV stations in the U.S. to make it economically feasible, and the idea was shelved.

Then, in 1983, when Kluge proposed to buy out all of the public shareholders of Metromedia and make it a private company, Diller and his team at Paramount considered a plan to overbid Kluge for the Metromedia stations, which would form the basis of a fourth TV network. Martin Davis had listened to a full-day presentation on the proposal and then impassively decided against it.

Now, on the eve of the cocktail party, Milken told Diller that there was an outside chance the Metromedia TV stations might be for sale. The rest of the company was not (at that time). In reality, Milken was being cagey. Milken and Kluge already knew that the cost of the junk bonds used by Kluge to make Metromedia a private company was so high that there was no way to meet the payments without a significant sale of assets. Kluge had then decided to keep Metromedia's cellular telephone businesses while selling off the radio and TV stations and most other properties.

Ironically, the leading bidder for the TV stations at the time was Paramount, under Frank Mancuso, who reported to Martin Davis. Paramount had again decided it made sense to own TV stations. Gulf + Western, Paramount's parent company, didn't offer all cash, however. It proposed to pay for the acquisition with a combination of cash and Gulf + Western stock. That didn't sit well with Kluge. He had a very high price in mind for the TV outlets—$2 billion—and he wanted it all in cash. He already had in hand an offer from the Hearst Corporation for the Boston TV station, should he decide to sell it.

There was no question that seventy-year-old John Werner Kluge, a short, stocky, balding man with a ridge of thinning gray hair around the back of his head, thin lips, a thick nose, and small eyes, had become one of the richest men in the world through his shrewd business dealings. Born in Chemnitz, Germany, in 1914, Kluge was eight years old when his family moved to Detroit. He attended Columbia University on a scholarship and then returned to Michigan, where he went to work for a paper company without salary. His deal was that if he could double sales, he would get a third of the company—which he did.

Dennis Stanfill, chairman and CEO of Twentieth Century–Fox from 1971 until 1981, when he was forced out by Marvin Davis. (Los Angeles Herald-Examiner)

Alan Hirschfield, who was chief operating officer of Fox from 1978 until he replaced Stanfill in 1981. (Los Angeles Herald-Examiner)

Norman Levy, head of distribution at Fox. A favorite of Davis's, he later added vice chairman to his responsibilities. (Los Angeles Herald-Examiner)

Marvin Davis. (Los Angeles Herald-Examiner)

Sherry Lansing, head of production at Twentieth Century–Fox. She became increasingly unhappy during Marvin Davis's tenure and left to form an independent production company with Stanley Jaffe. *(courtesy Jaffe/Lansing Productions)*

Marvin and Barbara Davis arrive for the New York premiere of *Taps*, one of the few hits for Fox during this period. *(AP/Wide World Photos)*

Charles Bluhdorn, mentor of Barry Diller and chairman and CEO of Gulf + Western until his death in 1983. *(courtesy Paramount Communications, Inc.)*

Martin Davis, who replaced Bluhdorn as head of Gulf + Western (now Paramount Communications). Davis clashed with Michael Eisner and Barry Diller, who went on to head Disney and Fox, respectively. *(courtesy Paramount Communications, Inc.)*

Barry Diller. *(courtesy Fox Broadcasting Company)*

Rupert Murdoch. *(courtesy Fox Broadcasting Company)*

John and Patricia Kluge. His sale of Metromedia television stations made the Fox network a viable possibility. *(Richmond Newspapers, Inc.)*

Jamie Kellner, president of FBC. *(courtesy Fox Broadcasting Company)*

Garth Ancier, first head of programming at Fox. *(courtesy Fox Broadcasting Company)*

Kevin Wendle was one of the first executives hired by Diller and filled various posts at the network. He left to become an independent producer. One of his first shows was Fox's "Totally Hidden Video." *(courtesy Fox Broadcasting Company)*

Scott Sassa, first head of publicity and promotion at the network. *(courtesy Fox Broadcasting Company)*

After serving in military intelligence during World War II, Kluge bought a radio station in Washington, D.C. He also began a food brokerage company, which would grow to over $500 million in sales by 1986. In 1959, after the short-lived Du Mont television network failed and its partner in station ownership, Paramount, pulled out, Kluge bought the money-losing Metropolitan station group, which included TV outlets in New York and Washington.

Kluge became a pioneer in independent TV-station operation, bunching his outlets in big cities, where he felt advertisers would concentrate their spending. He was right, and he made a fortune. But he was frustrated repeatedly in efforts to use his stations to launch a fourth TV network.

Kluge used his profits over the following twenty-five years to buy all kinds of things, ranging from a personnel agency to the Harlem Globetrotters to the Ice Capades. Along the way Kluge fulfilled a lifelong dream—to own the most expensive stock on the New York Stock Exchange. Unfortunately, a negative article in *Barron's,* a business publication, came out when the stock was peaking, and Metromedia fell from $550 a share to $300. Many observers felt that that was when Kluge decided to make his company private in a leveraged buyout.

As it turned out, Kluge's piecemeal sale of various parts of Metromedia eventually returned about four times what the buyout had cost—all of which was borrowed money anyway. The sale raised questions about just how fair Kluge had been with public stockholders when he initially valued the company for his own purchase.

Kluge, with a fortune *Forbes* estimated at $3.5 billion by 1987, went into semiretirement, living like the royalty of another age. In 1981 Kluge married his third wife, Patricia Rose Gay, a trim, attractive brunette. They were married in St. Patrick's Cathedral in New York. Her father was English and her mother Scottish-Iraqi. She had been raised in Iraq. As a young woman she'd moved to England, worked as a belly dancer, and, in the late 1960s, married the publisher of a sexually explicit magazine called *Knave.* She frequently posed nude in the magazine and wrote a raunchy sexual advice column. She also produced some soft-core pornographic movies. Her lurid past life came back to haunt the Kluges when they were to help host an event for Prince Charles and Princess Diana during a U.S. visit. When the English tabloids ran pictures of Mrs. Kluge in the buff from her earlier career, the Kluges suddenly announced that they would have to be out of the country during the royal visit. There are some things even a billionaire can't buy.

The Kluges moved to rural Virginia, where they adopted a baby boy, John Jr., to live with them on their 6,000-acre plantation, Albemarle Farms. They built a 45-room brick manor house in the Georgian style as well as numerous outbuildings, including a Gothic chapel, stables, and cottages for a staff of 120. There are also tennis courts, a golf course, and a log cabin in the woods, John Kluge's private office. *Town and Country* magazine in 1987 called Albemarle Farms "grander and more ambitious than anything that has been built in America since the 1920s."

As an investment, Kluge also went on to purchase a controlling interest in Orion Pictures and to finance an outdoor billboard company with a new technology that allows the use of billboard-sized color photographs.

When he came to Fox for the 1985 Drexel Burnham Lambert investors' conference, Kluge was still in the process of selling off pieces of Metromedia.

Cocktails were scheduled for 6:00 P.M. in Diller's conference room. Murdoch arrived first. He passed through the outer area where Diller's two secretaries sit and into the next room, an almost completely white office, and found Diller seated at his desk. Diller popped up and greeted Murdoch warmly. They had known each other for several years, but not well. Now Diller looked to Murdoch as his salvation in his battles with Marvin Davis. Diller and Murdoch walked together through another smaller room, near Diller's private bathroom, and then into the comfortable conference room. A long mahogany table dominated the room, which was tastefully decorated with a print wallpaper and reproductions of old English oil paintings.

A few minutes later, Marvin Davis walked down the hall from his office and joined them. Diller cringed when he saw Davis, his 300-pound girth in a charcoal-gray suit. Diller froze a half smile on his face as he softly shook Davis's hand. Davis, rolling his eyes, quickly made his way over to Murdoch and began to chat. Just then the phone buzzer sounded and Diller, relieved, moved quickly to the receiver. A secretary informed him that the Fox guard at the front gate had called and that Kluge was on his way.

Kluge, short and balding, had a slight screen of sweat on his forehead as he marched in, accompanied by his taller, thinner associate, Stuart Subotnick. Diller ushered them both into the back conference room and began making introductions.

It was Diller's impression that Murdoch knew Kluge only slightly when he introduced them and that Davis did not know Kluge at all. Davis, however, said later that he not only knew Kluge but had already met with him privately to discuss buying the Metromedia television stations.

Drinks were served as they all sat around one end of the conference table and on a nearby couch. The mood was cordial and the conversation light at first. Diller, playing the role of host, was attentive to each of his guests. He took the lead in making conversation with Kluge. They both recalled the meeting with Marvin Josephson about a possible fourth TV network. Kluge said he'd always been sorry they had not gone forward with it at the time.

That provided Diller with an opening to ask Kluge about the rumor that he might be selling the TV stations, although he made it a point not to mention his conversations with Milken. Kluge said it was true that he would be willing to part with some stations, but not the one in New York. He also said that Boston was already promised to Hearst. That left the stations in Los Angeles, Chicago, Dallas–Fort Worth, Houston, and Washington, D.C.

Murdoch, perking up, was interested immediately, and he said so. Davis was unusually quiet, nursing his drink in a corner, but seemed interested as well. Diller suggested to Kluge that if he really was serious, they should meet again the next day to discuss it further. They agreed. Outside the window they could already see a stream of cars heading toward the back of the lot, where a dinner and stage for entertainment had been set up for the Drexel Burnham Lambert guests.

Davis was the first to look at his watch and note that it was getting late. Kluge quickly bounced out of his chair and said he and Subotnick had to go. The cocktail party in Diller's conference room was over in just under an hour, but it had started something that would last long after that evening.

The next day they were all back for a brief meeting in Diller's office, which also was attended by Milken and executives from Drexel Burnham Lambert. Kluge again said that he wanted to sell the TV stations, with the exception of New York and Boston. He then stated his price: $1.05 billion. If he were to sell all of the stations, including New York and Boston, Kluge said the price would be $2 billion. Diller was taken aback, not just by the high price, but also by the magnitude of what was being discussed. Murdoch told him not to worry about the price. "I just thought it was crazy," Diller recalls.

Still, he agreed to fly to New York the following week to continue the discussions with Murdoch. Marvin Davis said he had to be in Denver but asked to be kept informed.

At that point, Diller didn't know Murdoch very well, so he really couldn't gauge his sincerity. Later he would realize that it was exactly the kind of opportunity Murdoch lived for, that would keep him up all night putting it together. Although there were serious obstacles to the purchase, Murdoch's mind was spinning with ideas.

The two most obvious problems had to do with U.S. laws regarding TV-station ownership. First, any significant owner had to be a U.S. citizen. Murdoch was an Australian citizen. Second, it was in violation of cross-ownership rules to own TV stations and newspapers in the same cities. Murdoch already owned major newspapers in New York and Chicago, where Metromedia had TV outlets.

None of these obstacles was going to stop Murdoch.

The following Monday afternoon, Diller was in lower Manhattan in Murdoch's modest corporate offices in the New York Post building along with Murdoch and some of his key executives. The office was neat and functional but small, with a window looking out over the Hudson River. They sat around talking about the TV stations while Murdoch and Richard Sarazen doodled numbers on yellow legal pads. What Kluge had proposed represented a price of about fifteen to seventeen times the station's annual earnings at a time when similar properties were going for about ten to twelve times their annual earnings.

That didn't bother Murdoch. He argued that the Metromedia stations represented a unique franchise. There would be very few times, he said, when a group of mostly VHF stations, all unaffiliated with any network, would be available in the largest cities all at once. He said it was certainly worth a unique premium.

Diller already was talking in theoretical terms about using the stations as the basis of a fourth TV network, or at least a program service (a limited but regularly scheduled programming network) to start. Other options, he noted, might be an ad hoc network of stations that would run programs for free in return for carrying "barter" advertisements (commercials inserted into the program by the network that have been sold to advertisers who want to reach a lot of independent stations at once).

Drexel Burnham Lambert executives, meanwhile, had been calling to warn the Fox group that Paramount was a serious bidder and that Coca-Cola, which owned Columbia Pictures, also was considering the purchase. Murdoch recognized it as the kind of talk salesmen use to push someone into a purchase; still, he didn't feel they should wait.

What about the citizenship question? Diller wanted to know. "It's not a problem," Murdoch assured him. "I can take care of it." And the cross-ownership problem? Murdoch said they would ask for a temporary waiver from the FCC rules and figure out how to handle it later.

What about the TV network in Australia that would have to be sold if Murdoch gave up his citizenship there? Murdoch's feeling was that they should just go ahead and say yes, and then work out all the details.

"Then what should we do next?" asked Diller.

Murdoch answered by picking up the phone and placing a call to Kluge at his apartment in the Waldorf Towers. "If you're still serious," Murdoch told Kluge, "we're ready to come over right now and make the deal."

"I'll be expecting you," replied Kluge.

They shared a cab uptown and were greeted by Kluge and Subotnick, who also had an apartment at the Waldorf. Kluge ushered them into the living room and asked if anyone wanted coffee or drinks, which were served by his small staff of domestic help. Kluge was expansive as he talked about how much the stations had meant to him, often looking longingly out the window at the grand view of Manhattan.

Murdoch, impatient to get on with it, said right away that there couldn't be any deal without including the New York station. If they were to start a network, or even a program service, they had to have New York. Kluge said he would guarantee to carry any such service on his New York station, although he wouldn't put it in writing, and would give them an option to buy WNEW-TV upon his death. Murdoch insisted. There could be no deal without New York. Kluge quickly caved in.

Murdoch said they would be willing to resell Boston to Hearst immediately for $450 million. That meant that the Fox group would set up a separate corporation to buy the six remaining stations for approximately $1.55 billion.

The price was settled that afternoon, but it still took days of intense negotiations to work out many of the details. The biggest obstacle was the $1.35 billion in debt and accumulated interest on the junk bonds (in at least four different forms) that Drexel had issued in December 1984 for Kluge's leveraged buyout. The bonds had been issued against the assets of the entire Metromedia corporation, including the radio stations and cellular telephone properties. To separate them so that the collateral would be only the six TV stations, the bondholders would have to agree. Kluge turned the problem over to Milken. Within a couple of days, Milken and his Drexel team provided assurances that they could get the necessary agreements. That meant that if Murdoch put in about $450 million in cash, which he was prepared to do, then the bonds could simply be assumed and paid off later.

As the negotiations wore on, both sides began to bring in outside experts to help. A key advisor who joined the Murdoch-Diller-team was I. Martin Pompadur, who had spent seventeen years as a business executive at the ABC network before leaving in 1977 to form his own company, which was acquiring cable TV systems and other media properties. Pompadur had met Murdoch years before, when ABC entered a joint venture with him for a record company in Australia. Murdoch's Metromedia purchase marked the first time that Pompadur had acted as a consultant.

Pompadur was not only part of the negotiations, he also held separate meetings that at times included Murdoch, Diller, Jon Dolgen, Robert Krieg (a Fox executive with a TV background), and Michael Lambert (the well-thought-of head of Fox's TV syndication division). They began doing proformas, which are projections of different ways things might turn out financially, depending on differing factors.

In other words, they looked at the revenue from the stations and immediately saw that it would not be enough to cover the interest payments on the purchase debt.

Murdoch recalled later that he knew right from the start that they would have to do more than just operate the stations in order to support the price they had paid. The advantage of creating a network lay in the way advertisers and advertising agencies value television viewers. Generally, advertising is sold based on a cost for each one thousand pairs of eyes that are watching. Advertisers pay a premium price for network viewers, a somewhat lower price for those watching syndicated shows, and an even lower price for locally originated TV programs. In other words, to use a simple example, the same minute that a local TV station can sell for $100 for each thousand viewers, the syndicated program can sell for

$150 and the network can sell for over $200. So the value of time on a network is worth far more.

Pompadur also warned Murdoch that if Twentieth Century–Fox did own a network by the FCC definition (at least fifteen hours a week of programming), it couldn't be in the TV-syndication business, which was where Fox was making much of its money. Murdoch said they would start slowly and would not officially be a network for quite a while. "That will be at least five years down the road," he told Pompadur. "Don't worry about it. We'll change it or something else will happen by then."

Marvin Davis, meanwhile, sent his associate Gerald Gray to New York to study the deal being shaped. Gray, a former Denver accountant, listened in on one meeting and shortly afterward returned to Denver to report to Davis. Davis and Gray didn't tell Diller or Murdoch, but they had already done their own financial analysis. What Gray heard that day simply reinforced what they had already concluded: Kluge was asking $600 million more than the stations were worth. It was far too expensive for Davis's taste.

Davis told Murdoch by phone that if he did go in, he would not be a long-term player. He would want to cash out fairly quickly. Murdoch said that in that case, he wanted an option to buy out Davis in the stations and the studio. Davis tentatively agreed and set an option price. A few hours later, Davis called back. He had changed his mind about selling the studio, and if he did decide to sell, it would be at a much higher price. They went back and forth for days, without coming to any final decision.

Diller, Murdoch, and Kluge, in the meantime, were ready to conclude the deal. The only thing holding it up was the question of Marvin Davis's participation.

Finally it seemed clear, at least to Diller, that Davis would not join in on the station purchase. Rather than wait for a decision, however, they decided to give Davis an option to join in on the station purchase later, while the deal went forward.

Diller personally approved a press release announcing the purchase, which was already the subject of speculation in the financial press. It suggested that Davis and Murdoch were in the purchase together, although Murdoch and Diller knew that Davis was out. "We felt to announce it any other way would be a nightmare," says Diller, "because the speculation would be ridiculous. Davis was happy because he got his name in the paper as if he bought something, and he didn't have to put up any money. I knew though, there was no chance [Davis would be a partner in the TV stations] because it would have cost real money."

When it was obvious that Davis would not be in on the deal, Pompadur asked Murdoch if he had enough money to go it alone. "Funny you should ask that," was Murdoch's reply, yanking a yellow sheet of paper out of his pocket.

It was a profit-and-loss statement for News Corp. listing all of Murdoch's properties. There would be plenty of money, Murdoch said. His only real concern was that he might be forced to sell the *New York Post,* which was losing about $20 million a year. He said that even though it wasn't a prestige paper, it had given him great access to U.S. politicians, which he didn't want to lose. Later he would realize that a TV network could give him even more clout.

Murdoch and Kluge signed the agreement. Within a few days, however, Drexel Burnham Lambert dropped a bombshell. It was unable to get all of the bondholders to agree to the new terms. There was no way that Murdoch could assume Kluge's junk bonds.

Instead, Milken suggested that the new Fox TV-station company issue $1.15 billion in convertible preferred stock. It would be due in three years and would carry an interest rate of 13 percent the first year, 14 percent the second year, and 15 percent the third year. If not paid off by the end of three years, it would convert into News Corp. stock, which would lead to a major dilution of Murdoch's ownership of his company. It appeared to be a tremendous risk for Murdoch. If he guessed wrong, or if there was an economic downturn, he could lose control of the company he had spent his life building.

Murdoch was angry. He believed that he had been misled by Milken and Drexel and that now they were trying to manipulate him. He thought briefly about just walking away from the whole thing, but then he realized that there was a lot more at stake than whether or not he had been misled. This was the fulfillment of a dream. This was the kind of giant opportunity that came along once in a lifetime. He decided to do whatever it would take.

Even after Murdoch agreed to the new preferred stock issue, some Metromedia bondholders refused to trade, so Fox also had to assume about $100 million worth of Kluge's junk bonds.

Murdoch's displeasure didn't stem only from the fact that Drexel's guarantee had been worthless. He and Sarazen also noted that Drexel's fee from issuing the new preferred stock would be about $50 million, far in excess of what Drexel would have collected had Murdoch just assumed the Kluge junk bonds. There was a feeling that Drexel had put one over on them.

Murdoch and Sarazen would never forgive Drexel and would refuse to work with them ever again (although Diller and Fox would separately use the firm).

Sarazen did come up with a couple of novel twists from a tax accounting point of view to help with the purchase. First, the Drexel fee of $50 million—which by usual U.S. accounting standards had to be written off the year it occurred—was treated instead as part of the purchase expense by News Corp. That meant it could be used as a tax write-off for forty years, providing a small tax shelter. News Corp. recouped one-fortieth of that amount each year for forty years, tax-free.

Second, for accounting purposes, Sarazen was able to treat the interest payments on the preferred stock differently in the U.S. and in Australia. While it was just paper shuffling, it was crucial to Murdoch's ability to finance the purchase. Here is how it worked: in the United States, News Corp. treated the interest charges as a form of debt—money owed to someone else. Under U.S. tax law, then, it could be written off each year as a business expense.

In Australia, however, it was legal to treat it for accounting purposes as an asset, as something they already owned. So immediately they could act as if the News Corp. assets had increased by approximately $1.6 billion, which meant that News Corp. could borrow that much more money against its assets.

At the time, it was a terribly controversial move, but through tax savings, it provided much-needed cash to News Corp. in the two years immediately after the deal was made. Sarazen estimates that they saved 46 percent on taxes.

To pay off the cost of the preferred stock, News Corp. also began disposing of some of its assets including a stake in Reuters, the profitable European-based news wire service; the *Village Voice,* which went for an astounding $55 million; and the *Chicago Sun– Times,* which was acquired for $80 million in 1984 and sold for $145 million in early 1986, a profit of $65 million in less than two years.

Sarazen next began negotiating for new credit from a group of banks in the United States and abroad. Within a year Sarazen was able to float a new bond issue in Europe that was at a lower interest rate and had no risk of diluting Murdoch's ownership of News Corp. That money was used to pay off the purchase debt from the Metromedia junk bonds. As it turned out, all of Fox's preferred stock was paid off by July 1, 1987, two years after the purchase. Murdoch's ownership of News Corp. wasn't diluted, while the value of his holdings was greatly increased.

Three years after the purchase, the IRS still had not done anything about the questionable way News Corp. had accounted for the preferred stock. By then Sarazen could laugh about it. The amount in question was no more than $25 million, as it turned out, which wasn't a big deal as News Corp. continued to grow. At the time of the purchase, however, it had been crucial to Murdoch.

Once the Metromedia deal was set, Murdoch and Diller became closer, while Davis grew more upset. Davis officially pulled out of the TV-station purchase in June, while trading threats of legal action with Barry Diller. It was now obvious to everyone involved that Diller and Davis hated each other and couldn't stay in business together. At the studio they no longer spoke to each other, except when absolutely necessary. Diller had given orders that Davis be billed for every single thing he used, and Davis bristled each time he was told about a new charge.

Davis was in an increasingly isolated and difficult position. His only option seemed to be to sell his half of Fox. As he had so many times, Davis was determined to turn adversity to his advantage.

Davis came up with a new strategy. Now that Murdoch had bought the TV stations, he needed Diller desperately to run them. Through his attorney, Davis took the position that Diller, as chairman of Fox, had no automatic right to spend time working on Murdoch's TV stations. He charged that Diller was breaching his Fox contract. Davis felt that this gave him leverage over Murdoch, and he pushed up his asking price for his half of Fox.

After weeks of dragged-out, acrimonious negotiations, they finally cut a deal. Murdoch agreed to pay Davis $325 million for the rest of Fox, but that included the $88 million he had put in already as a loan to the studio. The cash to Davis, then, was $237 million. In addition, however, a real estate partnership controlled by Davis got the entire Fox interest in Pebble Beach and Aspen and half of the newly constructed Fox Plaza office building. In return, Murdoch's News Corp. was left with 100 percent of the fifty-six-acre Twentieth Century–Fox studio lot.

At the last minute, Davis also insisted on some added concessions for his son John, who had proven himself a capable Fox executive and now was becoming an independent film producer. To settle the sale contract, Murdoch and Diller agreed to give John Davis's production company office space on the Fox lot for five years, along with a promise that the studio would distribute three movies that Davis would finance fully. Murdoch and Diller also agreed to give John Davis an interest in several other films, including *Predator,* which became a huge hit. John Davis went on to become an able and active producer, even winning the grudging respect of Barry Diller.

Marvin Davis had sold his half of Fox for several reasons. First, with Diller around, Fox was no longer any fun. Second, he didn't want to inject more money. Third, he didn't want to face angry bankers, and possibly lawsuits, if Diller left. Finally, he really did feel he was getting a premium price for assets that he had on his books at no cost. Since he had long before gotten out his entire initial investment and then some.

Still, Marvin Davis left angry at Diller and bitter about his entire Fox experience. "My mistake was in going after the wrong Paramount executive," Davis would say two years later. "If I had only gone after Michael Eisner and got him to run the studio . . . it would be successful and I would still own Twentieth Century–Fox."

Of course, Davis never said that to Diller's face. Instead, Davis stalled on signing the final sale papers until Barry Diller personally drove his black Corvette up to Davis's enormous Bel Air home. Diller stood there impatiently as Davis signed on the dotted line. The last words Davis spoke to Diller were intended to rub a little salt in an old wound. "Thanks pal," said Davis to Diller. "You just made me an awful lot of money."

Murdoch had some unfinished business as well.

Shortly before lunchtime on September 4, 1985, Rupert Murdoch stood in a crowd of immigrants in a lower Manhattan courthouse, raised his right hand, and swore an oath. He renounced his Australian citizenship and promised that from that time forward, he would uphold the laws and constitution of the United States of America.

Now Keith Rupert Murdoch, U.S. citizen and 100 percent owner of Twentieth Century–Fox, officially could become a television broadcaster and network pioneer.

12

NETWORKING

ON A COOL, clear day in early December 1985, Barry Diller, wearing a cream-colored suit, white shirt, and pale-yellow silk tie, stood near the entryway to his three-room suite of offices in the Twentieth Century–Fox executive office building, warmly welcoming his half dozen luncheon guests. After exchanging a brief greeting with each one, he turned and introduced them individually to Rupert Murdoch, who stood nearby in his dark business suit wearing a friendly smile. As they chatted and waited for everyone to arrive, a waiter in a white linen jacket circulated among them, offering drinks or coffee.

Diller's guests, most dressed with casual elegance but a few in suits and ties, were a very select group of show-business elite. Each was a top writer, producer, or studio executive deeply involved in the production of programming for America's three existing television networks. Most had a laundry list of credits that included the most popular shows on the boob tube. Several, including producer Stephen J. Cannell, had names and faces that had become better known than those of most of the actors on their shows.

After a few minutes, Diller invited his guests and Murdoch to join him in the conference room for a catered lunch. Diller sat at the head of the table, acting as host, while Murdoch took a seat off to the side, where he could watch and listen. He took occasional notes on a legal-sized yellow pad.

As the plates were cleared, Diller rose and again greeted his guests warmly. He turned on all of his famous charm and affability, in sharp contrast to his reputation among some for being cold and distant. Diller was determined to win this crowd over. He wanted them to leave excited about the ideas he was about to present.

This was one in a series of luncheons Diller had arranged throughout the fall and winter of 1985–86 so that Murdoch could meet the top movers, shakers, and creators in American television. Each time he knew Murdoch was going to be in Los Angeles, Diller would select another group of four to eight guests, always concentrating on the creative producers of the very best, most successful network TV shows.

This was Diller's way of laying the groundwork for the fourth television network that Fox was about to begin. He felt that if the new venture was going to succeed, they would need the help of experienced producers; and in order to get them, Diller believed that his first job had to be to show them that Murdoch was someone they would want to be associated with. Diller knew that Murdoch's media image was terrible, particularly because of the *New York Post.* He also believed that if they could meet Murdoch, they would think otherwise.

By the time coffee was served, Diller was into his pitch. He told his guests about the purchase of the Metromedia TV stations and a bit about the overall growth of the News Corp. interests in entertainment. Then he revealed that he and Murdoch planned to start a fourth television network, but one with a difference. They intended to put a lot more emphasis on the creative aspects. They wanted to give the top producers a chance to do their best work without the petty hassles and power struggles that so often marked their relationships with the three major networks. "What we will be doing will start on only a few nights at first," Diller told them. "But then we expect it to grow and add nights as we build our franchise."

Murdoch spoke briefly, making clear his intention was to give the new venture unlimited support. He displayed an expertise in television born out of his long ownership of TV interests in Australia and England, but he made it clear that Barry Diller would be running the new network.

When Diller concluded by promising that the license fees Fox's network would pay for shows would be equal to what the networks paid, that Fox would provide a guaranteed commitment in advance to put shows on the air for an entire season, and that they also would give the top producers almost total artistic freedom, most of those present indicated an interest in talking further.

Within two hours the lunch was over. As he had at almost every one of the luncheons, it seemed that Diller had accomplished both of his goals. He had gotten the word out that there was going to be a serious new player in the network race and that Murdoch was a sane, sensible, intelligent executive. Murdoch was someone who the top creative people could work with without concern for their reputations or their freedom of expression.

Murdoch went public for the first time with plans for the new network on January 5, 1986, in a speech before the convention of the Independent Television Association (INTV) at the Century Plaza Hotel in Los Angeles. Speaking in a low monotone, his voice tinted with an Australian accent, Murdoch promised "programming initiatives which will excite and embolden those who join us in this great and timely venture."

Speaking as owner of a movie studio as well as founder of a new TV network, Murdoch added:

> This may sound hypocritical, given the quite provable assertion that I am also in the business of offering you syndicated programming. But I am a realist, and I know that it is only the foolish who assume the ability of broadcasters to continue the escalation of program prices. The only hope for the syndicator and the broadcaster is a saner and more reasonable marketplace. And the only hope for growth in either sector is that the programs offered perform in that marketplace with increasing competitiveness and cost efficiency. . . . It is our aim to deliver these programs at a cost that will be an amiable companion to its ability to attract audiences.

Murdoch also had a surprise for Murdoch in the first quarter of 1986—a new contract. Murdoch didn't like the deal Diller had signed with Davis. He felt it was too open-ended, given the fact that it was dependent on the appreciation of certain assets over a period of time. Murdoch knew that he couldn't just take that away, so he offered Murdoch a whole new package.

The five-year contract signed on March 10 provided Diller with his base salary of $3 million, and vested him with 25 percent of the voting control of Fox in the form of Fox preferred stock. In return for dropping the Davis bonus plan, Murdoch also gave Diller two million shares of News Corp. stock, fully registered on the Australian exchange, and agreed to pay him 5 percent of any gain in profits during his term. Other perks and incentives were based on the performance of the studio and TV stations.

Diller and Murdoch also agreed to keep the three entities they now controlled separate, at least legally. Diller called it "keeping up the Chinese walls." In other words, they wouldn't simply merge the stations and network into the studio. Each would be a separate legal entity, owned by Murdoch and run by Diller.

It was reassurance for Diller at a time when things had gotten a bit bumpy at the studio. In the fall of 1985, Larry Gordon had gone to his doctor for a routine checkup and had been diagnosed as having a blocked artery leading to his heart. After additional tests it was determined that Gordon had blockages in two of the three main arteries entering his heart. His doctors, while deciding if surgery was the best way to treat Gordon, had strongly suggested that he quit his high-pressure job as president of Twentieth Century–Fox.

Gordon had lived with concern about his heart for years because his father had died of a heart attack at age fifty-six. So he took his doctor's warnings seriously.

After a sleepless night, Gordon told Barry Diller over lunch that he had to resign. It couldn't have come at a worse time from Diller's point of view. He was deeply involved with the new TV-station group and the planning for the new network. After a long run of flop movies, the studio had just begun a turnaround with hits like *Commando* and *Cocoon*.

Gordon agreed to stay on for a few months more, but the pressure was on Diller to find a replacement. It took until nearly the end of 1985 before Diller hired Alan Horn, a youthful executive who had just left Embassy Communications following its sale to Coca-Cola. Diller had courted Horn and promised him the opportunity to run the movie and TV divisions. It wasn't destined to work out, however. By the spring of 1986, the Diller-Horn relationship had gone sour. While Diller expected his executives to fight for their movie projects, Horn thought he had the authority to just do the job. Horn soon found that he could get his movies made only if Diller agreed, and there was almost nothing that he and Diller could agree on. Recalls Horn, "We could never agree on the allocation of responsibility."

The result was paralysis. For almost a year, Twentieth Century–

Fox hardly put any new movies into production. For a studio that needed to plan product flow eighteen months in advance, that was disastrous.

Horn finally became fed up with junior executives openly jockeying for his job and with the abuse he was taking from Diller, who had lost any semblence of respect for the young executive. Horn quit.

Diller had no choice but to buckle down and take on the responsibility for running the movie division, as well as the TV stations and planning for the network himself while searching for another executive to replace Horn. The one bright spot for Diller was the rapid development of the new network.

As he searched for executives for the new enterprise, Diller was surprised one day to receive a call from a top show-business attorney. Diller was at his desk in the front room of his office, the strong afternoon sun streaming through the window, when his secretary, Ruth Haley, buzzed on the intercom with word that Peter Dekom, one of the best known attorneys in Hollywood, was on the line. Diller lifted the receiver, still paging through a script on the desk in front of him. After a warm exchange of greetings, Diller made it clear that he was in a hurry.

"We've heard you're starting a new network," said Dekom. "I have a client that might interest you. She isn't available right now, but she might be available soon."

"Who are we talking about?" Diller finally asked.

"I'm speaking on behalf of Joan Rivers and Edgar Rosenberg," said the attorney.

Diller stopped paging through the script. He immediately could see the possibilities of a relationship with Joan Rivers, then the permanent guest host of NBC's top-rated "Tonight Show" starring Johnny Carson.

"We'd be interested in discussing it," said Diller coolly. "Why not set up a meeting."

"Good idea," said Dekom. "But I'm sure you understand it wouldn't do for any of this to get around. Joan is still under contract to NBC and . . ."

"I understand. Tell Miss Rivers I just wanted to know, 'Can we talk?' " said Diller, parodying the comedienne's famous line.

"It could take a little while," said the attorney. "There are some complications. If we can get together, it is going to take some negotiating. But I'm glad to hear you're interested. We'll be in touch."

As Diller hung up, he recalled another conversation he'd had with his close friend Sandy Gallin, a producer and personal manager who at one time had represented Joan Rivers. Gallin had suggested that Rivers was just the kind of person Diller would need to launch a late night talk show on his new network. Diller had filed that thought away but never done anything about it. The call from the attorney moved it to the front burner on Diller's priority list.

This is exactly what we need, Diller thought to himself. Stealing Joan Rivers away from NBC would have great drama and tremendous marquee value. It was also the kind of show that could be put on the air very, very quickly.

Later that afternoon, Diller discussed it over the phone with Murdoch, who, it seemed, didn't know who Rivers was. Still, on the basis of Diller's enthusiasm, Murdoch agreed that they should see what could be worked out.

Diller knew that Rivers would have to be convinced. After all, it wouldn't be easy jumping from an established network at the top of the ratings heap to a new network without any form, substance, or affiliates. Diller decided he had to convince her that the reward would be worth the risk.

At the same time, Diller was making his first hire for the new network. Jamie Kellner, who officially was named president on February 1, 1986, was an odd choice in some ways. An intense forty-year-old with boy-next-door good looks, wavy light-brown hair, clear blue eyes, and an athletic build, Kellner was very different in temperament and personality from Diller. As it turned out, they shared an important characteristic—the tenacity to stick with a project until the job was done.

Jamie Kellner was born in Brooklyn and raised on Long Island, where his passion in life was sailing. His father was a commodities broker on Wall Street who lived a boom-and-bust existence. Kellner began working at part-time jobs in high school—including pumping gas—and continued to do so through college.

It was the 1960s, a time of idealism and the Vietnam War. Kellner went off to a state university to become a teacher but by his junior year was looking for a profession that would pay a lot better. He switched to C. W. Post College on Long Island to major in marketing and graduated in 1969.

While at Post, Kellner had taken a night job managing the bar of a local yacht club. He had turned around a money-losing operation, impressing the private club member whose committee oversaw the operation. The club member had told Kellner that he worked at CBS and that if he ever wanted a job, to call him.

Kellner's main concern after graduation was being drafted to fight in Vietnam. Then fate intervened. Kellner badly injured his left knee and had to have surgery. That made him 4-F and ineligible for the army.

While he was limping around recuperating, Kellner remembered the man from the yacht club. He called him at CBS and was hired that day into the CBS management-training program.

As a trainee, Kellner was moved from one department to the next to see where he might fit in. In special products, he learned that CBS had a laminated paper record that could be made cheaply and played on any record player. Soon afterward, he saw comic Red Skelton doing his own special patriotic, sentimental version of the Pledge of Allegiance. Shortly after that he convinced Burger King, the fast-food restaurant chain, to hand out paper records of Skelton as a promotion. When he returned with an order for 5 million, Kellner became a hot young executive to watch.

Eventually Kellner moved to CBS Enterprises, which took shows that appeared on the network and resold them to independent stations (later this was called syndication). When CBS agreed, along with ABC and NBC, to a consent decree in 1972 that took them out of the used program business, Kellner stayed on as the division was detached from CBS and set up as a new, independent company called Viacom Enterprises.

In 1978 Kellner jumped to Filmways, which was under new management. Kellner's big contribution was finding a way to take the ninety-minute "Saturday Night Live" shows done for NBC and recut them into thirty-minute comedy shows for syndication. When Filmways was taken over by Orion in 1982, Kellner was one of the few executives invited to stay on.

Kellner supervised both network and syndicated production at Orion, including the hit cop show "Cagney and Lacey" (CBS). He also spent a lot of time looking for shows that Orion could mount directly for syndication. One project about which he was very enthusiastic was a daytime talk show starring Joan Rivers. Orion had done a lot of research that showed that Rivers's main appeal was to women, who were heavy daytime TV viewers. He went so far as to offer Rivers $3.5 million for one year, but against the advice of Bernie Brillstein, her consultant, Rivers turned it down. She said she liked the glamour of late night too much, and that she felt she would have to tone down her act for daytime TV.

Kellner did get a new version of "Hollywood Squares" on the air. Shortly afterward he got a call from Robert Fell, an executive recruiter in Century City. Fell had called Kellner several times before with various offers, but nothing had ever worked out. This time Kellner was intrigued as Fell told him he represented people who planned to start a fourth television network.

At thirty-eight, Kellner was already financially secure thanks to profit participations in a number of Filmways/Orion shows. It was clear that what Fell was talking about wouldn't pay as much as he presently was making, but it was the idea of taking on the major networks that Kellner loved. He felt very strongly at the time that the network-TV game was changing, and he didn't think the existing networks were smart enough or fast enough on their feet to keep up with the changes. He felt that very shortly, the networks were going to find themselves seriously challenged for viewers.

In late October 1985, shortly after sharing his views with Fell, Kellner got a call from Barry Diller, who invited him to his house for coffee the following Saturday morning.

Although Diller could provide few details, Kellner immediately felt that the plan to start a new network was feasible. He also saw the purchase of the six Metromedia stations as a dramatic commitment. He knew enough about Diller and Murdoch to know that they wouldn't have bought those stations just to operate them as independents.

After three meetings with Diller, Kellner had breakfast at the Bel Air Hotel one morning with Murdoch. He recalls his initial impression:

> I'd never met him before. I thought he was gentle, reserved, and rather charming. And very pleasant. He certainly didn't think twice about the fact that he wanted to build a competitive national company that would strive toward excellence, not just play at the game. He really wanted to get in there and make it happen. As did Barry.

Kellner's contract with Orion didn't expire for a few months, and he already had an offer from Orion to renew for five more years at attractive terms. Instead he decided to go with Fox. "I was thirty-eight, thirty-nine and I'd made a lot of money already," says Kellner. "It was my treat to myself to do something that was sort of like the ultimate challenge."

Before making his final decision, Kellner flew to New York to meet with Arthur Krim, the chairman of Orion and Kellner's longtime friend. "He said, 'Well, if I tell you not to do it, and someone else does it and it's successful, then you'll hate me,' " recalls Kellner. " 'So I'll tell you to do it and wish you luck. If it doesn't work, call me.' "

So the new network, which didn't have a name, a concept, or a time frame in which to operate, now had a president.

Unlike Alan Horn, however, this president arrived with full knowledge of who really made the decisions. Says Kellner:

Barry's a difficult guy in some ways, but I think he does have a brilliant mind and he is visionary. Yes, a number of people told me I should not go to work for him. But I think they were wrong because the experience of having been one of the team that is building this company, through all the painful moments as well as the joyful ones, when you add it all up, it certainly comes out on the positive side. If this was supposed to be easy, then there would be ten or twelve networks. This is supposed to be hard and painful and expensive.

13

BREAKING THE NETWORK MONOPOLY

BARRY DILLER HAD been hiring and firing people since his years at ABC, when he was barely old enough to vote, but it remained one of the most difficult things he had to do. Suddenly, with the birth of the new network, he had to make many hiring decisions very rapidly. It didn't take him long to decide that he didn't want people who would try to impose the system from any existing network on his new operation. He wanted to reinvent the broadcasting wheel.

Diller explained his hiring philosophy in an interview one day in the rear conference room of his Twentieth Century–Fox office.

I believe the worst mistake you can make is to hire somebody based on a meeting with them or based upon their reputation. I think the only way you can effectively hire people—and it's not full-proof even then—is to hire people into the company in middle positions, not senior positions. If you have a choice, hire people who don't qualify rather than people who do, because your ability to mate with them is better than it would be if you'd follow a process of hiring a "star" from some other company who has built up his own rhythm of life and the way he likes to function, which may not be in rhythm

119

with your own. A company is, in the final analysis, the combined rhythms of intelligent people rather than any one person's particular expertise or brains. I think that's the right thing to do, but it is, like anything, a theory. Sometimes it works. Sometimes it doesn't. I'm more comfortable with it than with another process.

There was no one who could tell Diller he was wrong. After all, no one had succeeded in starting a network in forty years, despite repeated attempts.

The last serious attempt at a fourth network had floundered and died in 1955. Started by Allen B. Du Mont, a pioneering TV-set manufacturer and broadcaster, it was called the Du Mont Network.

Beginning before World War II, the Allen B. Du Mont Laboratories manufactured picture tubes and TV receivers. Much of the work on television was being done by RCA, but Du Mont made several major engineering contributions. His most notable achievement was an improvement in cathode-ray picture tubes, which had been notoriously unreliable. After the war, Du Mont took the lead in making sets with larger screens and better definition. He also worked aggressively against a CBS proposal for a field-sequential color-TV system, which he felt would be obsolete before it got off the ground.

Du Mont's first TV stations were WABD in New York City (which had first signed on as W3XWT) and WDTV in Pittsburgh. Paramount Pictures Corporation purchased a half interest in Du Mont's TV stations in 1938 and then in 1946 linked some (but not all) other stations it owned to form the Du Mont Network.

Paramount was the only major Hollywood studio that had shown an interest in working with the new electronic medium. All of the others, including Twentieth Century–Fox and MGM, refused to even sell programming to the new medium, which they considered a threat to their theatrical business.

Instead, most TV licenses were grabbed up by existing radio broadcasters, who tended to affiliate their TV operations with the network owned by their radio-network partners. That meant that RCA and CBS had an immediate foothold in the new industry when they began in the late 1940s.

RCA, the most powerful company in broadcasting (both as a programmer and a TV-set manufacturer), was forced by federal trustbusters in 1943 to divest one of its two radio networks. It chose to spin off the weaker of its operations, which then became the ABC network. "There was really only room for about two and a half networks at that time, so ABC and Du Mont were each ending up with about a quarter," says Leonard Goldenson, who founded and ran the ABC network from the early 1950s until the mid-1980s.

The way the federal government initially distributed TV-station licenses also lent itself to a very limited number of networks. The FCC rules adopted in 1952 emphasized a desire for local TV-station ownership and a mix of VHF and UHF stations. VHF (or very high frequency) had a very limited spectrum, which meant a limited number of stations, but it offered excellent signal quality and was easier to pinpoint on a TV's tuner dial. UHF (ultra high frequency) had a broader spectrum, but the signal was easily impacted by weather and required a much greater amount of electricity, which made it more expensive to operate.

That meant that despite the good intentions of the FCC, most station owners opted for VHF. The TV-set manufacturers followed suit, and on most sets, the viewer could tune in only VHF signals.

The idea of local ownership was also a bust. The reality was that local owners soon sold out to better capitalized group station owners, especially in the largest markets. By both FCC design and the economics of the marketplace new stations came on the scene very slowly. In most cities there was one, and no more than two, stations available to affiliate with any network. That limited the development of new networks.

Statistics kept by the Association of Independent Television Stations indicate that in 1952 there were only seven cities in the United States with a fourth VHF station that might be available to join a network. It was only slightly better for the third network, ABC, which didn't really reach parity in the number of affiliates and audience reach until the 1960s.

The Columbia Broadcasting System run by William Paley, a brilliant executive with incredible programming instincts, and RCA, which called its network the National Broadcasting Company, weren't troubled by Hollywood's refusal to provide programming. They simply moved the old vaudeville stars who had worked for them on radio over to television—including such household names as Bob Hope, Bing Crosby, Edgar Bergen, Jack Benny, George Burns, and Jimmy Durante.

Du Mont and ABC, on the other hand, were continually starved for programming. Du Mont decided to make do by creating new live shows that would be broadcast from New York. In 1953 it opened a $5 million video-production facility, the most extravagant the young medium had ever seen. Its mainstays were Jackie Gleason, Bishop Fulton J. Sheen, and Monday night boxing. Du Mont also took chances to find an audience. For instance, it drew enormous attention by covering the historic Army-McCarthy hearings.

Still, Du Mont never could get enough affiliated stations to make itself economically feasible. At various times it reported that it had as many as 178 affiliates, but many of them took only selected shows. The problem was, all programming had to be delivered over land-based telephone lines that were enormously expensive. Network economics only made sense if there were a lot of affiliates drawing a lot of viewers, so that advertisers could be persuaded to spend big bucks as sponsors.

Du Mont finally collapsed in 1955. The lab and manufacturing operations were spun off as a separate company, and the Du Mont stations became the Metropolitan stations. They were acquired in 1959 by John W. Kluge, who renamed them the Metromedia stations. That was the name they kept until 1985, when they became the Fox stations and the basis of yet another TV network.

During the year after Du Mont's demise, advertising billings at ABC jumped 68 percent. It was widely assumed that it was because of what had happened to Du Mont. To an extent, it was. But it was also the result of a little guy trying harder to avoid extinction.

ABC was really the result of two government-forced divestitures. First, as mentioned, was the spin-off of the weaker of RCA's two radio networks in 1943. Then, in 1951 Paramount was forced to divest its profitable circuit of movie theaters, which were run by young attorney Leonard Goldenson. He recalls that when the opportunity arose a short time later to buy the ABC network for $25 million in stock (half preferred, half common stock), he was very enthusiastic but his board of directors was not. Only after a late night meeting and an offer of outside financing to pull off the deal did they relent.

Goldenson had hinged his pitch for ABC on his belief that he could get Hollywood to provide programming. He felt that since his Paramount theater circuit was the largest single buyer of movies in the world at the time, they would have to listen. When old Hollywood hands called him a traitor for even trying, Goldenson told them that they soon would be using the new medium to promote their movies—that they would have to work together.

General David Sarnoff, founder and longtime chairman of powerful RCA, called Goldenson and suggested that ABC specialize in running shows after they had run on ABC and CBS, to save money.

Goldenson told the general that he had not entered broadcasting to be a second-run network.

Finally, after pleading his way through a five-hour lunch in a Hollywood restaurant, Goldenson got Jack Warner, whose studio, Warner Bros., was in deep financial trouble, to agree to make a few TV series. That led to "Cheyenne" and a wave of Westerns on TV.

Still, most studios refused to sell to TV. Then one day Walt and Roy Disney paid a visit to Goldenson looking for investors for a new theme park they wanted to build in southern California that would be called Disneyland. The Disneys were mortgaged up to their eyeballs and had already been turned down by NBC and CBS. Goldenson said he would be interested if they could also produce a one-hour weekly TV show for his network. They agreed, and an eight-year deal was worked out that gave ABC a 35 percent interest in The Disney Company as well. The park in Anaheim, California, and the TV show were both a huge success.

Incidentally, ABC, was so unhappy seven years later, when Disney jumped to NBC so that the show could be in color, that it sold the Disney stock for a $10 million profit—which in retrospect is a fraction of what it was worth.

By 1960 Hollywood was ready and willing to provide all the programming television wanted, if only to keep its expensive soundstages busy. However, even though programming was no longer a bar to forming a fourth network, some major obstacles remained. The biggest was the cost of those telephone lines. The second biggest was the lack of independent stations to carry the programs of a fourth network.

Still, there were attempts. In May 1967, for eleven nights, the United Network broadcast the "Las Vegas Show" for two hours nightly over 127 network affiliates and independent stations. It quickly collapsed because of the high cost of telephone lines for transcontinental transmission.

In 1976 a number of station groups joined together to form Operation Prime Time, which agreed to carry miniseries and specials in the prime evening hours, with all advertising sold by a central source. That led to the formation of other ad hoc networks, some placing programs in return for cash, most operating with barter advertising, where the station gets the show free in return for agreeing to carry a certain number of national advertisements.

Then, in the mid-1970s, a technological change caught up with broadcasting, forever altering the rules. It was the beginning of satellite transmission of TV programming. If it had never happened, there would have been no attempt at a Fox network. Nor would there have been the fantastic growth of cable-TV services that began to blossom in the late 1970s.

In October 1945 a science fiction article by Arthur C. Clarke had appeared in a British technical magazine called *Wireless World.* In it, Clarke suggested that it was possible to place reflectors in orbit 22,300 miles above the earth, positioned just over the equator, that would bounce radio signals back to earth. The distance and the idea were not just haphazard guesses. Clarke understood the principle of the geosynchronous orbit. Just as the earth orbits around the sun, objects can continuously circle the earth. Depending on how far up they are, that circle can be faster, slower, or exactly in tune with the speed at which the earth is rotating. To be perfectly in tune, the object must orbit at about 22,300 miles in the sky.

The miracle of this idea was that when one signal went up, it could be received, once it was reflected, over a very wide area—or footprint, as scientists called it. This meant that a single TV picture could be broadcast to a huge number of locations equipped with receiving dishes.

Another invention soon followed that moved communications technology even farther. On December 23, 1947, the Bell Telephone Laboratories in Murray Hill, New Jersey, held a secret demonstration of what scientists dubbed the "transistor." This was a device that allowed several electrical signals to be moved and switched with great simplicity. It opened the way for the miniaturization of all electronics and made possible the modern computer.

It also made possible the space race between the Soviet Union and the United States. On October 4, 1957, the Russians became the first to launch a man-made satellite into space, the *Sputnik 1.* The Americans followed in January 1958 with *Explorer 1,* and then in December 1958 with *Score,* the first artificial satellite used for voice communication. That led, in 1962, to the launching by the United States of *Telstar,* a satellite owned by AT & T, which was the first designed to handle communications transmissions. That was followed in 1963 by *Syncom,* the first satellite to use the geosynchronous orbit predicted by Clarke.

Over the following twenty years, tremendous scientific advances were made, including such innovations as a tiny silicon chip that could do the job of many transistors, and digital processing, which gave much greater control over video picture quality. By the mid-

1980s, when Rupert Murdoch bought the Fox stations, signal transmission was no longer a prohibitive expense to starting a fourth network.

Another obstacle also had been removed by the middle of the eighties.

In 1980 Ronald Wilson Reagan was elected president of the United States. One of the basic tenets of his Republican philosophy was that government should not be in any business that can be operated more efficiently by private enterprise. In broadcasting this led to a new era of deregulation. The FCC would no longer regulate programming; rather, it would limit itself to the role of electronic "traffic cop" to insure that one kind of communications transmission didn't interfere with another.

This led to several developments in television. First, the FCC began the rapid licensing of new TV stations all over the United States, both on the more popular VHF broadcast spectrum (encompassing channels 2 to 13) and on the UHF spectrum (channels 14 to 83). Most of these stations became independents, since lucrative network affiliations already were taken in their markets. The number of unaffiliated TV stations in the United States, according to INTV, rose from 112 to 1980 to 272 in 1986, the year the new Fox network was launched. There were, for the first time, enough independent stations to support a fourth over-the-air broadcast television network.

The FCC under President Reagan also provided new incentive for investing in broadcasting. It dropped rules requiring a licensee to hold a station for a minimum of three years. This made TV stations much more interesting to investors, who began pushing up station values and pumping in new capital that encouraged even more stations to go on the air.

The FCC also changed its rules to allow any one station group to own up to twelve TV stations, as long as its total reach was no greater than 25 percent of TV homes in the United States. This opened the way for larger station groups with more economic clout, resulting in an increase in programming made by station groups themselves.

Cable TV also was helping to pave the way for a fourth network. For years big advertisers had seen the three networks as their only outlet. Cable TV, both on a national level and on a local level, showed them an alternative and got ad agencies thinking about ways to target consumers. In other words, rather than paying a large sum to reach everyone who watched a CBS show, they could pay less to reach a smaller group of upscale, educated consumers who watched, as an example, the news on Turner Broadcasting's Cable News Network. This switch from mass numbers to targeted demographics, which also was boosted by improving audience-measurement technology, made it possible to think in terms of a network that would reach fewer people but still be profitable by reaching those most desired by advertisers.

Cable TV also gave new viability to fledgling UHF stations. For viewers with cable TV, the UHF station was no longer that fuzzy orphan signal that required a separate antenna and a knowledge of engineering to find. It was now just another button on the cable box.

All of this set the stage for the arrival of a fourth TV network, even as other voices insisted that it couldn't be done. They noted that with the advent of cable TV and the VCR, the share of the audience watching existing network shows was dropping—from a high of over 93 percent in 1970 to under 70 percent by 1986. They said that this meant it was the wrong time to start a network and that there simply would not be enough advertising revenue to support a fourth.

Researchers at NBC and CBS both told the press why a fourth network made up of struggling independent VHF stations and backwater UHF stations never could pull together enough of an audience to succeed with advertisers. An executive at a prominent syndication company told *Daily Variety,* the Hollywood-based trade paper, that

> For Fox to make money its programming would have to attract three times the primetime audience the [same] stations got in the February 1986 sweeps [when audiences are measured to set ad rates for the following quarter of the year]. . . . That kind of explosive increase on a regular-series basis has never happened before in the history of TV.

As he hired his first corps of executives in early 1986, Barry Diller had heard all of these arguments and more. That was why he was determined not to hire old network hands who would just tell him what couldn't be done. He needed either people with some experience who could share his vision or young executives not tainted by the doomsayers.

As it turned out, he found some of each.

David Johnson first read about the Fox network in the *Wall Street*

Journal while sitting at home in Greenwich, Connecticut, where he was trying to put together financing to buy a group of TV stations. A tall, broad-shouldered forty-six year old with sandy hair and a long, clean-shaven face, Johnson had risen through the ranks in administration and sales at ABC. He had been fired by the network as part of the cutbacks associated with the 1986 sale to Capital Cities. A short time later, while working as a consultant from his home in Connecticut, Johnson wrote a letter to Barry Diller that said, "Whatever you do don't hire network people to run your network because they're going to make all the same mistakes over again." Johnson then listed a number of errors he felt the networks were making.

A few days later Johnson got a call from Jamie Kellner, who said he was going to be flying east shortly and wanted to set up a meeting. Johnson soon became the third employee of the new, still unnamed network, after Diller and Kellner. He was put in charge of advertising and affiliate relations.

Johnson brought Fox a thorough knowledge of network economics as well as a highly iconoclastic spirit, which was exactly what Diller and Murdoch were looking for.

A native of Cleveland, he had attended Amherst College and then gotten a master's degree at the Harvard Business School. He began at ABC as a management trainee and then worked his way up the ladder in administration and sales. It was an exciting time at ABC, as the network moved from last place to first place in the ratings in the late 1970s. Johnson moved around from general manager of a local ABC-owned station to a corporate post overseeing the entire station group. At various times he tried to convince ABC to make acquisitions that he considered promising, including the purchase of half of Twentieth Century–Fox and of a broadcaster, Capital Cities, both rejected by senior management as too large. Later, of course, little Capital Cities would swallow up giant ABC for $3.5 billion. By that time, Johnson had been fired.

Johnson believed that TV networks were increasingly just programming engines that governed the value of the rest of the company—especially the network's owned and operated stations. He instinctively knew that Murdoch's purchase of Metromedia would require a similar kind of engine. Said Johnson shortly after joining Fox:

As long as I live I'll never understand Cap Cities and General Electric [owner of NBC] thinking the network business is anything but a low-margin, high-risk venture. When you're number one, you may make $300 million in profit, but you're not number one every year. When you're number three, you're losing a lot of money. However, what you don't read about is that the network's owned stations are still making $300 million. And the only reason they can do that is because the network can afford to give them programs because they've achieved these economies of scale by laying off those programming costs over 200-plus stations.

After Johnson, who was experienced but not locked into the old, established network systems, came Fox's fourth employee, who fit Diller's definition of an executive a year too young for the job but ready to grow.

Scott Sassa, an Asian-American with curly dark hair, eyes that shone, and an easy smile, had just passed his twenty-seventh birthday in the spring of 1986. He worked in programming for the Playboy Channel during a brief period when there was an effort to make it broader and more appealing to Yuppies. Although he was relatively young, Sassa had enjoyed a varied career that had included brief stints at the Walt Disney Company, the Rogers and Cowan public relations agency, and Turner Broadcasting. It was at Turner that Sassa had first seriously studied the possibility of a fourth broadcast network. Ted Turner, the flamboyant head of Turner Broadcasting, had suggested a way to start such a network without paying for programming. Turner executives called it the "condo network." The idea was to create a program service that would sell blocks of time to existing programmers, such as movie studios, who could do with it as they wanted and make as much from it by selling advertising as the market would bear. Turner, along with Sassa and his other executives, had met with top Hollywood executives, but the idea had never gone anywhere.

Sassa was then asked by Turner to start a cable music channel to compete with MTV. A month after it went on the air, Turner sold it to its arch competitor, MTV, which of course promptly pulled it off the air. That's when Sassa moved to Playboy.

After Murdoch's speech at INTV, Sassa had read about the Fox attempt at a fourth network and was intrigued. Unsure who to approach, he wrote to Alan Horn, whom he knew slightly, asking about openings at the new venture. Horn referred him to Kellner, who took Sassa to lunch on February 10, 1986. "We argued for two hours," recalls Sassa. "I told him why he would fail miserably in this task and . . . he gave me back good answers."

By the end of February, Sassa was employee number four. His assignment was to do a little of whatever was needed, ranging from helping Johnson write the business plan to advertising and public relations. His little portable MacIntosh computer became the central data bank of the new network, providing projections of advertising revenue based on various audience sizes and much more. "We were creating models that taught us what the business was about, what we could control," says Sassa. "We questioned everything. What was a rating point worth? How much will we have to spend on programming? What kind of [station lineup] clearances could we expect? All those things that we didn't know but over time became more comfortable with."

At Diller and Kellner's insistence, Johnson and Sassa created a preliminary business plan. It envisioned a "network" that would operate one or two nights a week in prime time (8:00 to 11:00 P.M.) and would aim at an upscale, urban audience. Johnson and Sassa projected that the new service would reach about 70 percent of U.S. television homes and might draw about 4 to 6 percent of these as viewers initially. "It was done on a rainy night on a MacIntosh over at Scott's house," recalls Johnson. "It was just bullshit. We did it in an hour, and then we used it. And later they wanted to hold us to those numbers. Like, 'This is your sales target.' Hey, wait a minute. We just made this up. We stated these were just assumptions."

Diller, however, was determined to achieve this goal and to do it more quickly than any of them had ever imagined possible. "You didn't have time to do what you had to do, but you also didn't have time to interview and hire others," says Sassa about those first crazy weeks. "It's different than a normal company. We had nobody. The one profound lesson I learned was you just have to stop, find the people you need, hire those people, and get them on board."

The boldest attempt at a fourth U.S. television network since the fall of Du Mont was beginning to take shape.

OUT BY NOON

AS THE NEW network began to take form, it became imperative to find a head of programming as quickly as possible. This person would be responsible for developing shows, working with producers, writers, and others. His or her taste would shape the outside world's first impression of the new venture and determine whether its future would be long term.

Recalls Jamie Kellner:

> The criteria at that point, since we were not going to be as involved in the production of shows as networks tend to be, just by the nature of the fact that we were going to be a low-overhead, smaller operation, and because we were going to bring in producers and give them the mandate, we wanted someone with more ideas than production background. . . . We were really looking for bright people who we felt had the right kind of personality to develop relationships and to represent us in the creative community.

Diller and Kellner, through their own contacts and candidates suggested by an executive recruiter, had gone through a long list of names and interviewed a number of people. They had offered the job to an executive at Warner Bros. Television, but he had decided to accept another offer instead. That's when Scott Sassa, who had just joined Fox as a vice president involved in public relations, administration, and affiliate relations, got into the act. One of the first people he called for suggestions was his friend Garth Ancier. Ancier worked in comedy development at NBC, which had just become the most-watched network—primarily because of the success of its comedies, such as "The Golden Girls" and "The Cosby Show."

Sassa had known Ancier, whom he met through a mutual friend at Cable News Network, for several years. They would chat on the phone occasionally or meet for dinner. Although both were in their twenties, Ancier seemed very mature to Sassa. Tall and lean, with a head full of shaggy, light-brown hair and a long, boyish face, Ancier constantly amazed Sassa with his knowledge of television history. "To me Garth was unbelievable," says Sassa. "He was such a student of broadcasting."

When Sassa called, Ancier offered a few suggestions for the programming position. As soon as he hung up, Sassa picked up the phone and called right back. "Garth, you know I did something really rude," said Sassa. "I didn't ask if you'd be interested. I guess I didn't think you'd want to give up what you have at NBC. You've put in a lot of time, they really like you, and you have a shot at being *the* guy, so I figured you'd probably want to stay there."

Sassa had always kidded Ancier that while he was very risk oriented, Ancier was risk adverse. "This Fox thing is kind of risky," continued Sassa. "Who knows if it'll even work. It'll probably just be a pinpoint in history. . . . But you know, how many presidents do they have at NBC? You could be the ninth or tenth—or the first president of programming at Fox. Would you be interested?"

Ancier had read about the Fox venture in the paper and wasn't sure, but he said if they wanted to talk to him, he was willing to at least discuss it. But the next day when Sassa called, Ancier had changed his mind. He would pass.

Sassa, however, kept talking about Ancier to others at Fox. During one meeting when Ancier's name came up, and Diller told Murdoch that he was just a lower-level programming executive at NBC, Sassa jumped in to point out that Ancier was actually only a few slots away from Brandon Tartikoff, the head of programming.

At another meeting there was discussion about doing a live news-oriented comedy show, and Sassa suggested they talk to Kevin Wendle, director of drama development at NBC, who had a background in local TV news. Wendle, although in a much more junior position at NBC, also happened to be quite friendly with Ancier.

Kellner set up a breakfast with Wendle in the Polo Lounge of the Beverly Hills Hotel, a legendary gathering place for those in show business. The hotel, then owned in part by the wife of notorious investor Ivan Boesky, was a large, pink baroque building set back behind a forest of palm trees on Sunset Boulevard in the heart of a residential area of Beverly Hills. Kevin Wendle arrived first and gave the keys to his sports car to the valet parking attendant. His light-brown hair neatly trimmed, Wendle had a high forehead and was solidly built and square jawed. Wearing a light-colored sport jacket and tie, he walked through the tiled lobby and took a right turn toward the Polo Lounge, which got its name in the 1940s when a group of polo-playing movie stars made it their hangout.

At the entrance, Wendle encountered Bernice, the pleasant and efficient woman who seated each guest. She escorted him to a plush dark-red leather booth in the front of the restaurant. Behind him was a glass wall looking back into another room, where Wendle recognized several of the top executives in Hollywood sipping coffee as they gossiped and made deals.

Jamie Kellner, deeply tanned and radiating health in his light-tan suit and iridescent blue tie, slid into the seat across from Wendle. The men exchanged greetings and quickly got down to business. "We aren't sure exactly how many people we're going to need or when, but Scott [Sassa] felt you might be the kind of person who could fit into this kind of start-up situation."

Kevin Wendle spoke rapidly, his cleanly shaven face bronzed by a dark tan. He talked a bit about himself, how he had begun his career while still a schoolboy, passing for eighteen years of age when he was really only fifteen. He told Kellner about his experience in local TV news and his job at NBC, where he was a very junior executive in the programming department.

"Kevin was very smart and very honest about how much experience he had," Kellner recalled later. "Next I set up a meeting with Barry, and Barry also though very highly of him. But not for the number-one job."

What Diller and Kellner said was that if he was to be offered a job, it would be as the number-two person in the programming department. Kevin was interested but unsure about what to do. First, he didn't want to make any decision until he knew for whom he actually would be working for. Second, he felt he still had a lot to learn and a great deal of opportunity to do so at NBC.

Feeling confused after his breakfast with Kellner, Wendle turned for advice to his colleague at NBC, Garth Ancier, the one person he felt would fully grasp the opportunity being presented while keeping it absolutely secret. Ancier readily agreed that it was a tempting offer and a fascinating challenge.

After another long meeting with Diller, Wendle got a call from Kellner offering him the number-two job in programming. Wendle said it would depend on who was chosen as number one. "I hear you might be interested in Garth Ancier," said Wendle. "If that's true, then you'd have me in a second."

"I'm so relieved," answered Kellner. "I thought you'd say 'if you're thinking about Garth, then I'm not interested.' "

Ancier, meanwhile, had agreed to at least listen to what Fox had to offer. Over the next four days, Ancier met with Kellner and Diller again and was offered the job. Ancier then told his immediate superior at NBC, Warren Littlefield, who was number two to Tartikoff, about the Fox offer. Ancier was then called in to discuss it with Tartikoff. "You shouldn't do this," Tartikoff told Ancier. "They just have a lot of weak UHF stations. It would be a mistake. We're going to do big things at NBC. . . . I'm going to put you on the phone with Grant [Tinker, president of the network], and he'll tell you how important you are to the future of NBC."

A short time later Tinker called Ancier and made a counteroffer with a raise in pay that made his salary equal to Fox's offer. Ancier then decided to stay at NBC, so he called Kellner and said the Fox offer wasn't good enough financially. Kellner, however, refused to accept that as an answer. He insisted that Ancier come over that very night and meet once more with Diller, Murdoch, and himself.

By the end of cocktails at Fox, Ancier had agreed to a deal—for significantly more money than had been offered the first time around.

That night Ancier called Wendle, who agreed to move to Fox as well. "We were like kids set loose in a candy store," says Wendle. "All of a sudden we were going to be running a network programming department."

The next morning at NBC, Ancier pondered how to resign. Before he could do anything, he got a call requesting that he come to Fox for lunch. Sitting in the studio commissary with Diller, Murdoch, Kellner, and Johnson, Ancier saw "L.A. Law" producer Steven Bochco and Warren Littlefield of NBC walk in and sit at another table. He knew Littlefield had seen him.

Later, when Ancier called his secretary at NBC, she told him that the word was out in the halls and they were all wondering what was going on. Ancier said he would see her the next morning at NBC in Burbank.

Later in the afternoon, Kevin Wendle arrived to join the all-day meeting that Diller and Murdoch had been holding with their new network team. Wendle remembers that they "talked about the vaguest kind of things—what satellites should we be on, the kind of people we were going to hire."

Wendle recalls how surprised he was that Murdoch was so soft-spoken yet so keenly aware of every detail of what was going on. "He was like 'Father Knows Best,'" says Wendle. "He was so warm. I just felt like this was the best move I'd ever made. I felt like part of a family."

Wendle's instant association with "Father Knows Best," a classic situation comedy from TV's first generation, wasn't just a casual reference. Both Wendle and Ancier, although quite different in many respects, had been heavy television watchers throughout childhood, often using the TV families to fill voids in their own lives.

"My father was in sales and so we moved around a lot to various towns in northern New Jersey when I was growing up," Wendle explains. "I didn't have a lot of friends. . . . So my best friends were Gilligan on 'Gilligan's Island,' Will from 'Lost in Space,' Samantha on 'Bewitched,' and Jeannie on 'I Dream of Jeannie.' I watched a lot of TV. I just sort of devoured it."

In the spring of 1974, when Wendle was fourteen, a TV-news crew from channel 5 in New York, the Metromedia station, came to his school to work on a story. Wendle followed them around all day in awe. He asked if there was any chance he could get a summer job at the station. He said he would work for free and would do anything, even shine shoes. The reporter, Chris Jones, told him that when the time came he should give him a call.

Wendle didn't believe it would ever happen, but Jones's offer stayed in the back of his mind. Four months later, in July 1974, Wendle had a fight with his best friend and was bored. He decided to call Jones, who promptly invited him to come to the station the next day around noon.

Wendle was so excited he couldn't sleep. He got a ride into the city with his neighbor at 7:30 A.M. and then sat in the lobby of channel 5 until noon so Jones wouldn't think he was too anxious. Jones, the station's "action news reporter," immediately put Wendle to work opening mail and trying to answer some of the complaints people sent in. Wendle was fascinated by every detail of the operation.

Jones had told Wendle to come in for about three hours a day. Instead he began arriving early in the morning and staying until late at night. When summer ended, Wendle continued working there every day after school. Soon he met Ron Van Dor, a production assistant who was only a few years older than Wendle. Van Dor showed him the ropes and taught him how to write a news script. Shortly after that, Van Dor quit and went to work for channel 11 news.

A few months later, during the Christmas holiday, Van Dor called Wendle and told him there was a paying job for a copyboy available at WINS, an all-news radio station. Wendle got the job, his first paying position in the media, and soon was filling in on the radio, giving sports scores and doing the weather forecast.

In mid-1975, six months after his arrival, Wendle's supervisor discovered that Wendle was underage. He said the child labor laws prohibited anyone his age from working over four hours a day. A few months later Wendle went to the station manager and announced that he had just turned eighteen. The station manager said fine and put him back on a full forty-hour workweek. Actually, Wendle had just turned fifteen.

The following Christmas, in 1976, Wendle got another call from Van Dor, who told him it was time to move out of radio and into television as his assistant at channel 11, the *New York Daily News* television station. Wendle moved there on a free-lance basis and began writing news copy. One day the boss came out and asked if anyone was available to write sports reports on Saturdays. Wendle piped up and said he had experience from WINS. He got the job. "I've never watched a football game from beginning to end to this day," laughs Wendle, "but I got it done. I'd rip it off the wire, get a sense of it, look for the big names, and then go to the tape and show the great plays."

After a year writing about sports, Wendle was asked if he could fill in as producer of the late, late news, which was a summary of the day's events read by an announcer while slides were shown. Shortly after he started, a hurricane hit the New York City area. Wendle set up a live hookup to the National Weather Service and went on the air to ask questions and provide updated information. The station's news director was so impressed that he asked Wendle to become the producer of the midday news show. Wendle took the job, although he never told his boss that it meant he would have to skip the second half of his senior year in high school. He took an apartment on Thirty-seventh Street in Manhattan, signed up for enough courses at New York University to qualify for a high school diploma, and set to work. It was 1978. He was sixteen years old.

Wendle never got around to going to college, but over the next two years he got an intense education in television. He tried everything from writing to on-air reporting. He found that he preferred being the producer, the one in control, rather than the person on the air. Working with Van Dor on the evening news show, they won an Emmy for the best newscast, beating out the network-affiliated stations in New York. That led ABC to hire Van Dor to produce its news show at WLS in Chicago. A year later Van Dor recruited Wendle to join him. Soon Wendle was producing the number-one news show in the Windy City, using a chatty, "happy talk" format. There was just one problem. When the newscasters wanted to buy Wendle a drink to celebrate being number one in the ratings, they discovered he wasn't yet old enough to drink in Illinois. "That was a great source of amusement in the newsroom," he recalls.

When the WLS general manager was moved to New York, he brought Wendle back to produce the six o'clock news at WABC, the network's flagship station. It remained number one throughout his tenure there.

By 1982 Wendle was bored. He considered trying sales and research but finally decided to move into local programming at WABC. At the time, MTV, the rock music cable-TV service, had just come on, amid controversy over the lack of black musicians it showcased. Wendle decided to produce a late night black music video show, working with a tiny budget. "New York Hot Tracks," on Friday night, almost immediately became a hit, and it was expanded from thirty minutes to ninety minutes. The show later moved into national syndication and won an Emmy for a special on break dancing.

Wendle now knew enough about television to know that he wanted to do a lot more. Everybody he talked to told him he needed to move to California if he really wanted to be in production. After a short visit to Los Angeles, Wendle decided to take the chance. He quit his job, gave up his apartment, and moved west in October 1984. After several months of producing free-lance TV-magazine segments, he got a job at NBC as manager of drama development. Less than eighteen months later he was headed for Fox.

Leaving NBC was much more traumatic for Ancier, for several reasons. First, he had been there much longer. Second, Ancier was much more conservative and had a harder time dealing with constant change. He liked routines and he liked to work with the same people. Third, Ancier truly was in line to succeed Tartikoff some day, while Wendle was just another junior executive.

Garth Ancier had grown up in much greater affluence than Wendle had, in an upper-class suburban community called Lawrenceville, in New Jersey. His parents were both accountants, and his father also taught at a local college.

Ancier, too, had been a heavy TV watcher and had been fascinated with every aspect of the medium. At age twelve he was accepted as an unpaid intern at a public television station that had just opened in New Jersey. There he leaned about cameras, scripts, and what went into making a program. He also spent a lot of time hanging out at the campus radio station at Ryder College, where his father was a professor. "I was just very attracted to broadcasting," said Ancier during an interview a year after moving to Fox, running a hand through his tousled brown hair. "It still intrigues me that two of us can talk on a microphone in a room and you can broadcast it to everyone in the country. It's sort of magical."

Ancier had gotten his first paying job in broadcasting at age fourteen, when he became a part-time engineer at an NBC affiliated radio station in Trenton, New Jersey. He would flick the dials to open the microphone for the disc jockey, insert commercials, and fill in the log for the show. For the first time in his life Ancier felt like he was growing into something important. "I was always pretty shy and introverted as a kid," Ancier recalls. "I was never a good student. It's not that I couldn't do it, I just wasn't academically inclined."

Ancier dreamed of becoming a disc jockey, which he was sure would impress everyone he knew, even though his voice was still shrill and squeaky. Then, in April 1974, he got his chance. The station needed a public affairs program to meet some FCC requirements, so it gave Ancier a half hour early on Sunday morning to talk about young people.

"It was called 'Focus on Youth,'" says Ancier. "Kids on the issues. Youth on parade. It was me and some other kids interviewing a guest."

By then Ancier was enrolled in the Lawrenceville School, a prestigious boarding school for children of the upper class (Michael Eisner and Brandon Tartikoff were alumni). Using school equipment, he would head for Trenton on weekends to produce and host his radio show.

Ancier kept trying for bigger name guests. After about six months he convinced the governor of New Jersey to be on the show. At that point, Ancier decided that his show deserved more exposure, so he approached the NBC radio network. They weren't interested, but they did refer him to WNBC in New York City. In part because it had been accused of not giving New Jersey adequate coverage, WNBC put Ancier on the air early on Sunday mornings beginning in January 1975.

That was so easy, Ancier figured he might as well keep going. He then syndicated "Focus on Youth" to stations in Philadelphia, Los Angeles, Washington, D.C., and Boston. He kept upgrading the guest list and called the show, "America's student press conference of the air."

Despite his poor grades, Ancier's success with the show helped get him into Princeton University, where he continued to do the program until graduation. When he left, a "Focus" board was set up to continue the show. By the time Ancier (who had remained a board member) got to Fox, it was still on four hundred stations each week all over the United States. It was another "Focus" veteran who introduced Ancier to Sassa, leading to his job at Fox.

After graduating Princeton with a degree in politics, Ancier wanted to be in television programming. He wrote to all three networks but put special effort into a letter to his hero in life, Fred Silverman, who was then head of the NBC television network. On a trip to Los Angeles to interview actor Jimmy Stewart for his radio show, Ancier talked his way into the office of NBC programming head Brandon Tartikoff. He didn't have a resume with him, but he did have a "Focus" press kit, which included an article done on Ancier in *People* magazine. Tartikoff was impressed enough to hire Ancier for a management-training program in Burbank.

A year later Tartikoff moved to New York as head of the NBC network, taking Ancier along as his assistant. Later Ancier was moved back to Burbank to work in comedy development, just as NBC was heading for number one. He had been with NBC seven years when Fox came calling.

So on a cool afternoon at the end of March 1986, Ancier and Wendle found themselves in a room with Diller, one of the most legendary studio executives in Hollywood history; Murdoch, the world-famous head of a multinational communications and publishing empire; Kellner; Johnson; and Sassa. The next day Ancier and

Wendle would both march into NBC and resign, and Warren Littlefield would tell them that as they were moving to a competitor, it would be best if they would pack up immediately and be "out by noon."

Wendle joked to Ancier that if they ever wrote a book, they should call it *Out by Noon.*

It was indeed a time for jokes and joy. These two young men, neither yet thirty years old, would now be given many millions of dollars to buy programming that would make or break the bold new venture Murdoch and Diller were launching. They felt a sense of euphoria and almost electric anticipation.

"One of the things we spent a lot of time trying to decide was what to call this thing," says Ancier. "We looked at ABC, CBS, and NBC. We came up with Century Television Corporation and Century Broadcasting Company, but that would have the same initials as the Canadian Broadcasting Company, so we couldn't use it. We also considered UBC [United Broadcasting Company], UBS [United Broadcasting System], and IBC, the Independent Broadcasting Company."

Eventually they settled on FBC, the Fox Broadcasting Company.

All things seemed possible that March afternoon. As Rupert Murdoch put it, the core team of the new network venture was now assembled. That night would be the real beginning.

As darkness fell over Twentieth Century–Fox, Diller suggested that they all continue their discussions over dinner. He said he had made a reservation for them at the Mandarin, a Chinese restaurant in Beverly Hills.

15

JOAN'S FOXY MOVES

ON A FLIGHT from London to New York early in 1986, Edgar Rosenberg was seated in the first-class section of the wide-body jet, next to his wife Joan Rivers and her manager, Bill Sammeth. Rosenberg was reading *Newsweek*. Rosenberg told Rivers and Sammeth about an article written after Rupert Murdoch's speech at the INTV convention in Los Angeles. It said that Murdoch was planning to start a fourth U.S. television network, using the TV stations recently acquired from Metromedia as a base.

The article went on to speculate that Murdoch's new programming service might also be beamed to Western Europe over his Sky Channel satellite-delivered programming service and to Australia, where he had TV interests.

The story sparked an idea in Rosenberg's mind. Since his wife had just concluded a series of very popular talk show specials in England and had a big following in Australia—as well as in the United States, of course—perhaps Murdoch and Barry Diller might be interested in doing a show starring Joan Rivers. Even if they eventually decided it wasn't feasible, it might just provide Rivers with some negotiating leverage with NBC and Carson Productions,

140

which had been stalling on her new contract as permanent guest host of "The Tonight Show Starring Johnny Carson."

Rosenberg told his wife and Sammeth that he would have their attorney put out a feeler and see what happened. Rivers really wanted to stay with NBC, but she agreed it couldn't hurt to see what Murdoch and Diller would say and to have more than one bidder in the game during her delicate contract negotiations.

All three of them remembered the last time they had been in a delicate negotiation with Barry Diller. It hadn't really been with Diller. Rather, he had come in as an intermediary to help settle a legal war.

In a way, that, too, had begun on an airplane. In 1983 Barry Diller was flying home to Los Angeles after a brief vacation, accompanied by one of his closest friends, personal manager Sandy Gallin. Gallin and his partner Ray Katz's clients had included, over the years, Joan Rivers, Neil Diamond, Dolly Parton, Cher, Mac Davis, Anthony Newly, and nearly two dozen other well-known performers.

Gallin and Diller had agreed that there wasn't a good variety show on TV anymore, something with the impact of the "Ed Sullivan Show" during the 1950s and 1960s. Diller, as chairman of Paramount, suggested that they mount such a show together. Gallin said that it would be difficult to find a host. "You should be the host," Diller told Gallin.

That conversation led to a pilot and three shows that aired on NBC in late September 1983.

It was called "Live and In Person," and Gallin pulled out all the stops to offer a superstar lineup. Naturally, as host and one of the creators of such a huge undertaking, Gallin was consumed with details, which didn't leave much time for clients.

As it happened, one of his oldest clients, Joan Rivers—she'd been with him since 1972, when Gallin was a talent agent—needed a lot of management support that week. She had cohosted the Emmys with Eddie Murphy, and there had been a huge flap about the way she kept changing outfits and, particularly, about some of the political jokes she made.

It was also Rivers's week to guest host "The Tonight Show" under a contract Gallin had negotiated about a year earlier. At the last minute on Monday, the primary guest who had been booked, Linda Gray, had an accident and had to cancel. Joan needed her manager to help book another guest—fast. Gallin's assistant who was assigned to Rivers, Bill Sammeth, managed to get Shelley Winters, but Rivers still wasn't satisfied.

Although Rivers had been a guest on "Live and In Person," it irritated her and Rosenberg to think that her own manager was booking so many superstars that it left them slim pickings when she guest hosted for Johnny. Her manager had become her competitor.

Rivers was fed up. She instructed her attorney to notify Gallin that he was no longer her manager because he had breached his contract, which nullified the remaining year on their deal.

Despite all of the stars, "Live and In Person" bombed in the ratings, instantly ending Gallin's career in front of the camera. He turned back to his clients—and Rivers. In December Gallin filed suit demanding $30 million from Rivers in fees he was due and for damages. Rivers then countersued, and acrimony flowed from both sides.

Shortly after Rivers left Gallin, Sammeth quit his job at Katz-Gallin. A few weeks later he became Rivers new personal manager (and went on to manage Cher and others). Gallin made it obvious that he resented Sammeth's "stealing" Rivers.

A preliminary trial date was set for June. As it neared, there was a huge swell of interest from the press, especially the supermarket tabloids. Barry Diller, unhappy that his friend "Sandy" was under stress and about to be dragged through the public mud, contacted Sammeth and told him they had to engineer an out-of-court settlement.

Sammeth felt no obligation, but he set the wheels in motion that led to a settlement. Diller worked out the details in a phone call with Bert Fields, an attorney for Rivers. Rivers paid Gallin an undisclosed amount of money (nowhere near $30 million) representing his share of her income for the last year of the contract.

In the three years since leaving Gallin, Rivers also had retained personable personal manager and producer Bernie Brillstein as a consultant. Brillstein had encouraged her to seriously consider two talk show offers: one from ABC, which wanted Rivers to host a late morning talk show; and the other from Orion Television, under Jamie Kellner, to host a daytime talk show that would be syndicated nationally. In both cases Rivers had said no because she preferred to do a late night talk show, which she felt lent itself to a more glamorous image and nicer clothes.

After Edgar Rosenberg arranged for their attorney, Peter Dekom, to contact Diller about the new Fox network, he discussed it with Bernie Brillstein. He told Brillstein he was sending Diller the research done by Orion that showed Rivers's strong appeal to women and young adults.

Brillstein thought Rivers would be better off remaining as permanent guest host of ''The Tonight Show.'' He said it kept her in the public eye and supported her heavy concert and nightclub appearances nicely. It was a no-lose situation. The Fox idea, on the other hand, would lead into uncharted waters with the risk that she could fail simply because the network was so new that it didn't have its act together.

Brillstein also pointed out that the research was proprietary information that belonged to Orion. When Rosenberg persisted and sent it to Fox anyway, Brillstein resigned as their consultant. Rosenberg didn't tell Rivers what had transpired. He just said that Brillstein was so busy that he wasn't doing enough to justify what they were paying him (Rivers insists that Brillstein had been fired before any of this happened, but others involved corroborate the story).

Diller, who had been thinking about luring Rivers to Fox since the call from her attorney, was telling Murdoch that taking a high-profile performer like Rivers away from NBC would give the network instant credibility and attract independent TV stations to affiliate. Murdoch saw some tapes of her on ''The Tonight Show'' and gave his blessing.

Rivers, however, was increasingly cool toward the whole initiative, which her husband kept pushing. Throughout her life she had been extremely insecure, and that insecurity made her want to stick with the tried and true. She liked having a permanent home at NBC. She ordered Peter Dekom to tell Diller that she had changed her mind.

The attorney reported back that Diller was very upset. Rivers was making him look bad with Murdoch after he had just sold him on the idea. He just wanted a chance to meet and talk. At least they owed him that much.

Rivers didn't know what to do. She wanted to stay at NBC, but she couldn't stand feeling insulted. She felt that Carson and his people were not treating her fairly and that NBC had been too slow in making a gesture to show her that she was part of their family. Her old insecurity began to surface.

Rivers had been appearing on and guest hosting ''The Tonight Show'' since the mid-1970s. She had been named permanent guest host in August 1983, but since then, several things had happened to make her wonder about her position. First, an NBC memo was leaked to the press with a list of names of comics who were candidates to replace Johnny Carson if he decided to retire. Rivers's name was not on it. NBC disavowed the memo, but the psychological damage had been done.

Then there was the problem of her contract. Each year Rivers would wait for Carson to decide that he wasn't going to retire. If his new contract was for one year, she would then be offered a one-year contract as guest host. If it was for two years, then she would be offered two years as well. In early 1986, however, when Carson signed on for two more years, NBC and Carson Productions, which produced the show, offered Rivers only one year. This was immediately taken as a bad sign by Rivers, Rosenberg, and Sammeth.

Sammeth called the head of business affairs at NBC, John Aggolia, to find out what was going on. Rosenberg wanted a larger overall deal, so that Rivers would know she had a home at the network. Even if there was no "Tonight Show," she wanted some assurance that NBC would keep her in the family doing specials, TV movies, and series.

Aggolia, in New York on other business, didn't return repeated calls from Sammeth.

Sammeth also called Henry Bushkin, Carson's longtime personal attorney. Bushkin didn't return his calls, either. Sammeth and his clients then assumed that Bushkin and Carson were still mad at them. Sammeth's last conversation with Bushkin had been six months earlier. Carson's attorney had called to ask Rivers to take a lower fee than her contract called for on the sale of "The Tonight Show" to Australia. The contractual fee was triggered by a single foreign sale and then covered all subsequent sales. But this deal was only for a single country, argued Bushkin, so Rivers should take less. Sammeth said they would stick by the contract and invited Bushkin to go out and sell the show elsewhere now that the payment was to be made. In the end the Australian deal was killed, at least in part because of Rivers's refusal to take less money.

The feeling in the Carson camp was that Rivers was ungrateful.

Finally, Sammeth called Brandon Tartikoff in Burbank and told him what was happening. Tartikoff promised to help. That afternoon Aggolia finally called Sammeth, apologizing for having been out of town, and said they were ready to sign a one-year contract. Sammeth told him he wanted a bigger, overall deal, including assurances that whatever happened with "The Tonight Show," Rivers would remain a part of the NBC family. Aggolia assured him that they wanted to keep Rivers at NBC. However, Aggolia added, because of some unhappy experiences in the past, the network had a policy against long-term agreements that stipulate what a performer's status would be if certain things occurred. He said they wanted to sign a contract for "The Tonight Show" first, and then Rivers could discuss with Tartikoff other things she might do at NBC.

When Sammeth relayed the NBC position, Rivers agreed to meet with Barry Diller and hear what he had to offer.

Diller came for coffee at the Rivers-Rosenberg home in Bel Air, where he proceeded to charm Rivers, Rosenberg, Sammeth, and attorney Peter Dekom. He was surprisingly warm, friendly, upbeat. This was part of the complex nature of Diller's personality. As much as he could be tough and ruthless in business, he also could be incredibly engaging and attentive when he chose to turn on the charm.

Diller told them that he and Murdoch were starting a new network and that they needed Rivers immediately to help launch it. He said they might not need her in a year, and that "The Tonight Show" would never really need her. He reminded them that he knew Carson quite well from their monthly poker games at Dan Melnick's house and that his impression was that Johnny was tired and wouldn't go on with his show much longer. That meant, said Diller, that Rivers's new talk show would be competitive and ready to fill the void. It also meant a new host for the NBC show, and, Diller added, it was very unlikely that that host would be Rivers. Diller concluded by saying that he just wanted to keep the lines of communication open.

At that point, Rivers was ready to call off discussions. But at Rosenberg's and Sammeth's suggestion, she agreed to meet again. This time Diller invited the trio to visit him at his home on a Saturday morning. It was a short drive from the Rivers-Rosenberg home in Bel Air to Coldwater Canyon, where Diller lived. As their car snaked up the trail through the canyon, Sammeth strained to catch the house numbers. He finally found Diller's mailbox and narrow driveway in what otherwise appeared to be a thick forest of trees and shrubbery. The long private driveway turned from paved road into a gravel trail after a few yards, as it wound higher and higher up a hill though thick vegetation. At the top of the hill the car stopped in the circular drive directly in front of the massive front doors.

Rivers and Rosenberg both commented as they pulled up on the contrast between the nearly wild growth of trees and plants all around and the carefully manicured state around the house itself. Every bush and flower seemed to have been placed with great thought. Every hedge was carefully shaped and trimmed, and every lawn edged with the precision of a well-cared-for estate.

Diller greeted his guests graciously and ushered them into his spacious living room, where Fox network president Jamie Kellner waited. A large glass window offered a view of the gardens in back, which also were neatly fixed and bursting with colorful flowers and plants. From one angle, there was also a view of the large swimming pool filled with clear, bluish water.

What surprised Rivers was the tree growing out of the ground and up through the middle of the living room. It shot up through the roof and broadened out into long spines of thick green leaves.

There was a bar on one side of the uncluttered room, which was furnished in light-colored fabrics. Diller's server brought coffee and offered other refreshments. They finally sat in the living room, which was separated from the nearby den by several couches and other furniture.

Jamie Kellner jumped into the conversation immediately, as Diller moved around, finishing his duties as host. Although Kellner had tried to sign Rivers for a show while he was at Orion, most of his negotiations had been with Bernie Brillstein, so he didn't know Rivers or Rosenberg well. As soon as Diller was settled, Kellner let him take the lead in talking about the new talk show Fox had in mind for Rivers to host. By the time the luncheon dishes were cleared, Diller had offered Rivers a two-year deal. Still insisting she wasn't ready to make a decision, Rivers said that if they did get together, she wouldn't consider anything less than three years. She needed more security.

Over the next few weeks, negotiations continued. Peter Dekom talked to people at Fox, and then got on the phone with Rivers, Rosenberg, and Sammeth to make decisions. Rivers held a strong hand and won total creative control over the show. Rosenberg and Sammeth were to be executive producers. Fox also promised to build a theater setting for the new show that would duplicate "The Tonight Show" set in Burbank. The key, said Rivers, was to have the seats going up at a sharp angle, because it makes the laughs roll back down like thunder.

Fox finally agreed to a three-year contract. If the show performed as expected, Fox would pay $15 million, or $5 million each year.

In the meantime, NBC's Aggolia was calling Sammeth, Rivers, and Rosenberg and now *his* calls weren't being returned. Rivers and her husband were stalling while they tried to decide whether or not to really go with Fox.

On the night of the Academy Awards, Joan Rivers and Edgar Rosenberg met for cocktails at Diller's home with Diller and Murdoch, who was accompanied by his wife Anna. The Murdochs assured Rivers that she was one of their favorites. Diller and Murdoch openly wooed Rivers to join the family.

They all then went to agent Irving "Swifty" Lazar's annual Oscar night party at Spago, sitting at separate tables. Later, Rivers would recall bitterly how she watched Diller and Murdoch warmly greet Johnny Carson and his longtime producer Freddy De Cordova. "They stood there kiss, kiss, kiss, knowing they had just fucked them an hour earlier," Rivers said long after the event. "Those are the things I find fascinating, how they all just kill each other off."

The next decision was when to launch the show—and the network. Murdoch and Diller wanted to move quickly. At the pre-Oscars cocktail party in March, Murdoch asked Rivers if she could start work in May and be ready to go on the air by August. Rivers felt she needed a lot more time to prepare. There was also another problem. Her heaviest concert-touring period was summer, and she already was booked for almost every night until after Labor Day. Canceling would cost her millions of dollars and result in a lot of bad publicity.

Then Fox suggested starting in September or early October. Rivers said she would not work on the Jewish high holy days but that she would start right after that in October. She also agreed to announce the show in May, although she asked that it be kept secret until the last minute so that she could complete her hosting chores on "The Tonight Show" and have a chance to say good-bye properly.

Later, Rivers would be taken to task for the way she handled her severance from Carson, but at the time there seemed to be little choice. Rivers was one of Carson's regular guests one Friday night in mid-April, just before her last scheduled week as guest host. Some Fox executives wanted her to announce on the air that she was leaving, but Rivers was adamantly opposed. She felt that while it might help them, it would hurt her career.

She was nervous enough already about the big changes ahead. On the night that she was Carson's guest for the last time, she never gave a hint of what was coming. When she got in her car in the parking lot of the NBC studio in Burbank, however, she began to sob uncontrollably. In her heart, she really believed the dedication she had included in the front of the autobiography she had recently published called *Enter Talking* (written with *People* magazine writer Richard Meryman), which read: "To Johnny Carson, who made it 'all' happen."

Joan Rivers, born Joan Molansky in Brooklyn, New York, had always been overly sensitive about her looks, her talent, and her ability to hold on to the rewards life handed her. So she prepared longer and worked harder than anyone else. Her last week on "The Tonight Show" was typical. She would prepare for the show all day. For one thing, she actually tried to read the books of the authors she would be interviewing. Then, after the taping the show, she would race to the airport and fly to Las Vegas to do two shows, in accordance with her long-term pact with Caesar's Palace. Then Rivers would sleep for a few hours and fly back to Los Angeles in the morning. It left her exhausted, but at least she was satisfied that she was doing everything possible to insure success.

By chance, on the last night she hosted "The Tonight Show," famed photographer David Kennerly was there taking pictures for a book called, *A Day in the Life of America.* Rivers's final hour behind Carson's desk is immortalized in a full-page shot in the book.

The press conference was set for Tuesday, May 6, in the garden of Fox Square, the KTTV (the Fox station in Los Angeles) complex in Hollywood. Both Rivers and Fox had kept it a secret through more than two months of discussions, but the pressure was building—and inevitably, there were leaks.

Louis Chunovic, who covered TV for the *Hollywood Reporter,* knew the basic outline of the announcement about five days before it was to be made public. When he called to check it out, the Fox executives stalled him while trying to decide what to do. The *Hollywood Reporter*'s recently appointed editor, Paul Wilner, had been beefing up coverage. For years the *Reporter* had taken a backseat to its competitor, the *Daily Variety,* in breaking important stories. Wilner had another problem, however. There had been a lot of bad blood between the trade paper and the studio. Under Norman Levy, Fox had pulled all of its advertising from the *Reporter* for several months because of unhappiness over certain stories. After Diller arrived at Fox, he almost always had his press people leak the important stories first to *Variety.* Now, with Fox in a panic, Wilner offered a compromise. If Fox would guarantee certain other exclusives to the *Reporter,* as well as parity with *Variety* in the future on all stories, he would hold off on naming Rivers as host of a new late night show. Fox gratefully accepted.

Rona Barrett, who did daily radio entertainment reports for the Mutual Network, also found out about Rivers. Fox also convinced her that if she wanted to remain in the studio's favor, it would be best to hold the story, at least until the morning of the press conference. She did.

The big problem happened the night before the press conference, when Garth Ancier got a call from Brandon Tartikoff, his former boss. Tartikoff started talking about a recent visit he had made to Lawrenceville Academy in New Jersey, which they had both attended. Ancier knew instinctively that Lawrenceville was not the real reason for the call. Finally Tartikoff told him what was on his mind. Everyone knew that Fox was planning a late night show, but no one knew who would host it. Tartikoff had analyzed who made the most sense and decided it was Rivers. Suddenly, Tartikoff told Ancier, he'd understood why Rivers was stalling on signing her new contract. Tartikoff had called Aggolia, and they had both come to the conclusion that Rivers was going to Fox. Ancier wouldn't confirm it, but he wouldn't deny it, either. He just couldn't lie to Tartikoff. Tartikoff knew immediately from Ancier's reaction that his guess was correct. Tartikoff told Ancier that to protect NBC's relationship with its star, Johnny Carson, Tartikoff would have to tell him immediately what was happening.

Ancier quickly called Diller, who then called Rivers. The plan had been for her to call Carson an hour before the announcement, but now that wouldn't work. When Rivers called back Carson's secretary answered. Rivers identified herself. The secretary came back after a minute and said that Carson was out, and that she didn't know when he might be available.

Another subject of debate was the question of how to handle the press conference. It fell into Scott Sassa's area, but from the start he had been consulting with Brenda Mutchnick, an advertising, marketing, and public relations specialist whom Diller had brought over from Paramount to head up Fox's corporate public relations. Mutchnick, in turn, had hired Buffy Shutt, another veteran of the Paramount movie division, on a free-lance basis to set the announcement. And Sassa had recruited Michael Binkow, whom he had worked with at the big Rogers and Cowan public relations firm in Beverly Hills, also on a temporary basis.

When they all met with Diller a week before the announcement, he said he didn't want to make the press conference a circus. He suggested that the way to handle the announcement was simply to tell the press that Fox executives would be on hand to talk about the new network. Then they would just calmly announce that Rivers was the host of their first show, a late night talk and variety program.

Binkow, tall and broad shouldered with a round face and longish light-brown hair, was reluctant to argue, but he couldn't remain silent. He piped up to tell Diller that he thought this was much bigger news than that. He felt it would have tremendous impact.

The consensus, however, was to follow Diller's lead.

Then Rivers showed up for the meeting, accompanied by her husband Edgar, manager Bill Sammeth, and public relations counsel, Richard Grant. When she was told that Fox had decided to make the announcement in a "casual" fashion, both Rivers and her husband became upset. Rosenberg started to question whether Fox knew what it was doing. At one point, Diller told Rosenberg to shut up, and then immediately apologized. Finally Rivers, her face red, exploded, "Then have your press conference without me. You don't need me if you're doing something 'subtle.' "

Richard Grant stepped in and suggested that this was big news and needed to be treated that way. Diller reassured Rivers and the others that he understood. As soon as Rivers and her advisors left, Diller turned to his assembled executives, rolled his eyes, and said, "Okay, make it a zoo, make it a circus. Just go and do it."

Fox told the press that it was invited to hear about plans for the new, fourth network. The most important media outlets also were told that there would be a major surprise announcement. The press was wary of the Fox executives' pitch. They wanted firm assurances that something really important was going to be announced. One reporter told Binkow, "Last week we got a call from Universal about this big, big deal and it turned out to be a new version of 'Leave It to Beaver.' We don't want to be burned again."

On the day of the press conference, the Fox team had scripted everything the way it wanted it to go. As the press arrived at the Fox Television Center, almost all knew what was going on. Either they had been told or they had heard it from Rona Barrett that morning on the radio. Still, the anticipation was intense.

The KTTV garden was surrounded by sculptures and fountains collected by John Kluge during his years of ownership. It filled rapidly with Fox executives, about two dozen news reporters, ten camera crews, and an aggressive pack of photographers. As they arrived, the members of the fourth estate served themselves breakfast from tables on the back patio laden with fresh fruit, pastries, canapés, coffee, and other refreshments.

The plan laid out by Fox executives called for Diller to come out first and introduce some of the other Fox executives. He would speak briefly about the plans for the new network and then introduce Rivers, who would make her grand entrance.

That's not the way it turned out, however.

Rivers had arrived with her husband and Bill Sammeth still very concerned about her relationship with Carson. She had called a number of other key figures, including Brandon Tartikoff of NBC and Bernie Brillstein to let them know about her new show, but she had not been able to reach Johnny Carson. She decided to try calling him again from the KTTV studio. Rivers's assistant placed the call and a maid answered. The assistant handed the phone to Rivers, who says she heard Carson's voice on the line as well. River's quickly said, "Johnny, its Joan." Rivers says Carson then immediately hung up on her. He wouldn't take her call.

Rivers couldn't stop the tears from flooding her eyes. Rosenberg and Sammeth tried to comfort her, but she was visibly upset. She began wondering again if she had done the right thing. She felt confused and unhappy.

A Fox executive who came by to check on Rivers realized there was a problem when he saw that her eyes were red with tears. He rushed down the hall to warn Diller about what was going on. Diller immediately went to Rivers and began trying to soothe her feelings. At their urging, she composed herself and put on fresh makeup. Diller decided that the best thing would be for them to stay together, to make Rivers feel they were being supportive. So Diller took her arm and at the appointed moment walked Rivers out into the bright sunshine, where the media surged forward to greet them.

Diller and Jamie Kellner seated Rivers at a long table set up in the forward part of the garden that was heavily laden with microphones. Across the front of the cloth-covered table were glittery cutouts of the FBC initials and the words: Fox Broadcasting Company.

The questions began to fly. Rivers, always the trooper, immediately perked up and began to banter with the questioners. Diller and Kellner took a straightforward approach but clearly were very optimistic about the prospects for their new venture.

"Joan Rivers has brought a real sense of adventure and audacity to television," Diller said in response to a question. "This spirit embodies the approach we will continue to take in achieving our goals for this network."

Rivers declined to reveal the terms of her three-year contract with Fox. "[We made] a great handshake," she joked.

Rivers said her new show would be "full of surprises" and promised it would feature the kind of performers she had not been allowed to have as guests on NBC's "The Tonight Show" because they were too young, too hip, or not Johnny Carson's kind of guest. Among the performers she said she'd had to "fight to get on" the NBC program Rivers listed Lily Tomlin, Pee Wee Herman, David Lee Roth, and Boy George.

Later Rivers would lament that she had sounded too negative when discussing Johnny Carson and the reasons for the change. She also carried a deep hurt regarding the way Carson had treated her. She wondered why he didn't see that it was simply business.

Kellner said that Fox was not going to be a network, at least not at first, but rather would be a "satellite-delivered program service."

Diller said that Rupert Murdoch and Fox had made "a commitment of $100 million [to launch the new network] regardless of whether anybody other than our owned-and-operated stations sign up. . . . Nobody has really tried to [create a fourth network] who is a major broadcaster in their own right."

The press conference was over in just under an hour.

The announcement, primarily because of Joan Rivers's involvement, landed like a nuclear explosion in the media. It went out over both major U.S. wire services and was played on page one of many newspapers around the country. *The New York Times* tucked it inside the back of the first section.

The Rivers announcement had impact beyond Fox's hopes. It gave the new entity instant credibility and, for the first time, a real public profile. David Johnson, who as the new vice president of marketing for Fox was working on rounding up affiliates for the new network, suddenly found his job much easier. Station managers in markets he hadn't even approached yet were calling Fox and asking how they could become affiliated.

According to Kellner,

It was a good idea for us for a lot of reasons. If it worked, it would have been an incredibly positive revenue source both for our stations and for the network. It would give us nice visibility very quickly and help start growing our affiliated stations. It also could have given us an opportunity to promote our own shows and our own stars (by appearing with Rivers). Joan certainly was someone who, at the time, had enormous popularity and was worthy of a lot of press coverage.

Once the announcement was made, they turned their attention to the format of the show and dozens of other production-related details. For a start, they needed a producer. Fox had suggestions and so did Rivers and Rosenberg, but neither liked the other's candidates. As it turned out, it would take more than three months for them to agree on a producer, who would arrive just before the show aired.

Inside Fox, Diller put Kevin Wendle in charge of "The Late Show Starring Joan Rivers." Wendle, in turn, hired an executive who couldn't get along with Rivers, and then, for a replacement, turned to his old friend Ron Van Dor. Unfortunately, Van Dor and Rivers and her husband didn't get along, either. Over the next few weeks, Van Dor became a symbol of everything the couple disliked about Fox. At one meeting, in her dressing room suite just before the show, Rivers became so angry that she hurled whatever objects were within her reach at Van Dor, who quickly retreated.

There were some things they all agreed on, however. "Joan wanted to do the show she had done with Johnny but on our air. She wanted 'The Tonight Show' starring Joan Rivers," said Kevin Wendle. "That's also what Fox wanted. We thought, Hey, when she does the 'Tonight Show' she gets higher numbers than Johnny. So why not just do that every night of the week?"

Sammeth went to work, almost full time, lining up guests for the show, just as he had booked most of Rivers's guests on "The Tonight Show." The difference was that he now had a lot more freedom. As she had mentioned at the press conference, Rivers had frequently complained that "The Tonight Show" producers wouldn't let her bring on acts, including both comics and musicians, with an appeal to younger audiences. Now she could book anyone she wanted.

Rivers felt that she needed four guests and a musical act for each sixty-minute show. It quickly became obvious that it wasn't going to be easy. While "The Tonight Show" never made any public or official moves, word spread rapidly that anyone who appeared with Rivers would not be welcome on "The Tonight Show." That immediately eliminated most of the top comic talent in the nation, many of whom felt indebted to Carson because he had given so many comics their big career breaks over the years.

Fox suggested to Rivers that she tone down her act a bit, both to attract guests and to hold viewers. Apparently, it was all right for her to be full of bile when she was only an occasional guest host, but now she needed people to invite her back into their living rooms night after night.

Fox wanted Rivers to open each show with a monologue, but she was against it. She felt that she needed to just do a joke, say hello, and then get to the desk and the guests. Fox reluctantly agreed—at least in the beginning.

Both Fox and Rivers and her husband wanted music to be an integral part of the show. Both sides began looking for a musical director and a theme song. Some of the top names in music came up with ideas for a song, including singer-composer Barry Manilow and composer Henry Mancini. One of those who contacted Sammeth about submitting a song was Mark Hudson, one of the singing Hudson Brothers, who had also worked as an actor on a TV series shortly before called "Sara." Hudson submitted three songs and met with Sammeth and several Fox executives, including Ancier and Wendle, to play them.

Eventually the songs were played as a blind test, without any of them knowing which one was written by which artist or writer. That narrowed the field to eleven songs, but none were right. A few days later Hudson got a call at home. It was Joan Rivers. She had come up with an idea for a beginning of the theme song with a swing feel, something Frank Sinatra might sing. The next day Hudson worked with a writer and developed it into a demo tape. When it was played along with the other songs a few days later at another blind test, the song was chosen.

Hudson, with an upbeat, bubbling personality and a posthippie beard, was also a hit. He was chosen to be the music director of the show. Things went fine for the next few weeks, until Fox announced that it wanted all publishing rights to the theme song— which, over time, could become worth thousands of dollars. Rivers, who had come up with the initial idea for the song, felt that she and Rosenberg should own the rights. Hudson, who had developed and cowritten it, felt that he and his writing partner should own the song.

"I got put in the middle of it, and it was a very difficult time for me," recalled Hudson long after the fact. "My primary allegiance was to Joan, but at the same time I felt an allegiance to Fox, who had given me everything I wanted to put together the best possible band. The pressure just got to be too much."

It became obvious to the staff that Edgar Rosenberg was putting constant pressure on Hudson to give in on the publishing rights issue. Hudson was angry and unhappy but then realized that the flap could cost him his position as director. "I found out I might make $7,000 a year from it," recalls Hudson. "That just wasn't worth it for what I was going through emotionally, personally, politically. It wasn't worth it, just for job security alone."

Shortly after the show first went on the air, Hudson went to Rosenberg and conceded on the theme song: "I'm giving you whatever you need." Despite the battle, Hudson maintained his close relationship and respect for Rivers and her husband.

In the end, neither Hudson nor Rivers got the publishing rights, all of which went to Fox Broadcasting Company.

In the meantime, construction had begun on the offices and new studio at KTTV in Hollywood. This was Fox's first show, and no detail was too small to be discussed by the key Fox executives, often including Diller. They spent over $2 million just on construction of the 420-seat studio and had to battle the fire marshal over the sharp angle of the seats that Rivers had demanded.

A green room, which holds special visitors and guests waiting to go on, was created. Actually, it was a two-room suite, one room for guests and the other for visiting VIP's and Fox executives. Diller hated the way it was furnished. Just before the show went on the air, he had his personal decorator come in and completely redo it, raising the cost for the two rooms to over $35,000.

Rivers had asked for at least two rooms as her dressing room, one for makeup and meetings and one for a private bedroom. Fox created a 1,000-square-foot, five-room suite, which held not only Rivers but also her makeup artist, hairdresser, wardrobe aide, and other staff. There was even a safe, which typically held over $350,000 worth of jewelry borrowed for Rivers to wear.

Early on, Fox had decided that to give the show a real edge, it should be live, at least in the eastern United States. Murdoch heartily endorsed the idea. Rivers wasn't as enthusiastic, because it meant that she wouldn't get away from the studio until about 8:30 P.M. On the other hand, if they taped at five o'clock or so, she could be finished by a little after six o'clock. When she flew to Las Vegas after the show, she wouldn't be cutting it as close.

Fox insisted, and Rivers agreed. The show would be live. The decision meant that they had to spend an extra $200,000 for a special machine that delayed the signal just a few seconds, allowing for instant censorship when necessary.

Including Rivers's salary, the show was budgeted at about $400,000 a week. However, there was not a single week during which it didn't go at least $4,000 over budget. One problem was that staff was hired as needed, without any budget plan in advance.

By August, nine writers had been hired, including head writer Hank Bradford, whom Rivers knew from "The Tonight Show." Although it was a live interview show, Rivers wanted the writers to help with funny openings, clever questions, occasional skits, and other bits. She chose and approved each writer personally and met with them for one to two hours daily, reworking almost everything to fit her style.

As the days of August passed, the battle over who would be producer continued. Fox would come up with a candidate, and then have Rivers and Rosenberg meet him or her. If they approved, Diller would meet the potential producer. And he would say no. This went on for weeks. Finally, Bruce McKay, a veteran producer who had also worked on "The Tonight Show," was chosen as a compromise candidate. Fox immediately considered him Rivers's person.

Diller had promised to help secure top guests for the new show, but the task fell primarily to Sammeth.

Sammeth called in favors, used every contact, and tapped every resource to line up good guests. For the first show he got Cher, one of his clients; Elton John, who had never done a talk show in America before; and two guests whom "The Tonight Show" had refused to book because they appealed to too young a crowd, Pee Wee Herman and singer David Lee Roth.

This was the group for opening night, October 9, 1986. Thus Fox launched the show on ninety-five stations, reaching around 85 percent of all U.S. television homes—well in excess of the 65 percent originally projected.

Was Fox really reaching 85 percent of all American TV homes? A secret analysis by CBS at the time indicated that because many Fox affiliates were weak UHF stations with limited reach, it really reached only about 55 percent of TV homes.

David Johnson and Scott Sassa looked deep into the little MacIntosh computer once more and decided that "The Late Show" would attract 4 percent of all American TV homes on average each night, about half the number that watched Johnny Carson. Advertising was then sold on that basis, with a guarantee that if it was not met, Fox would make up the difference with other ads for free.

Shortly before the first show was to air, Joan Rivers came to Fox for a meeting with Barry Diller. She was upset. There had been death threats against her and she felt that more security was needed at KTTV, where they did the shows. Rivers wanted Fox to hire a private outside security consultant and his guard service. She felt the Fox guards were not adequate. Diller assured her that there was already heavy security and that it wasn't necessary for her to hire outside security help at Fox's expense.

Rivers became angry. She couldn't believe that Diller seemed not to acknowledge that her life might be at stake. He appeared to be taking it so lightly. She felt a pain inside, wondering what kind of man she was in business with. Said Rivers much later:

> It was not a minor thing. I had a death threat. They were leaving notes in my mailbox. We had a show that was live, which meant anybody could know when I was there. So we asked for our own security guard to come in, which would make me secure. They wouldn't do it. It became blown up. It became a power play. I remember Barry said to me, 'The tail doesn't wag the dog.' "

Diller tried to remain cool, but he felt furious. Diller felt it was really an attempt by Rivers to exercise power. "It became an issue about control. That's all," said Diller later.

Diller couldn't believe that, when there were so many big, important issues to confront, Rivers was making this such a big deal. He finally got her to calm down and discuss some other points about the show.

At the end of the meeting, Rivers looked at Diller and said, "Now that I've been nice, do I get the extra guards?"

Rivers meant the remark as a joke, but Diller didn't take it that way.

Diller was incredulous. He suddenly realized that she had been trying to manipulate him the whole time. Later he would look back and mark that meeting as the point at which his relationship with Rivers, and his confidence in her, began to go sour. "Oh, I knew so quickly," Diller said months later. "That's the terrible part. I didn't tell anybody, but I knew."

16

VISIONS OF PRIME TIME DANCED IN THEIR HEADS

BARRY DILLER'S SLEEK black Corvette slid into the space reserved for the chairman of the board in front of the Twentieth Century–Fox executive office building on a warm late-winter morning in 1987. Dressed in a dark business suit, white shirt, and bright-blue silk tie, Diller bounded across the walkway and up a few steps, and then quickly darted into his office. He had been away for almost a week and was anxious to attack the pile of mail, messages, memos, and other items he knew awaited his attention.

Diller darted through the reception area and into his three-room office suite, immediately followed by Ruth Haley, the elegant, silvery gray–haired woman who was his longtime secretary. She pointed out a stack of papers that needed attending to and began reeling off a list of callers. Diller said he would get back to some later, some not at all, and named a few he wanted to talk to as soon as possible. Haley also reminded Diller of several appointments he had scheduled that afternoon and of a screening set for later in the evening.

Diller was already sitting behind the off-white desk in the center of his light, airy office. Across the way, inset cases in the wall held pot after pot overflowing with freshly cut flowers. The entire decor

158

was in white or shades of beige, including the couches, end tables, and lamps. Immediately beyond the office area was a sitting room and bath. Beyond that was Diller's private conference room, dominated by the long, brown, polished wooden table and high-backed leather chairs.

Diller didn't look up from the stack of papers as his secretary spoke, but at the mention of a screening of a new Fox film that evening, his head shot up. He told Haley that he also would need to speak with Leonard Goldberg later that morning and that he wanted Garth Ancier to send down the tapes from the first week of shooting in Canada on "Jump Street Chapel," one of the new series being prepared for the launch of the Fox Broadcasting Company's first evening of prime-time programming, to start in early April 1987.

Diller began jotting notes on a movie-production memo. It was such a relief for him to see so many movies in progress after the long, dry year he had spent with Alan Horn. After a lengthy search, Diller finally had convinced his old friend and mentor Leonard Goldberg to come aboard as president of the studio, which really meant head of all movie and television production. Goldberg, who had continued on successfully as an independent television producer after ending his long association with producer Aaron Spelling, had almost taken positions with two different TV networks, but in the end had never been able to cut a deal that would give him the independence he felt necessary. Now he had come to Fox, and he had quickly stepped up production.

In Goldberg, Diller finally had a friend whom he also could respect professionally. Diller still would challenge every major project and expenditure, but he knew he could trust Goldberg's judgment and his ability to fulfill whatever he promised.

Now Diller really could hunker down and spend all of his time shaping the new network. There was certainly plenty to do. "The Late Show Starring Joan Rivers" had been launched in October with a spectacular wave of publicity and promotion, but it had never grown in audience ratings or production content as Diller had hoped. Instead of progress, all that Diller ever seemed to hear from Rivers, Rosenberg, the Fox executives on the show, and the outside critics was that there were problems. It had become a constant source of irritation. Diller knew that radical changes would be necessary, and now he intended to begin figuring out what they were.

First, however, he needed to get back up to speed on the progress toward the prime-time launch. He felt that the process of signing more affiliates and lining up advertisers was moving along; but he was concerned about progress in promoting the new program service and, especially, about shaping the first wave of programming.

In a way, FBC had tied its own hands. Once the decision had been made to start with prime evening programming on the two weekend nights, all involved agreed that they needed to hit the ground running. That meant shows as good or better than what aired on NBC, ABC, and CBS. Since FBC had only a tiny production staff, two key decisions had been made. First, they would not lean heavily on the production capability of Twentieth Century–Fox. It was crucial to convince the rest of Hollywood that FBC was more than an arm of the studio. It had to be seen as an independent network that licensed shows only for a certain number of runs and was not always going to look first to its affiliated operations at Fox.

The second decision, which flowed from the first, was to seek out the top network producers and essentially give them a free hand to create new shows. FBC would pay a license fee as high as what the existing networks paid and would make a series of unprecedented commitments to air a certain number of shows without seeing even a single pilot episode. The commitment was being made simply to hook these top producers and production companies. Said Ancier at the time,

> The key is to have people who know how to do it and say to them, "We aren't going to put any restrictions on you. We want you to think as creatively as you can. Don't try to do a show you think will please us. Try to do shows that you're going to have a passion about doing." I think when you ask producers to do that, you're going to get a better cut of show than when a network says, "Here's the idea, go execute it."

The very first commitment had been made to a show with nothing but a title and studio behind it. The year before, *Down and Out in Beverly Hills* starring Richard Dreyfuss, Nick Nolte, and Bette Midler, had become a big hit movie for the Walt Disney Company, the first of many hits to be produced under the new regime there led by Michael Eisner, Jeffrey Katzenberg, and Richard Frank, all of whom had gone there from Paramount after declining invitations from Diller to come to Fox. In a meeting between Diller and Eisner, Fox had committed to buy at least nine episodes of a half-hour situation comedy based on the movie, but without any of the original cast. It would be about a rich Beverly Hills family with a cute dog who take in a bum as a houseguest. It would be up to Disney to give it shape, form, and humor.

The second FBC program commitment was even more unusual and open-ended. One of the few top creative talents who had followed Diller from Paramount to Fox was James L. Brooks, the brilliant TV writer, director, and producer, who had branched into movies with the Academy Award–winning *Terms of Endearment.* He had come to Fox to make more movies and was at work on what would become another hit, *Broadcast News.* Diller, Kellner, Ancier, Wendle, and the rest of FBC now desperately wanted him to work with them in TV as well.

Brooks, who had won Emmys for his work on "Taxi" and other earlier shows, was hesitant. He didn't want to do anything that wasn't special, and he didn't want to be embarrassed by making a lot of announcements that never produced anything meaningful. The deal he finally agreed to was unprecedented in the history of broadcasting. FBC would create a generous TV-series-development fund to allow Brooks to experiment and make pilots, without any pressure to air his creations unless he was satisfied. Once he decided on either a half-hour or hour show (it was to be his choice), then Brooks would have a guarantee that the new network would immediately buy twenty-six episodes, sight unseen. While Brooks looked around for something suitable, Fox agreed to keep the entire agreement secret. That way, if Brooks felt there wasn't anything worth doing, he wouldn't have to be embarrassed or explain his "failure."

In early 1987, more than six months after the agreement was signed, Brooks felt he had a possibility. He had discovered a British comedienne named Tracey Ullman who could sing, dance, tell jokes, and do skits. Now Brooks was building a half-hour comedy-variety series around her that again would break new ground. It would have no continuing characters—at least not at first. Each week, Brooks explained to the FBC executives, Ullman would do a series of characters. Later, if any of them seemed to really be working, they might be repeated. She also would occasionally sing and dance, but only in the context of the skits, which would be done with a repertory company of regular actors who would support Ullman on every show.

The third FBC program commitment was for an untitled half-hour situation comedy with edge, to be produced by Michael Moye and Ron Leavitt, in association with Embassy Communications.

Moye and Leavitt had been executive producers on the hit CBS show "The Jeffersons," although they hadn't created it. They had helped develop the NBC hit "Silver Spoons" with David Duclon and had written for a long list of other shows. Embassy, founded by producers Norman Lear and Bud Yorkin and then sold to Coca-Cola, also had a long history of making hit comedies, including "Silver Spoons" for NBC and "Who's the Boss?" for ABC. Now FBC was promising a thirteen-show commitment for a half-hour series that they hoped would push the edge of comedy into new territory, much as Norman Lear's "All in the Family" had done on CBS in the early 1970s.

Moye and Leavitt had come up with an idea for a situation comedy about a modern-day blue-collar family whose squabbling and adventures would be in the tradition of "The Honeymooners" and "All in the Family." It was Diller and Ancier's feeling that it was time for a comedy that would play at the opposite end of the spectrum from the biggest hit in TV at the time, "The Cosby Show." Where Cosby was warm, loving, friendly, and full of moral lessons, the new FBC show would border on being mean-spirited and outrageous and never would worry about having a moral to the story. The working title among the producers and the network was "Not the Cosby Show."

Another show that was put into development was "Mr. President," a comedy-drama starring renowned actor George C. Scott, in his first TV series in many years. It had come about through Kevin Wendle's relationship with Ed Weinberger, a top producer who headed Johnny Carson's production company. It was helped along as well by Diller's friendship with Carson. Despite Carson's anger at Joan Rivers for the way she'd left his show, he and Diller had remained friends. In mid-1986, Carson's production company had developed a show for NBC starring Scott as the president, but NBC had delayed buying it because there was little time available on its schedule, which was then number one in the ratings. So Diller and Wendle convinced Carson Productions to put the show on Fox, with a guarantee of thirteen episodes in advance, again without any pilot show. Carson had brought in Gene Reynolds, who had made his reputation with "M*A*S*H," and Weinberger as producers and to direct some episodes. Weinberger, a tall, lanky man with an offbeat sense of humor, had become a legend in Hollywood working with Jim Brooks on such shows as "Taxi" and for his input on the hit "The Cosby Show."

Fox's other key open-ended commitment had been made to producer Stephan J. Cannell, creator of "The Rockford Files," "Riptide," "The A-Team," and many other hit shows. In 1979 Cannell had begun his own company. To keep costs down, he was shooting most of his shows in Vancouver, Canada. Not only were prices of almost everything from food to extras lower, but Canadian currency was also 10 percent cheaper than the U.S. dollar. So the new Fox show would be made there.

From the start, Ancier and Wendle pitched Cannell to create a show for a very specific, "protected" time slot. They wanted an action adventure program that would appeal to teenagers and young adults. It would air from 7:00 to 8:00 P.M. on Sunday night. That was the one hour of the week when the other networks were limited by a government-consent decree to only air programs that appealed to youngsters or were informational. Since by the FCC's strict definition, Fox would not be a TV network, it didn't have to live by the same rules. Which meant that it could counterprogram with a show that would appeal to an essentially disenfranchised audience—young males and, to a lesser extent, young females. "Young" in this case meant from about twelve years old up to about thirty-nine years old.

To actually go to Canada and produce the show, Cannell brought in a longtime associate, Patrick Hasburgh, who was just finishing three seasons as executive producer of another Cannell-backed action show, "Hardcastle and McCormick." As Hasburgh recalled two years later,

> We heard that a new fourth network was starting and they were going to allow all kinds of creative freedom. That appealed to me because I always had trouble working with authority. I'm a little bit like Woody Allen. You know. When a cop pulls me over to write me up on a ticket, I tear up my driver's license.

Together with Ancier and Wendle, Cannell and Hasburgh came up with an idea that held great appeal for Fox. They would create an hour-long action show about a group of undercover cops in high school. It would have a multiracial cast that would be reminiscent of the 1960s hit "Mod Squad," while dealing with such 1980s problems as drugs, gangs, rape, and even arson. The cops would hang out together in an old church, which led to the series title, "Jump Street Chapel."

It was to become one of Fox's most controversial and most successful shows, but it was not to be an easy birth. Right from the start, Hasburgh and the Fox executives seemed to have a different show in mind.

Patrick Hasburgh grew up in Buffalo, New York, and after high school graduation in 1969 took a job in a steel mill. He soon moved to Aspen, Colorado, where, for the next half-dozen years, Hasburgh was a ski instructor in the winter, white water rafting guide in the summer, and truck driver in between. He also began writing scripts, which he tried to place with the help of Hollywood celebrities he met on the slopes and in the ski classes he taught.

When he turned thirty, Hasburgh headed for Los Angeles, along with his new wife, who was a teacher. His wife had gone to the same school as Steven Cannell, who had become a successful TV producer. They all met at an alumni picnic in 1980. It turned out that Cannell's children also attended the school where Hasburgh's wife taught. That led Hasburgh to send some scripts he had written to Cannell, who immediately hired him as a story editor. They went on to cocreate "The A-Team," which became a huge hit on NBC. After a year there, Hasburgh created "Hardcastle and McCormick."

Hasburgh's first script for the pilot of "Jump Street Chapel," about a high school gym teacher who is a murderer and rapist, was seen as too dark and depressing by Fox. According to Hasburgh, Kevin Wendle told him that they wanted either an all-out action show or something more like the 1970s situation comedy "Happy Days." Wendle denies making any such demand.

Hasburgh wasn't satisfied with that particular script himself, but he wasn't about to give Fox another "Happy Days." Instead, within a week he had written a new pilot about a kid from a middle-class family with a drug problem. "It wasn't just about the drug problem," explains Hasburgh. "It was about high school in general."

It was designed to introduce a set of characters, the undercover cops and their mentor, an older cop. At first Ancier told Hasburgh that they loved his script. Then he said that they wanted it to take a different direction. Recalls Hasburgh:

The pressure on [the Fox executives] was so great that one week they'd say it was great and then they have to change it. We got into huge fights about this. I said, This is a terrific pilot. I'm not going to water it down. I had been told I could use words you couldn't use on network television, like "kick ass" or "screw off." The way kids really talk. Suddenly, I was being ordered to edit out all those words and I was just furious about it.

Fox also insisted on a new title. They felt the word *chapel* would make viewers think it was a religious show. So it was renamed "21 Jump Street."

Time was running out. If they were to make the scheduled air date, production had to begin. Hasburgh had spent weeks casting the new show, but he still couldn't find actors he thought perfect for every role. He picked a pretty black girl named Holly Robinson as his Judy Hoffs; Vietnamese immigrant Dustin Nguyen as a Japanese immigrant who becomes a cop; and Peter DeLuise, son of actor Dom DeLuise, as Doug Penhall, a young cop with fire in his belly. Frederick Forrest was chosen as the older cop who would shepherd this flock. The only role left unsettled was the central male lead.

"Fox said we had to deliver the show on such and such a date," Hasburgh recalls. "I said, 'Well, we've read about fifty kids, but none of them have drilled it. The best kid we've got is Jeff Yeager. If you want the show on this date, then Yeager must leave for Canada tomorrow for wardrobe fittings.' "

Hasburgh knew that Yeager was a competent actor but felt he was slightly miscast for the role of Tom Hanson, the good-looking young cop who really cares about his fellow man. He figured they could always recast after the pilot, although he didn't tell Yeager that. After all, they had recast a key role in "The A-Team" after the pilot was shot. Wendle didn't agree and urged him to immediately recast the lead role.

The first week of shooting in Vancouver, Canada, was nearing completion when Diller arrived at his office in his sleek black Corvette on that winter morning in early 1987. He had seen pictures of the cast members chosen for the new Cannell show, but now he was anxious to see how they actually played on camera.

Diller liked the show, but like Wendle he hated the lead character. He felt that Yeager looked like someone older trying to play a high school kid, instead of being someone in his twenties who could pass for a teenager. Diller immediately said it had to be recast. Ancier and Wendle called Cannell and made the demand.

"We called and they went crazy," said Diller long afterward. "They have this big investment. They're no longer objective."

Diller finally got on the phone with Cannell and cut a deal. Production would shut down while they found a new actor, and then Fox and Cannell would split the added cost, which was about $800,000. Yeager was told that although he was a fine actor, he wasn't really right for this part. He was paid his salary for the one show and let go.

Diller called in Scott Rudin, his head of movie production under Len Goldberg. He told him it was an emergency. Since Rudin was a former casting director, Diller wanted him to head a crash effort to find a new lead for "21 Jump Street."

Rudin sent out the call in Los Angeles for young actors to begin auditioning that very afternoon. He also arranged for a friend who was a casting director in New York to begin the search in Manhattan.

Hasburgh, who had flown back from Canada, recalls that it came down to Johnny Depp, a young actor with a smoldering look, and Josh Brolin, another young, muscular actor. Hasburgh strongly supported Depp, as did Kevin Wendle, but not everyone agreed. "I said, 'Trust me when I tell you I am not going to recast for anybody but Depp,' " said Hasburgh. "I said, 'You guys can fuck off,' and I walked out of the room. I threw a fucking tantrum and then came back about half an hour later and apologized. But I said, 'I'm still not going to do it.' "

Diller remembers it as having been simpler than that. "We sat and looked at them [on tape], and one guy popped to everybody, instantly," says Diller. "His name is Johnny Depp."

The next day Depp was on a plane to Vancouver, where all of the scenes with the Hanson character were reshot. From then on, Diller made a rule that every actor would have to be tested on tape before being cast.

According to Diller,

It was the cheapest $350,000 we ever spent. We did the right thing for the show, and it taught the staff something. We made a mistake. They picked themselves up off of the floor and learned something very significant. Once you make a decision, you have to look at it for a very long time. So don't let anyone give you pressure: It's costing thousands of dollars a day. Do it! Do it! No you don't. You do it right.

Later it became clear that the "21 Jump Street" recasting was symptomatic of many things. Hasburgh was just beginning his battles over creative control with Wendle and other Fox executives. The new network that wouldn't interfere had actually just moved the process of interfering to a higher executive level, mainly because the Fox production executives were too few in number and too inexperienced to do most of the job on the front lines. Finally, it set the tone for how Barry Diller would operate—and why he would drive many people nearly crazy.

Barry Diller was a perfectionist who didn't know what he liked until he saw it. In programming it meant that he might like a concept on paper but hate it on the screen. In advertising and promotion it meant that everything was fine-tuned over and over again—often at great expense, and often slowing down the process so much that it became difficult to meet deadlines for getting things in print or on the air.

During his Paramount years, Diller's constant tinkering had paid off with stronger marketing and advertising for movies. It had been somewhat hidden on the production side by the system of passionate advocacy. Movies took so long to slug their way through the system that those that made it met with everybody's approval—even Diller's.

In television, with so many more decisions to make and much shorter deadlines, Diller's need to fine-tune became a kind of bottleneck for every department in the new network. Diller himself was finally forced to confront it. Later he explained the problem:

> The truth of the matter is that everybody needs an editor. I need an editor. I'm also a very good editor. My form of editing is denial: No, it's not good enough. Bring it back. For those who like the process, it's great. For those who don't, I mean, you know, it's pick your horses.

It's also important, Diller realized, that he really understand where those horses were coming from. "I really need context," Diller says. "Taken out of context, I'm not good. I need to understand. I'm not good at abstract theory."

Nowhere did Diller's need for editing and for context create greater havoc than in the promotion and advertising of the new network. He would approve an ad one week, only to demand that it be revised the following week, just as it was about to be placed in newspapers all over the United States. He would see a TV promo spot cut to advertise a certain show and demand that it be recut a different way. Says Diller with a shrug:

> I've always believed I'm never good at the middle of the game You can't look at the stuff in the middle of the game because you don't get it. I'm only good at the very beginning and the very end of the process, looking over every shoulder.

A former Fox executive put it a bit differently:

> No matter what you do, Barry will push you and push you and push you to get it a little better. Barry's management style is to set up adversary situations because he believes out of that great ideas emerge. It's true. But when you are already working seven days a week, eighteen hours a day, you don't need adversaries."

Yet, the same executive called it

> a privilege to work with Barry Diller. . . . Underneath, there is a kindness and warmth that most people don't see. Sometimes he says something in a meeting that seems mean, but those who know him will say you've got to see what he's really saying.

Scott Sassa, the youthful Asian-American executive who came from the Playboy Channel to take charge of advertising and promotion, was feeling swamped by early 1987. After a huge expenditure on the launching of "The Late Show Starring Joan Rivers," he had been short of money for an additional push. When Fox did do advertising, it didn't seem to be working well. Even worse, Sassa felt that some of the young executives working under him weren't doing their jobs. Finally, he convinced Kellner, Johnson, and Diller that Fox needed a professional advertising agency's involvement.

After a prolonged search, Sassa hired Chiat Day, a Los Angeles agency known for outstanding creative work with such products as Apple computers and Nike running shoes.

Chiat Day did a thorough evaluation of everything the Fox Broadcasting Company had done up to that point. Their first suggestion was that the emphasis be placed not on the acronym *FBC* but on the name *Fox,* which could be identified with a tradition of great entertainment.

Chiat Day came up with a plan to spend $8 million for the launch of the Sunday night schedule in early April. It also helped devise a plan to repeat some of the first shows to encourage a wide audience to sample the new network.

It was Chiat Day that came up with a scheme to turn the famed HOLLYWOOD sign into the word *Fox* for the week of the prime-time launch. They handled negotiations with the city of Los Angeles (for a $25,000 payment), the Hollywood Chamber of Commerce, and the police, and they attended a hearing where some neighborhood groups opposed the deal. It was approved, and it turned out to be a brilliant publicity stunt that made page one of several local news-papers and received coverage in a national news magazine.

Still, Chiat Day ran into a familiar problem. After endless meet-ings, it would have an ad prepared and ready to go. The final proof would be shown to the Fox executives, and inevitably, Diller would want changes. While the Fox executives understood, it was very difficult for the people at Chiat Day.

Fox, on the other hand, began to feel that the agency wasn't responsive enough to their needs. And it certainly wasn't moving quickly enough on the requested changes.

Another battle was fought over how to spend the limited re-sources Fox did have. One side held that advertising money should be poured into the big markets where everyone felt they would do the most good. The other side said that the money needed to be sunk into markets where they had weak stations, to help build them up.

There was also a pressing need for experienced publicists who could plant favorable stories about the new network and its shows in the right publications and on the right news-and-information shows. Sassa knew he didn't have the time or the background, so around the same time that Rivers went on the air, he began his search. He turned to an old friend in January 1987. Brad Turell worked at Rogers and Cowan, the biggest public relations agency in Hollywood.

Like Diller, Turell had grown up in Beverly Hills. He attended the University of California at Santa Barbara, graduating with a degree in economics in 1979, and became a page at CBS and then a radio reporter for a small public radio station. He also did some modeling and drove a limousine to make a living. Then he got a job in public relations in Dallas. After his father's death, Turell returned to Beverly Hills to be with his mother and got the job at Rogers and Cowan. Despite losing some internal political battles, he did well there, representing such actors as Mr. T, Shelly Long ("Cheers"), Kirk Douglas, and Lucille Ball.

When Sassa asked him to meet with Diller, Turell remembers being frightened. But when Diller asked him what it would take to turn around the public relations problem at Fox, he didn't hesitate. "This isn't brain surgery," Turell told Diller. "You put the right story with the right publication and you have good relations with the writers and reporters and you make sure they know you're in it for the long term."

Diller hired him on the spot. Turell returned to Rogers and

Cowan and gave two weeks' notice. He was looking forward to working closely with his old friend, Scott Sassa.

Sassa, however, was having his own problems. With Kellner, Johnson, and others frequently out of town soliciting affiliated stations or advertisers, a tremendous load fell on his shoulders. It wasn't unusual for Diller to call him at home as well as at the office. His entire life was becoming one big blur of work and more work.

Recalls Sassa:

> Jamie [Kellner] called me one day [from New York City] and said, "What do you think of the latest ads?" I was getting bloodied, killed by Barry, about everything. I was so stressed out. It was all so difficult. I was always behind. I replied, "I don't think about that anymore. I just think about making deadlines. I'm too close to this. I'm doing a lousy job for you. You should replace me."

Kellner told him to "think it over . . . you're just tired" and promised that he'd talk to Diller when he got back to town.

A week later, on February 2, his birthday, Sassa was at home sick and exhausted. The phone rang. Brenda Mutchnick, who had been head of corporate public relations, was taking over the job as head of advertising and promotion for FBC. Sassa was being moved to "operations," where he would handle whatever details needed tending in affiliate relations, sales, marketing, and production administration.

Sassa breathed a sigh of relief, but he also knew his days at Fox were now numbered. Barry Diller had lost confidence in him. There would be no more promotions, no more invitations to top-level meetings. Diller would barely talk to him over the next few weeks, and within a few months, Sassa would be forced out. However, he would move on to other jobs, where he would prove himself all over again.

Diller's philosophy of putting a person in a job before they were really ready had taken its toll. In some cases, like Kevin Wendle's, the person would grow and change with each assignment. For Sassa, however, it had led to burnout and unhappiness.

Diller was a lot more comfortable with Brenda Mutchnick, whom he had worked with at Paramount, but she didn't find life at Fox particularly easy, either.

Mutchnick's style was to tackle each task enthusiastically. As the budget for the launch of Fox's prime-time programming mushroomed from the original $8 million toward the eventual real cost of $24 million, the pressure became intense. For the last two weeks before the April 11 start, Mutchnick was in her office continuously, including weekends, trying to make all of the last-minute changes Diller wanted and get everything else done. At the last minute, one of the other Fox executives came into her office and began criticizing everything. He didn't like the advertising, the promotion, or where the ads were scheduled to run. When he walked out, Mutchnick was ready to burst into tears.

"I called Barry," she recalls, "and said, 'If it's all so terrible, maybe you should get somebody else.' He said, 'Brenda, it's terrific. You're working hard. Don't do this to yourself. . . .' That's Barry. When you get to that brink, he's there for you."

To herald the launch, Fox executives asked Mutchnick—again at the last minute—to organize a huge party on the top floor of the uncompleted highrise Fox Plaza building. She arranged for the construction tools to be removed and had tables set up. A caterer brought in food and drinks. On the eve of the launch, hundreds of people, including all of the Fox executives and the stars of the new Fox shows, crowded into elevators and rode up to the top floor.

There were advertisers, journalists, friends, members of the Hollywood creative community, and others, all crowded together as the lights were dimmed. In the distance, on a signal from Jamie Kellner, the Hollywood sign was illuminated by powerful lights—only now it said FOX, in giant letters. The crowd let out a huge cheer, and Brenda Mutchnick breathed a sigh of relief.

Prime-time Fox was finally on the air.

17

IT'S LATER
THAN THEY THINK

AMID CONSIDERABLE PRESS attention and a multimillion-dollar promotional campaign, *The Late Show Starring Joan Rivers* got off to a promising start during the second week of October 1986. Of all those watching television after 11:00 P.M., between 3 percent and 4 percent tuned in to sample the new network's first show. By the end of October, however, the average number of viewers each night had fallen slightly to about 2 percent of the viewing audience. It then maintained that level.

That was less than half the audience "The Tonight Show" was averaging on NBC, but it was an improvement over what most of the small, independent stations that carried it had enjoyed previously. The problem was that Fox Broadcasting, gazing into its crystal ball, had sold advertising time based on reaching an audience representing about a 5 percent share of the viewing public. It quickly became apparent to Jamie Kellner and others inside Fox that there would be a significant shortfall to be made up. Fox was going to have to give free ad time to sponsors to make up for the difference between what it had promised and what Rivers's show delivered. Which meant that the show would produce lower revenues and the network would sustain higher losses than had been anticipated.

With the show regularly running over budget, Fox quickly became concerned about controlling costs more effectively. That meant exercising a greater degree of control over the producers as well as the star and her husband, who also was an executive producer. To Rivers and Rosenberg, when Fox said it wanted to control costs, it really meant that the network wanted to take charge of the creative direction of the program, which they felt was contrary to their understanding with Fox.

As the point man for business dealings with Fox, Rosenberg was constantly in the position of arguing over what he, Rivers, and Bill Sammeth could and could not do. Rosenberg's position was that their contract guaranteed them total control, while the Fox people felt that it was their show, so they should be able to shape it as they saw fit. Ron Van Dor, the Fox executive on the show, never seemed to be able to enforce the new network's wishes. So a succession of upper-level Fox executives—including Ancier, Wendle, and Kellner—carried that message to producer Bruce McKay, the man helplessly stuck in the middle of a growing power struggle. Usually, even when changes were made, neither side was satisfied.

Before the show even went on the air, Fox was distressed that Rosenberg, as one of the show's executive producers, played such a major role. They blamed him for problems in working out details with Rivers. They seemed to feel that if he had not been there, everything would have gone smoothly. In reality, Rosenberg discussed everything with Rivers. She was involved in every decision. Rosenberg's major affront to Fox seemed to be that he put his wife's interests ahead of every other consideration.

At a height of five feet eight, with gray hair and a closely cropped gray beard, Rosenberg was a powerful force with a strong voice, even though his body often showed signs of ill health. To some he was an almost comic figure, frequently wearing one pair of glasses on his head and another perched on his nose when he read. Yet he was also an object of fear. He wouldn't allow anyone to ever make any kind of joke concerning his wife, and he had no tolerance for stupidity, laziness, or, especially, drunkenness. Like Rivers, he really was quite a formal person who had a great deal of difficulty expressing real, open emotions—one of the contributing factors to his many health problems. Only two years earlier he had undergone open-heart surgery. On many days he looked pale and worn and walked slowly, as if it were a great struggle. Still, he was there each day, early in the morning, with his wife. While she would prepare for the day's show and meet for several hours with the writers, Rosenberg would attend to other details and make suggestions to members of the staff. "Edgar can be pretty hard to take sometimes," recalled a family friend in mid-1987. "He could lose his temper and get very angry. He really wasn't very popular on that show."

Still, he was respected. Each evening he would go out and warm up the audience for Rivers. He had been a comedian once himself, and he'd been a TV producer for many years before he married Rivers and became her second husband. After the show started, Rosenberg would sit on a chair just off camera signaling the guests when to walk on, making whispered suggestions to Rivers during commercial breaks, and generally keeping an eye on every aspect of the show. One of his favorite sayings was, "God is in the details," meaning to get to the top, and to stay there, you have to attend to every little item and make it as close to perfect as possible.

Rosenberg also fancied himself an authority on music, although he hated most popular contemporary music, including rock and roll and rap, but he loved classical and Broadway show tunes. To him, music was Cole Porter or Gershwin or Benny Goodman. He would regularly push bearded bandleader Mark Hudson to play more of his kind of music and less rock and roll. Hudson, a thin, amiable man who felt he owed his job to Rivers and Rosenberg, was willing; but then he constantly took flack from Fox, because the price to clear the music rights on some of the music Rosenberg requested was much higher than the alternative. The music Hudson chose could be cleared for a few hundred dollars a week with the music publishers group, whereas the music Rosenberg wanted would make the budget soar into the thousands of dollars.

One night about two weeks after "The Late Show" went on the air, Rosenberg was standing with Hudson in the band area about three minutes before airtime. Rosenberg had just finished the warm-up and, as usual, had made Hudson the butt of most of his jokes. It was a gambit other people constantly told Hudson they thought he should object to, but he took the stance that it was just Rosenberg's sense of humor and all part of the game.

What really hurt Hudson was how Rosenberg had forced him to drop his claim to the rights to the show's theme song, even though he had written and composed most of it. Hudson had tried to put it behind him, but it was always an irritant in the back of his mind whenever he dealt with Rosenberg.

So, with three minutes to airtime, Rosenberg, several heads shorter than Hudson, grabbed the bandleader firmly by the arm, peered over the reading glasses dangling off the end of his nose, and said in his throaty, almost-hoarse voice, "Maaarrrk, I want you to play more Cole Porter."

Hudson knew that Cole Porter's music was among the most expensive to use, and costing as much as forty times the available alternative. "Edgar," pleaded Hudson, "I don't think I should. Fox is already on my ass about the expense. I've got to cut back. Fox said so . . ."

Hudson, nervous about the approaching opening number for the show, began to ease himself away. But Rosenberg reached out and grabbed Hudson even more firmly by the arm, holding him in place. Rosenberg stared into Hudson's eyes and, like a parent scolding a difficult child, said again, "Maaarrrk, play more Cole Porter."

"Edgar," said Hudson, looking for a one-line reply that would be his exit line, "I'm just a pawn in the scheme of 'The Late Show.' " Then he pulled away.

Rosenberg moved with Hudson, grabbing him by the arm again, this time even more firmly. "Mark," he rasped, his eyes burning, "I'm a pawn as well. I'm just in a larger game."

As it turned out, it was a game that became bitter with surprising speed as the juggling for power between Rivers and her husband and Fox intensified. By the end of November, less than two months after the show premiered, both sides were doing much of their communicating through their attorneys, who also accompanied them at meetings.

One constant source of friction was over how many guests to book for each show. Rivers wanted four a night, the same as she had had when she guest hosted "The Tonight Show." Fox wanted her to have three, which would mean more in-depth interviews and less demand on the limited pool of available quality, high-profile guests. As Rivers said later:

> I'm a nervous Jewish lady. I'm full of insecurity. I thought, "Wouldn't it be great to have all the guests we wanted." I wanted that show. But I didn't want that dressing room and I didn't want

that green room. And I didn't want them to serve wine [to the guests]. Everything they worried about. All we wanted to do was mind our business.

Fox saw the situation quite differently, however. Recalls Jamie Kellner:

It was always a sore point with us because we wanted [the interviews] longer. There were a lot of kind of things, rumors that went around. One of the talent coordinators said a guest told her that he heard Joan say as she walked down the stairs, "That's the last time we'll have them on the show." Joan was turning some people off. I think we did the best we could.

There also was constant tension over who to book as a guest. Sammeth, Rivers, and Rosenberg thought that they would have a free hand to book young, hip, interesting guests of all kinds, particularly after years of frustration at "The Tonight Show," where they had been limited to the kind of guests Johnny Carson would approve of—as interpreted by his staff.

At one early meeting, Rupert Murdoch had suggested to Sammeth and Rivers that they should book Barbra Streisand. Sammeth agreed but knew it was totally impossible, so he just rolled his eyes at Rivers, who shrugged. Sammeth wanted to tell Murdoch that he was already booking as many top names as possible, but that it wasn't easy. First, there was the fear on the part of guests that they would be blackballed by Carson—a very real concern, especially for young comics. Second, there was fear of Rivers herself. Her sharp tongue and fearless questioning, especially about very personal matters, such as sex and marriage, combined with a truly quick, rapier wit, was what had made her famous; but it was intimidating to many celebrities.

It also angered Rivers and her husband that Fox kept pushing them to book obscure guests who just happened to be stars of either Twentieth Century–Fox series or new FBC shows. Rivers didn't mind having Chris Lemmon, star of Fox's "Duet" and son of actor Jack Lemmon, because his famous father made him an added attraction, but complained bitterly about booking someone like Katey Sagal, who played the housewife on "Married . . . With Children."

They also felt let down by Diller, who, they said, had promised to use all of his connections and power to help book top guests. One who Sammeth wanted was Arnold Schwarzenegger, who had just made the movie *Predator* for Twentieth Century–Fox. But it was never arranged. "He never delivered," Rivers said later, with open bitterness. "Not one." Diller claims that he did make some behind-the-scenes efforts but admitted that he achieved no significant results.

What upset Rivers even more was that Fox constantly seemed to be making demands and placing restrictions on what she could talk about. For starters, they demanded that she lay off jokes about Fox executives because they felt it put the new network in a bad light, while Rivers felt they made the perfect foil, just as Johnny Carson was always taunting the NBC executives. Rivers later charged:

> It was a lot of ego. I had no ego. I have a show. You bought me. Don't change me. Don't send a little boy to tell me ten minutes before a show we can't say this and can't do this and can't do that. Then you've got the wrong show. And don't beat me up because you promised ratings you can't achieve. . . . What they bought they wouldn't let me do. What they wanted me to do they finally did after I left, and look what happened. [The show did even worse in the ratings.]

Fox was deeply concerned that Rivers was turning off the target audience of young adults. Recalls Garth Ancier,

> We did try as best as we could to tone Joan down to more of a comfortable host, more acceptable five nights a week, as opposed to a person on once a month. Brandon [Tartikoff, of NBC] said to me when we first announced Joan was coming to Fox, "She's your problem now." Not in a mean way. He said, "You have to understand, she prepped the entire month for a week. And I think you're going to have a problem. It's going to be hard to make it work every week. It's hard for her or anyone to prepare that much material."

Joan felt just the opposite. She didn't mind the hard work, the hours of preparation, the endless meetings with the writers and staff—as long as she felt it was all going to make the best possible show. Rivers recalled:

> They were scared about everything. Every argument was, "You can't do this. You shouldn't do that. Why did you say that?" They began to try to censor the jokes. There was no honeymoon. I wasn't a pig in a poke. They knew what they bought. But they tried to

change me immediately. They didn't wait a day. It was the most unhappy experience I ever had in my life. And it wasn't me.

As the battle inside heated up, so did the barrage of criticism from outside. As one of Rivers's longtime friends recalls,

> The critics were just eating [Joan] for breakfast. She hated it. She was very thin-skinned, but who wouldn't be. The Fox executives seemed to take it even more badly. I don't think they really quite knew what they were getting. Diller was stuck with this woman who was suddenly being creamed by the critics and his friends. I think Diller would go out to dinner and the people in his chic crowd would say, "What the hell are you doing with 'that' woman?!" Joan isn't noted for taste. Diller's friends are taste.

One big point of contention was whether Rivers should do a monologue at the top of each show, as Johnny Carson did. Recalls Bill Sammeth,

> They said they didn't want her to be dirty. They said, "Why can't she be classier?" Joan never wanted to do a monologue. So we said, "Wait a second. This solves the problem, guys. This will only happen in a monologue. It doesn't happen when you question. It doesn't go that way unless the person being interviewed wants to do it."

In theory, Diller, Rivers, Rosenberg, and Sammeth all wanted the same thing—a successful show. But Diller's management style with Rivers, as with his young executives, was to push to get what he wanted, not to gently manipulate. A longtime friend of Rivers links the friction between Rivers and Fox to the comedienne's feelings of insecurity.

> Remember, despite the money and fame, this is a very insecure lady. So if you are for Joan, on her side, believe in her, she'll do anything for you. She is yours. Barry and company could have gotten all they wanted from Joan if they had shown her they were in her corner. Instead she felt terribly threatened by them from the first second. To her Fox was snakelike, macho, terrifying. Everything they did to control her just hurt morale instead of building it.

Diller, on the other hand, felt that Rivers and Rosenberg weren't willing to work with Fox to achieve their mutual ends. Said Diller:

Her attitude, for her own reasons, for her own needs, notwithstanding any agreement, was that she needed to be in such total control that she also needed to close her ears to even hear anything else. Meaning everything is a contest of will and winning. But when you're dealing with somebody to whom that is what is important, nothing else is important. There is no [saying] "Wait a minute, consider this." There's no considering anything. There's just, I have to win. In any issue, I have to win. Now that's done for reasons that have nothing to do with putting bacon on the table.

Fox wanted Rivers to concentrate exclusively on making "The Late Show" a success, which meant taking time off from touring and doing comedy concerts. Ancier feels that

> She did things that were not very smart. She still tried to do other things, even though "The Late Show" was very demanding. She ran and did shows around the country on weekends. I think it was too much for any human being. But that's what she wanted to do. I think everyone knew those were problems going in. And those were problems that eventually did hurt the show.

But to Joan Rivers, there was no other way to feel alive. Throughout her career she had worked almost beyond human endurance. It made her feel whole. After the debacle at Fox she went on to do a Broadway play and, at the same time, work the late shift at a New York City cabaret. Then she'd fly to Las Vegas to work on weekends.

The outside activity also was tremendously lucrative. That was one reason Rivers quickly soured on doing the show live for the eastern time zone. If taped, she would be able to leave for the airport in time to do two shows that same night in Las Vegas. However, Fox felt that it had sold affiliates and advertisers on the idea that a live Joan Rivers would be unpredictable and exciting. So that, too, became a constant source of tension. Kevin Wendle recalls that

> They kept reminding us about all the money she was losing to do the show live. It was really a mutual call. If it had been a real issue, I think they would have made their case when they made the deal. It was an issue, but not a big issue. It was one of those things they used to throw in our face.

Of course, by trying to tone Rivers down, Fox took away a lot of the same spontaneity it was after by going live, effectively nullifying its own strategy. Later, Fox's research showed that few viewers knew or cared that the show was live. Rivers had quickly realized that most of her guests didn't know, either. When guests were made aware that the show was live in the eastern time zone, it only served to make them nervous.

As a compromise, Rivers suggested occasionally taking the show on the road with her. She felt it would be exciting, vibrant, and give it a feel of specialness. Other shows did it. But Fox said it would cost too much. So Rivers and her nine writers (Fox constantly complained that there were too many) came up with theme-night shows about places they wished they could visit. The more difficult it became to book good guests, the more Rivers pushed such special ideas. There was Amazon Night, with a staff member dressed up as the Great White Hunter to protect her during the monologue; Africa Night; a costume party for Halloween; and turkey costumes for Thanksgiving. Fox hated it. They kept demanding a streamlined show that depended solely on Rivers's quick wit and her emotional connection with the guests.

Instead Rivers worked the staff even harder, trying to come up with a way to make the show more appealing. Meetings were now taking place not only in the mornings and afternoons before the show, but also after the show, late into the night.

Soon the long hours became the cause of yet another battle. The home of "The Late Show" was in Fox Square, situated in a seedy part of the Hollywood section of Los Angeles. It also housed Fox's local station, KTTV. It was an area with few good restaurants nearby. The choice, then, was either to give the staff a long lunch hour right in the middle of preparing for that night's show, or bring food in. Fox reluctantly agreed to provide a "snack" for the executives and others in management, according to Courtney Conti, one of the youthful production executives who worked under producer Bruce McKay. The problem became one of defining just who was allowed to eat and how to handle staffers who took plates of food to others who, according to Fox, were not allowed to share the food.

Bandleader Hudson became adamant about the need to feed everyone who was there all day:

It wasn't "The Tonight Show." People didn't show up at 4:00 P.M. to go on at 5:30 P.M. We came in at 9:00 A.M. and often left at midnight. I was trying to be fair. If I'm there ten hours and you're there ten hours, why shouldn't you be eating the same food. I said that and got my butt kicked the next day by Ron Van Dor and Bruce McKay.

Eventually the talent, production staff, and Hudson were fed in one area, while musicians ate in another area. Fox remained adamant about not feeding the technical crew, however. Wendle claimed that if they did it for "The Late Show," it would set a bad precedent for crews on other shows that taped at the same facility.

Courtney Conti, who often seemed to be involved in every aspect of putting "The Late Show" on the air—always with infectious enthusiasm and the warmth of a teddy bear—took charge of finding a caterer. At first it was just snacks, but after a while he found someone who would bring in a hot meal for the same cost. He thought it was a great idea. Fox thought it was excessive. Recalled Conti:

> I'd made a deal with the caterer to feed the staff of about sixty-two people for $7.50 a head per day, instead of the usual $11 or $12 a head, by promising them a steady volume of work. Fox said the meal was too elaborate and ordered a cutback to a hot snack or high tea kind of thing. I said, "These people need a hot meal. They're here twelve hours a day." So they insisted on cold cuts, hot dogs, that kind of thing.

Fox also complained about the cost of free sodas being provided to the staff in a large refrigerator that was open to anyone and everyone. When their complaints went unheeded, Fox ordered the refrigerator removed and replaced with a Pepsi machine. Their compromise was to charge only 50 cents for each soda, which they said was cost, instead of the normal 75 cents. The Pepsi machine became a symbol among Rivers and the staff of everything they didn't like about Fox. Nobody would use it. Someone even painted a target on it and hung funny signs off it.

Instead, Rosenberg bought another refrigerator and each week would write a personal check for about $100 to keep it stocked with cold soft drinks and Perrier water for everyone.

Fox found no humor in either the Pepsi machine or the attitude it represented. Says Kevin Wendle,

> Every time we tried to come in with some constructive input, it was rudely rejected. And sometimes there is certain input, when you're responsible for the production of the show, that must happen or not

happen. Joan used the word *shit* several times on the air. Don't get me wrong. It wasn't just a little issue. We were on live and there were certain things that we had to do as our responsibility to our affiliates. So one directive was, "Don't say shit on television." On that she said, "You're right. I can't do that." Then a short time later she did it again.

Diller was growing increasingly concerned about the budget overruns, the audience ratings shortfall, the on-air jokes about Fox, and reports that his executives were being snubbed by Rivers and Rosenberg. It particularly annoyed him—and struck him as totally unprofessional—when Rivers accidentally gave out "Dallas" actress Victoria Principal's telephone number over the air. Principal, already upset because she felt that Rivers, as guest hostess, had asked too many personal questions during a "Tonight Show" appearance, immediately filed a lawsuit against Rivers and Fox demanding $3 million in damages. Recalls Diller,

> I went right after [Bruce] McKay and I said, "You're handling it all wrong. I went to their [Rivers and Rosenberg's] house and I sat there and I said, "It's very early in the game. No real damage has been done, but this is not being on a nightclub stage. You need every friend you can get. You need the people on this show to love you. You need them to support you and to protect you. And you're alienating every one of them, one by one, and it's terrible."

Thus the lines had been drawn in a high-stakes standoff. Both sides were convinced they were right. Both sides felt they had the power to enforce their point of view. Each was rapidly losing respect for the other. Each was convinced that his or her position would prevail.

A showdown had become inevitable.

18

JOAN'S RIVER
OF TEARS

IN EARLY FEBRUARY 1987, Joan Rivers and Edgar Rosenberg were asked to come to a meeting at Twentieth Century–Fox with the top executives of the Fox Broadcasting Company. The exact purpose of the gathering wasn't spelled out, but Rivers and her husband assumed it would be an effort to clear the air of increasing tension. They welcomed the opportunity to confront the mounting problems and declining ratings, and in particular wanted to use this meeting as an opportunity to convince Fox that "The Late Show" should no longer be done live.

The meeting was set for a cloudy Friday afternoon in one of the small conference rooms on the ground floor of Fox's executive office building. Rivers and her husband accompanied by attorney Peter Dekom arrived promptly and soon found themselves at a long, polished oak table surrounded by the top Fox executives, including Barry Diller, Jamie Kellner, Kevin Wendle, and one of Fox's attorneys. Both sides tried to be cordial, but it was obviously an effort. Emotions were running high and there was an almost palpable sense of tension in the air.

Rivers was dressed casually in a blazer and slacks, but wore full makeup because she was already made up for the show that night.

Her husband's attire was a navy blue Dunhill sports jacket and slate-blue shirt with a patterned silk tie. Diller and the other Fox executives were dressed more formally. Almost all of them wore starched white shirts with dark ties.

Rivers later said the budget complaint was particularly irritating to them because they could never get Fox to give them a copy of the show's budget—despite repeated requests. "We have lawyer letters saying you must show us the budget," says Rivers. "We begged for the budget. They would never show it to us."

Jamie Kellner began the conversation, reviewing the situation as Fox saw it. He talked about the budget overruns and how much Fox had paid back in free commercials to advertisers the previous month to make up for the shortfall in the ratings.

Rosenberg cut in to talk about how much the show had been improving in recent weeks, and to note how unfair it was to blame them for a drop in ratings during the first week of February, when local TV stations around the United States do special promotions as part of sweeps month, one of several months each year when ratings are used to set advertising rates.

Diller, standing against the wall, his face flushed, cut Rosenberg off. His eyes were like blue steel and his tone was icy. They weren't just talking about one week, or even one month, Diller said, but about the long-term ratings trend that had been established. It appeared that people had sampled the show in great numbers in the early weeks but that many fewer than had been expected were returning each evening. Diller said the show was losing the support of affiliates and advertisers. Things were not going well. Fox had no choice but to make certain changes.

Rivers, who had expected a frank discussion and open exchange of views, suddenly realized that they were in the midst of yet another power play. These men don't want to hear what Edgar and I have to say, she thought. They just want to dictate the terms of our surrender.

Kellner tried to keep it on a calm, businesslike level, but it wasn't easy. His razor-cut blonde-brown hair, boyish face, and athletic build seemed at odds with the tough words coming out of his mouth and the hard, unyielding glint in his eyes. Fox was taking back control of "The Late Show" from this point forward, Kellner said. There would be no more questions about who was in charge. Fox had to be the ultimate authority. "We owe it to our affiliates," said Kellner, "and we can no longer live with the rising losses and the falling level of audience."

Rivers and Rosenberg glared back at Kellner and Diller. Rivers fought the tears welling up in her eyes. She didn't want to give them the satisfaction of seeing her cry. She felt as if she were about to explode as the Fox executives went down the list of items they wanted changed.

When they got to Bruce McKay, Rivers tried to put in a good word for him. She thought he was a nice guy who was doing his best in a difficult position. Jamie Kellner didn't agree. McKay was fired, Kellner informed them, as of that very afternoon.

Then Kellner dropped the big one. Fox felt that Edgar Rosenberg was interfering with the operation of the show on every level and had assumed far more responsibility than they had ever intended to give him. Fox felt it would be impossible to get a first-rate producer to replace McKay as long as Rosenberg was playing a day-to-day role in the show. While they wanted Bill Sammeth, the other executive producer, to continue booking guests—and in fact play an expanded role—they didn't want Rosenberg to play any role. Kellner told them that Rosenberg no longer would be allowed to run things, to make any important decisions, or to dictate to Fox executives on any issue. In fact, they preferred that he not come to the stage at all but, if he did, they wanted him to stay in the background—deep in the background.

Rivers and her husband were furious. Rivers threatened a lawsuit for violating her contract. Barry Diller told her that he hoped a suit would not be necessary, but that ultimately it was Fox's show, Fox's network, and Fox's responsibility, and from that moment forward they would exercise that responsibility to the hilt.

When Rivers and Rosenberg stumbled outside after the meeting, even the sky had turned dark and threatening. It was as if the whole world were conspiring against them. Rivers was nearly hysterical with outrage. Rosenberg could feel his heart thumping in his chest as they drove from the studio toward Fox Square for the taping of that night's "The Late Show."

Rivers was most upset about Fox's insistence that her husband stay away from the show, especially considering that he had worked so long and hard to make it a success. Rosenberg downplayed his own situation but kept returning to how unfair and insulting it was for Fox to dictate to Joan Rivers after they had used her reputation to draw in the advertisers and affiliates that gave life and form to their new network.

It was raining by the time they pulled into their parking space at Fox Square. Rivers and Rosenberg somberly made their way down to the dressing room suite and slammed the door shut behind them. How could she possibly prepare for the show? How could she go out and be up and full of energy and witty when her insides felt like they had been ripped apart. Finally she decided that it would, in fact, be impossible to go on. She was not a machine on which Fox could punch a bunch of keys and get instant results. She was a sensitive, fragile human being, and she was devastated. Her enthusiasm had been drained, and she felt nothing but anger.

Rosenberg called Courtney Conti, the boyish, enthusiastic production executive who had become a family friend, and briefed him on what was going on. He told Conti that Joan Rivers would not be able to go on that night, and that he should let Fox and the staff know she was . . . too ill to perform. Conti immediately took their side and wanted to know what he could do to help. He thought about the time a few months before when he had been out sick with a bad cold and Rivers had shown up at his apartment bearing hot chicken soup and good cheer. He would have done anything for her, but he was helpless. He, too, was a pawn.

Upstairs on "The Late Show" soundstage, on the ground floor of the large studio building at Fox Square, Mark Hudson was just about to enter the final production meeting of the afternoon when one of the production assistants told him they had just gotten word that Rivers was too ill to go on that evening. Nobody knew whether or not there was going to be a show, but they were supposed to continue preparing as if the show would tape.

Hudson walked to the bandstand for a final rehearsal. Before they could start, however, Hudson got a phone call. He was needed upstairs in Bruce McKay's office immediately.

As soon as Hudson entered McKay's office, he knew something was wrong. McKay was sitting at his desk looking shell shocked, as if all of the blood had drained from his face. Hudson realized that something terrible must have happened. He stared at McKay, who said quietly, "I've been fired."

Also in the room were Jamie Kellner, Kevin Wendle, Garth Ancier, Ron Van Dor, Courtney Conti, director David Grossman, and one of the show segment producers. Kellner was the one who spoke first. He greeted Hudson and asked him to close the door behind him. As he did, he noticed how silent it was in the room, save for the sound of raindrops beating against the windows in the back of the room.

"Mark," Kellner began, "do you think you could guest host the show tonight?"

"Yeah," said Hudson without thinking. Inside, he was shaking, but he did his best to hide it. His head was swimming with what was happening. McKay was gone, Rivers had called in sick . . . What was next?

"We've had to make some changes, Mark, but we're very happy with what you've been doing. It was just time . . . for us to take charge of the situation here. We're going to be bringing in another producer," said Kellner, "but Kevin and Ron will be in charge for now. Everybody will just keep doing exactly what they've been doing."

Hudson was too numb to ask questions. Suddenly Grossman took him by the arm and led him out the door and downstairs for a run-through, his first as the host of "The Late Show."

For the next hour Grossman and Hudson worked out a routine to start the show and determined how they would handle various guests. Then another call came for Hudson from upstairs. Barry Diller had just called. He said they had decided not to do the show live this evening after all. They were going to use a rerun of a previous show. Everybody could go home and return Monday, when it would be business as usual.

In reality, it was never to be the same again. That day would later be remembered by "The Late Show" staff as Black Friday, the day Fox took over for real. Although it was far from the end, the spirit and enthusiasm that had been at the core of "The Late Show" was permanently diminished.

Rivers was back on the set on Monday, but Rosenberg didn't come in until late in the afternoon. He went directly to Rivers's dressing room until the taping, and then sat in his usual chair just off camera. Kevin Wendle was there throughout the day, riding herd over the staff. It was a subtle change, but it was one that every staff member felt.

As morale sank that week, and rumors flew about what really was going on, the Fox executives realized that they had to exercise some kind of damage control. On the following Thursday, after the show, the entire production staff and key department heads were asked to stay for a meeting.

It was held on the third floor of the adjacent building, which housed the producers' offices, amid a clutter of papers, telephones, and desks. It was a large, open area with pale walls and bulletin boards burdened with thousands of pieces of paper, pictures, schedules, memos, and notices. By the time Jamie Kellner, Kevin Wendle, and Ron Van Dor arrived, the room was already filled with staff members. Noticeably absent were Joan Rivers and Edgar Rosenberg.

Wendle, dressed in a dark suit, white shirt, and tie, began. "Thank you all for coming," he said. "We've asked you here because we know there has been a lot of discussion about what is happening to the show. There are going to be some changes. But I want to assure you that we do appreciate all of your hard work, and what we are doing is going to make this show really great. You've all done well, but we are making these changes. We just want you all to know the show is not going off, and you all are needed. Jamie, did you want to say something?"

Kellner, in a dark-tan lightweight suit, white shirt, and tie, stood up. "As you may have noticed, Kevin [Wendle] is taking a much more active role, and we will eventually be bringing in another producer. We are looking for a top person to come in and help us make this show even better. You may also have noticed that Mr. Rosenberg will not be playing a day-to-day role in the show any longer. So if there are any questions from now on, bring them to Kevin or Ron [Van Dor] and we will make sure everything is taken care of."

Kellner said that Fox wanted a simpler show, meaning Rivers just talking and interviewing guests. They didn't like theme or costume shows and hated amateurish gimmicks and skits. Fox was now taking a firm hand in all aspects of the show, and no matter who came in as producer, that would not change. Then he answered a few questions, and it was over. The staff, usually full of youthful exuberance, was unusually subdued. They walked out in small groups whispering among themselves. They did feel better that Kellner, the president of the network, had taken the trouble to reassure them, and he did seem like a surprisingly nice, warm man. Still, their hearts were torn.

"What people don't realize is everyone really loved Joan, they would have killed for her," Hudson explains. "Everyone thinks Joan is brash, but she's a very emotional person. And she drew very emotional reactions from everyone around her on the show."

Kellner certainly had not enjoyed what he'd had to do that day, but he felt there was no alternative.

It had become obvious that all the battling had to stop from our side and we had a responsibility to all the stations and to the advertisers for the product. It was our word to all these people, and not Joan Rivers. Barry and I felt a very strong responsibility. So we said, "If we're going to fail, let's fail, but let's be in charge of our own failure. If we're going to succeed, then now is the time." So I went in and explained to everybody that from now on this was not going to be decision by committee. That Fox was going to assume control of the show. We were going to bring in others, whom we would name soon, and they would have final say, yes or no, according to the contract. We told Joan and Edgar we would honor all parts of their contract, but from now on we were in charge. We would give her approvals but she was not going to run the show, and Edgar, as of that time, was not to render certain services on a daily basis, as per the original agreement.

It was Rivers and Rosenberg's habit after each show to return to the dressing room to change, talk with special guests, and unwind a bit before leaving. When they finally did go down the hall toward the exit, most of the staff would be waiting to chat briefly and say good night. Rivers would stick her head into some of the offices and the green room or angle down a hallway to make sure she didn't miss anyone. As she once told Mark Hudson, it would be inappropriate for her to actually sit and drink and fraternize with the staff, because it would be taken the wrong way, but she liked to let them all know that she did care about them. Rivers says she felt the staff would not be able to relax if "the boss" was around.

On the Friday night after Kellner had met with the staff, Rivers and her husband were rushing out to the airport to leave for a concert back east. Rivers saw how subdued many of the young staffers were and that there were tears in some eyes. It was all she could do to hold back her own tears. She realized that they were all sharing her pain, frustration, and outrage, and were as helpless as she felt to do anything about the situation.

Over the next two days, Rivers performed at an outdoor theater in upstate New York. It was chilly at night when she went on, and as she worked up a sweat on stage, she could feel the contrast of the cold air against her warm skin. She should have been more careful about getting a chill. She was always on the edge of exhaustion, but now, with all the stress and emotional turmoil in her life, it was as if some of the defenses had broken down.

On Monday morning there was a sudden snowstorm, delaying the return flight to Los Angeles. By the time the plane finally took off, Rivers's head was congested and she was having difficulty breathing. She coughed and choked as Edgar hovered nearby trying to convince her to take more medicine. She was feverish by the time the plane landed at Los Angeles International Airport and was rushed into a waiting limousine. It was already three o'clock by the time they got to their home in Bel Air.

Mechanically, Rivers forced herself to go into the bedroom and begin preparing to leave for the studio to tape the show. Her face was flush, her stomach upset, her head aching and feverish. Her husband finally insisted that she stay home and get into bed—there was no way she was going on that night. Usually, despite any health problems, she would have pushed him aside. But on this night, her morale as broken as her health, she shrugged and gave in. She undressed and slid into bed as Rosenberg went to the phone to notify Fox.

The news hit the Fox executive corps like an early warning of enemy bombers approaching the city. It wasn't just another night, or just another week. For more than a month Fox had been running a contest to find Joan Rivers look-alikes in each city where they had an affiliate. They had beaten the drum loudly, pushing hard to get all of the stations to publicize the event in their city. Then Fox had paid for airline tickets, hotel reservations, and other expenses to bring all of the winners to Los Angeles. They had been arriving all weekend and were scheduled to be on the show the next night, Tuesday. And now Rivers would not be there to greet them. To Diller, Kellner, and the other Fox executives, it smacked of a purposeful insult by Rivers and Rosenberg. They decided that it was their contractual right to make sure this wasn't just a display of temper. So they quickly dispatched a doctor to Joan Rivers's house to check her out. According to a paragraph deep in the boilerplate of their contract, they did have this right.

Rivers and Rosenberg were shocked and insulted when the Fox doctor appeared at their gate. Still, Rosenberg let the doctor in. After a thorough examination he told Rivers to stay in bed. He said there was no way she could work that night or for the rest of the week. She was very ill.

Fox, meanwhile, had scrambled to find a fill-in host and had come up with Rick Dees, a popular Los Angeles disc jockey who also hosted a Paramount syndicated music show called "Solid Gold." Dees showed up literally only minutes before airtime and proved an amiable host. It happened to be the night that the band, under Hudson's direction, was playing only Grammy-nominated tunes, in honor of the upcoming Grammy Awards. For Dees, who loved music, it was a natural transition.

Dees returned the next night and handled the Rivers look-alikes with easy charm. They were disappointed not to see Rivers, but it was still fun to be in Los Angeles.

On Wednesday Rivers told Fox that their doctor had been wrong. She would return that night. She wasn't completely well, but she was a trooper. She also agreed during the afternoon before the show to take the winner of the Rivers look-alike contest, a man, out shopping with her.

Things fell back into an uneasy pattern after that. Rivers still came each morning to prepare and work with the writers, but her husband didn't come in until later in the day. On some days he didn't come in at all. Word soon leaked out around town that all was not well between Rivers and Rosenberg and Fox. That led to an item in a gossip column in *People* that described Rosenberg as sitting forlornly in his wife's dressing room each day holding their little dog Spike on his lap.

Rivers was outraged. She decided to retaliate on the air. She told Fox in advance what she was going to do, and although they asked her not to, they couldn't stop her. She brought it up early in the show and made it clear that she only read *People* while in the bathroom. She finished by tossing the copy of the magazine onto the floor behind her.

Fox, without discussing it with Rivers, wrote a letter to *People* apologizing for its star's behavior and insisting that Fox had had nothing to do with it. The letter was written by a business affairs executive, but it clearly had been approved by Barry Diller. *People* printed Fox's letter in its next issue.

Rivers and her husband were furious. It was just one more problem in a long line of problems affecting the relationship between them and Fox.

Shortly afterward, Rivers went on a scheduled vacation to Europe, where she also did some concerts and taped several TV shows. While she was gone, Fox put on a series of guest hosts, including Pee Wee Herman and Howie Mandel, and much to their surprise, the ratings actually went up slightly. That created a sense that maybe there could be a "Late Show" without Joan Rivers. It planted a seed that was well fertilized by a lot of wishful thinking at Fox.

About a month after Black Friday, the new producer arrived. Joanne Goldberg was a tall, elegant woman with considerable experience. She had produced some Barbara Walters specials for ABC and had been involved with a long list of other shows, including the Tony Awards and "Baryshnikov on Broadway." Fox told her to use her vision to improve the show, but then put her on a short leash. She had a series of ten one-week contracts, which would then have to be renegotiated.

Goldberg (who declined to be interviewed for this book) apparently felt that she didn't have enough time to make massive changes in "The Late Show," at least not until her contract was renewed. She decided that the important thing was to develop a good relationship with Rivers and begin to fine-tune the show. She saw from the research that the show got a very high tune-in during the first ten minutes almost every night. People seemed to be checking to see who the guests would be, then switching to another station. Goldberg felt that the solution was to front-load the show with comedians who would draw those viewers in and keep the dial set on Fox.

After analyzing the difficulty of booking top guests in competition with Johnny Carson and studying tapes of the earlier shows, Goldberg also decided to change the kind of guests they were using. Instead of just celebrities, she started looking for authors, good conversationalists, and interesting people of all kinds. She believed that Rivers was best when just interacting with other interesting people, and that she was less likely to insult the intelligence of an intelligent person. It was a popular idea with both the staff and Rivers and Rosenberg.

Bill Sammeth began to show up less, deciding that it might be best to let Rivers and Goldberg work things out between themselves. They did seem to quickly develop a strong rapport that had the potential for growth. The only question was how much time they would have to develop it.

Barry Diller watched the changes at "The Late Show" with little enthusiasm or confidence. The ratings, he noted, were continuing in a slow downward trend. And even worse, new studies of the composition of the audience indicated that Rivers was losing ground among young adults, the very audience that Fox—and the advertisers—had wanted to reach.

Everywhere Diller turned, inside the company and outside, he kept hearing that something had to be done about "The Late Show." There was mounting concern among advertisers and affiliates that the ratings would continue to fall during the following month, May, another sweeps month, which would set the advertising rates for much of the rest of the year. If the ratings fell enough, Diller was told, it could threaten not only "The Late Show" but also the continued viability and existence of the whole network, which had just launched the Sunday night prime-time schedule to smaller-than-expected audiences.

At the weekly staff meeting, Garth Ancier, Brad Turell, and some others were very negative about Rivers. They didn't feel she was going to make the show grow significantly. They felt that it had been shown that her appeal was very limited and really reached only into the big cities. In small towns and rural America, she seemed to be turning off large numbers of people, according to Fox research.

Kevin Wendle kept reminding Diller how well they had done with the guest hosts for a week. He was confident that they could do it again and again, and then eventually find another host after on-air auditions.

At Fox Square, Courtney Conti, the young production executive who had become Rivers and Rosenberg's closest ally, was putting the final touches on one of the greatest coups in broadcasting history—or at least so he thought. Conti was working with producer Peter Greenberg to set up an interview, live via satellite, between Joan Rivers and Imelda Marcos, the wife of the recently deposed dictator of the Philippines. To Conti it was a natural. They could talk about their mutual love of shoes and their husbands. It would be great, live, event television. And it would cost Fox only a little over $20,000 extra to make it happen. Conti closed his eyes and envisioned a worldwide blast of publicity about the interview and a huge surge in the ratings.

As he finalized the details, Conti got the word from Ron Van Dor: Fox wasn't going to put up the money. There was to be no interview with Mrs. Marcos or anything else that would bust the budget. Conti argued, but Van Dor said he was just carrying the message from on high. There would be no further discussion.

At the same time, the Fox publicity machine under Michael Binkow and Brad Turell put out press releases hailing the growth of the "Late Show" audience. The press release showed that almost every affiliated station was doing better with Rivers than they had done previously.

In reality, other forces were also at work. In late April Diller was very concerned that if "The Tonight Show" did poorly in the upcoming May "sweeps"—when rates are set by audience size—Fox would begin loosing affiliate stations. That could jeopardize the network's continued existence. The final straw was a phone call from Frank Rothman, the former chairman of MGM/UA Entertainment, who was now in private law practice. He was acting as outside counsel for Fox in regard to Rivers and Rosenberg. Rothman recounted for Diller the history of the relationship. He noted that since November they had been sending letters to Rivers each time they felt she had done something to breach her contract. Diller recalls:

Rothman said that based on where we were at that point, Rivers was clearly in breach of her contract. I mean, we didn't put her in breach. She put herself in breach. And we believed it because we had the file [of threatening legal letters]. Every time she did something we had sent a letter to her lawyer because we knew this was inevitable. In other words, we would say, "We have warned you about this and we're telling you again." Now Rothman said she was clearly in breach, but if we let it continue to go on, we forgive the breach. We had only a certain window where legally we could deal with her. If we didn't, then we were forgiving the breach and we would have to start all over again.

That pushed Diller to make the decision: Rivers would have to go. Diller describes the situation:

It would be such a pleasure to get this albatross from around our necks. And we'll make up a new show every night. In my true dumbness, that's just what we did and that's why we did it. There's nothing more. I didn't speak to Joan Rivers previous to the final decision. There was no specific incident. There was no smoking gun, so to speak. It was just a mess. And I was concerned that if we didn't do it before the [May audience measurement] sweeps, we'd be pulled off the air [by affiliate defections].

In fact, the legal question was the smoking gun. And when it was fired, it shocked the public.

A Fox attorney notified Peter Dekom, Joan Rivers's attorney, on a Thursday, nine days after Joanne Goldberg's arrival, that the plug was being pulled and that they wanted an immediate resolution of her big-buck contract. Dekom called Rivers and Rosenberg. It was a crushing blow. "The stupidity is we could have given them a wonderful show and it still could have been on," Rivers said a year later, sitting in her tiny dressing room at Universal Studios, waiting to go on as the center square on "Hollywood Squares." The tears filling her eyes made her dark eye makeup run. "It was a very sad thing. They had promised too much. They didn't know what they

The top FBC executives and their key producers gathered together right before the network went on the air. Top row, from left to right: Michael Moye, Linda Marsh, Margie Peters, Patrick Hasburgh, Stephen J. Cannell, Howard Gewirtz, Ron Leavitt, Ruth Bennett. Bottom row, left to right: Ed. Weinberger, Garth Ancier, Barry Diller, Jamie Kellner, Gary David Goldberg. *(courtesy Fox Broadcasting Company)*

Jamie Kellner and Joan Rivers at an early network party. *(courtesy Fox Broadcasting Company)*

The Fox name replaced the famous Hollywood sign for the first week of April 1987, to mark the launch of Fox's prime-time programming. *(courtesy Fox Broadcasting Company)*

Joan Rivers applauds Joan Collins on "The Late Show." *(courtesy Fox Broadcasting Company)*

At a defiant celebratory party after Joan's relationship with "The Late Show" was severed, Joan Rivers is flanked, clockwise from left, by her husband Edgar Rosenberg, announcer Clint Holmes, musical director Mark Hudson, and daughter Melissa. *(AP/ Wide World Photos)*

Stephen J. Cannell, above, a network veteran with many successes to his credit, scored another one with "21 Jump Street," which was created and produced for its first two seasons by Patrick Hasburgh, below. *(courtesy Fox Broadcasting Company)*

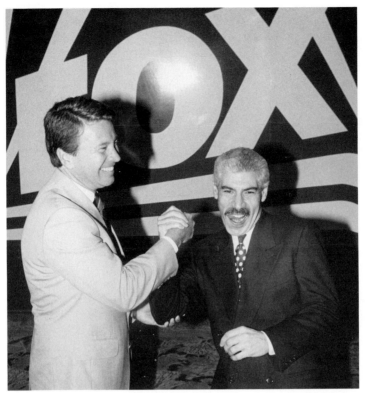

Kellner and heralded producer Barry Sand clasp hands shortly before Sand's "The Wilton North Report" began its three-week run. *(courtesy Fox Broadcasting Company)*

Ron Leavitt, left, and Michael Moye, co-creators and executive producers of the FBC hit "Married . . . with Children." *(courtesy Fox Broadcasting Company)*

John J. York and Chuck Connors in a scene from "Werewolf," a horror-action series for which FBC had high hopes. *(courtesy Fox Broadcasting Company)*

George C. Scott in "Mr. President," an ill-fated show from Johnny Carson's production company. *(courtesy Fox Broadcasting Company)*

Executive producer Michael Linder, left, and host John Walsh of "America's Most Wanted," Fox's revolutionary and successful series. *(courtesy Fox Broadcasting Company)*

Katey Sagal and Ed O'Neill as Peg and Al Bundy, who are definitely not the Cosbys in FBC's "Married . . . with Children," which has garnered high ratings and stirred controversy. *(courtesy Fox Broadcasting Company)*

Fox's first Emmy-winner, inventive comedienne Tracey
Ullman. *(courtesy Fox Broadcasting Company)*

Johnny Depp became a teen heartthrob for his portrayal
of undercover officer Tom Hanson on "21 Jump Street."
(courtesy Fox Broadcasting Company)

were doing. They had children running it. And I took the brunt of this. Then my husband took the brunt of it. It's just a shame."

The attorneys representing Fox made it clear there would be no last show without a settlement of Rivers's contract. It was part of the overall hard-line approach that Fox took toward the three-year agreement signed less than one year earlier. Their position was that Rivers was in breach of her contract, so they didn't really owe her anything. If she wanted to sue, they made it plain that the suit would probably drag through the courts for years; and in the end Rivers would still have to take only a fraction of the more than $10 million she was still owed under the agreement. Rivers had received about $3 million in her first seven months, and Fox pushed her to settle for little more than that. In addition, Fox demanded a gag order, which would mean that for at least one year Rivers would not be allowed to discuss her side of the story with the media. Rivers balked, but then consented only after Fox agreed to the same ban. On that Friday afternoon, it was finally over.

Bill Sammeth, in the meantime, was on the phone alerting some of Rivers's favorite guests that this was going to be her last night, if she was on at all. Among the first to insist on being with Rivers were comics Pee Wee Herman and Howie Mandel.

Rivers was gracious and elegant on the final show, much to Fox's relief. She said it was Fox's ball and bat and they had the right to call the game anytime they wished. She assured her audience that she had been around for a long time and would be there for them for a long time to come.

Rivers let a songwriter who was one of the production assistants on the show, have a chance to sing. It was Rivers's way of getting something positive out of a very negative experience.

At the end of the show, Rivers just sat back and let things run their course. Pee Wee Herman, Howie Mandel, singer Wendy O. Williams, and some others began jumping around to protest what had happened to Rivers. Rolls of toilet paper appeared and were wound around the set. Furniture tumbled and broke. It was the end to a short but exciting era.

When they were finally off the air, the audience stood and continued to applaud and applaud. They refused to leave. Almost the entire crew had slowly crept up to the edge of the set during the final minutes, and they all swept onto the stage at the end, hugging, kissing, and crying with Rivers.

One of those with teary eyes was Joanne Goldberg, who had been notified that day by Kevin Wendle that she, too, was fired, even though "The Late Show" would continue with a "host du jour," or different host each night. Wendle himself would be the producer. Fox felt that Goldberg was too close to Rivers. Within a week another twenty-four of the sixty-plus staffers would be fired, many of them directly associated with Rivers such as her hairdresser, makeup artist, and dresser.

Later that evening, when Rivers and Rosenberg were ready to leave, they began their slow procession to the parking lot down the hall lined with photographs of all of the guests who had appeared with Rivers. The whole staff was waiting, many of them in the previously off-limits green room, where the bar stocked by Fox was getting a heavy workout. Rivers had hugs and kisses and tears for them all as she slowly made her way out, trailed by Rosenberg, who carried their little dog Spike.

Looking back later, Rivers said that her main problem had been that she was the first to go on the network. They had used her to get affiliates and advertisers and then expected her to live up to their unrealistic expectations for ratings. In retrospect, she pointed out, the audience size she was averaging was respectable. As it turned out, "The Late Show" never did do as well after Rivers.

"They did what they did," said Rivers, still angry. "They lied. They cheated. They were dishonorable."

Fox president Jamie Kellner denied that the network had lied, cheated, or been dishonest. He said it was just business.

Rivers also placed blame for the next tragedy in her life directly on Fox during an interview for this book.

On August 11, 1987, Edgar Rosenberg went to Philadelphia, supposedly to conduct real estate and other business deals with a prominent local developer, Thomas Pillegi. He was scheduled to return to Los Angeles two days later and immediately check into Cedars-Sinai Medical Center for tests and treatment of his recurring heart and stomach ailments. Rivers, in the meantime, was already in the same hospital. She was scheduled for some corrective surgery and a procedure called liposuction (in which fat is literally vacuumed out of a certain part of the anatomy).

In Philadelphia, Rosenberg checked into $500-a-night suite 425–427 at the Four Seasons Hotel. He called Pillegi in Ocean City, New Jersey, that night just after ten o'clock. Pillegi, an old family friend, recalled later that Rosenberg had sounded very tired and depressed.

After sixty-three years of living, Rosenberg was indeed at the end of his psychological rope. Wracked with pain from his illness and guilt over the failure of the Fox show, Rosenberg decided that he no longer wanted to be a burden to his family. Wearing long-sleeved blue pajamas, he stared at pictures of Joan, his wife of twenty-two years and his daughter Melissa as he began to pop Valium tranquilizer pills into his mouth, gulping them down with a glass of water and miniature bottles of scotch and cognac from the suite's minibar. The coroner estimated Edgar Rosenberg's death at sometime around midnight. The body was found the next morning after Pillegi notified the hotel management and authorities that he was concerned about not being able to reach his friend.

There was speculation afterward that Rosenberg had purposely done it in Philadelphia so that his wife and daughter would not have to identify the body. Pillegi had that task.

Edgar Rosenberg left behind two hand-written notes and three audio cassettes, all in envelopes. One was addressed to whomever found the body, while the other items were addressed to Joan Rivers, Melissa Rosenberg, and Pillegi. Their contents have never been revealed.

Hours after his body was found, Melissa Rosenberg rushed into her mother's hospital room at Cedars-Sinai in Los Angeles and broke the tragic news. Mother and daughter cried long, bitter tears in each other's arms.

The tabloids screamed out with stories about how Rivers felt personally responsible for what had happened. " 'It's My Fault'— Why Joan Rivers Blames Herself for Hubby's Suicide" said page one of the *National Enquirer.*

Rivers, however, said during the interview that she blames Fox. "Look, I don't care how your book comes out at this point," said Rivers in her dressing room at Universal Studios. "Fox never did what they promised. They were totally dishonorable. And they got what they deserved. I'm still here. My husband is dead over it. Edgar killed himself over it."

Diller and Kellner said Fox had not done anything dishonorable. A Fox spokesman later insisted Rivers did not blame the network for her husband's death.

After Rosenberg's death, Rivers had taken several months off from public appearances. She had sued the author of an article in *GQ Magazine* over a story that appeared to be nonfiction but was in Rivers's view fiction, and which suggested that she was somehow happy about her husband's death. In a tearful press conference she and daughter Melissa denounced it bitterly as a pack of lies. It was eventually settled out of court. *GQ* magazine agreed to print a statement clarifying its article, and Ben Stein agreed to donate money to charities chosen by Rivers, without admitting any wrong-doing.

Rivers finally had reemerged, determined to throw herself back into her work so that she would be too busy to think about what had happened. Her first high-profile public appearance, ironically, was a brief walk-on at the Emmy Awards show in September 1987, where she received a thunderous ovation and then made a short award-presentation speech. The irony, of course, was that her appearance was a coup for the Emmys in the first year that the show was telecast over the Fox Broadcasting Company.

19

SATURDAY NIGHT FEVERED

DECISIONS AREN'T ALWAYS the result of brilliant planning. Often they arrive as the logical conclusion to a sequence of events. Seven months into late night programming, one month into prime time on Sunday night, one week after Joan Rivers had been fired, and just over two weeks before the anticipated launch of the Saturday night schedule, the fledgling Fox network was being swamped by events. No matter how fast Diller, Kellner, Ancier, and others hired new personnel, there was still too much to be done too fast by too few. At the same time, everything was costing more than had been budgeted, taking longer to come together, and, when the shows did air, performing below expectations. Add to that a young, inexperienced staff and a hands-on leader trying to run three complex companies at once, and it was easy to understand the undercurrent of tension among the key Fox network executives gathered in Barry Diller's small conference room on a bright, sunny southern California Tuesday morning in early May 1987.

As beams of hazy yellow sun flooded the room, a dozen or so neatly attired executives sipped coffee, chatted, and read through the stacks of notes piled at each place. They were mostly male and mostly white. One of the two women present was Brenda Mutchnick Farrier (her new married name) and the other was Marion Davis, who had joined the programming department from NBC. Barry Diller sat at the head of the table, with Jamie Kellner on his left and Rupert Murdoch, in town for his monthly visit, on his right. Others around the table included Garth Ancier, Kevin Wendle, David Johnson, and Brad Turrell.

Murdoch and Diller worked well together but made a visual contrast—Diller, with a receding hairline defined by a half moon of white-blond hair that turned gray at the sideburns, dark-blond eyebrows, thick features, and jutting jaw, sharply dressed in a light-gray suit, white shirt, and off-white tie; and Murdoch, neatly trimmed black hair with bolts of gray, long, craggy face, looking like a British banker in his dark blue pinstripe suit, high-collared white shirt, and striped maroon tie. Murdoch refused an offer of coffee, while Diller elected to have a cup of strongly brewed tea. Murdoch sat quietly, making notes on a legal-sized yellow pad and taking everything in, while Diller, looking like he hadn't slept well in a month, fidgeted impatiently in his seat.

It was a time of mixed emotions for the young network. The prime-time launch was behind them, but there was little proof that the venture was working. The ratings were generally below what had been anticipated, but the real problem was that it quickly had become evident that they were in real trouble in certain markets. While Washington, D.C., and New York City, where Fox owned and controlled the stations, were performing about as expected, many of the smaller affiliated stations in places like Pittsburgh and Tampa, Florida, were performing far below projections.

As the launch had approached, Diller had kept pushing for more and more advertising, raising the costs far above the original budget of about $12 million. Now that all of the bills were in, it looked like the real launch cost for advertising and promotion would be more like $24 million, more than half of what had been budgeted for the entire year. The launch of the Saturday night schedule was only two weeks away, and it had become obvious that things weren't falling into place in either programming or promotion.

There was some good news, however. Fox finally had achieved one of the secret aims on its opening agenda—to find "franchise" programming that would help raise the network's profile and build its credibility. Fox had stunned the entertainment world the previous week when it announced that the Academy of Television Arts and Sciences (ATAS) had awarded Fox broadcast rights to the Emmy Awards for the next three years, as well as the annual Television Academy Hall of Fame show. The news that Fox had won the rights to this prestigious industry event had made headlines, and for the first time, the three major networks were forced to think about Fox as a competitor. The network bosses had quickly cried foul.

For four decades the three major commercial networks had basically alternated showing the Emmys, always claiming that it was really more of a public service than a profit center. While it wasn't stated policy, on the night the Emmys were shown, the networks that were not carrying it would schedule reruns or less-than-killer programs. The idea was that it was in all of their best interests to encourage the public, on that one night, to watch the network carrying the program that honored all of television.

The TV academy, meanwhile, had grown unhappy about the size of the license fee it was paid for the three-hour show, which in the previous year had been $750,000, less than the networks typically paid to license a one-hour drama. Also, as the ATAS entered contract negotiations in early 1987, there was pressure from the networks to sharply cut the number of awards given out on the show, limiting it to only those in high-profile categories. That meant rewarding actors and a few other creative executives before a huge audience, while shuffling technical personnel and minor categories off to a separate, nontelevised event. The networks also were balking at carrying the ATAS new pet project, the Television Academy Hall of Fame, which each year installed a handful of TV pioneers. Inside the highly charged political atmosphere of ATAS, cutting awards and the hall of fame show wasn't a very popular notion.

There were many in the TV academy who didn't even want to give Fox a chance to bid. They felt that putting the Emmys on Fox would make it a second-class event. There was also a growing competitive jealousy on the part of the other three networks, who publicly said Fox wasn't competition but privately worried about the newest threat to their dominance of the airwaves.

The only reason Fox was finally allowed to get a foot in the door was the friendship between Barry Diller and Richard Frank, the president of ATAS, who was also president of Disney's movie- and TV-production arm. Frank had worked for Diller at Paramount and was now doing business with him on several shows, including a TV version of the Disney/Touchstone movie *Down and Out in Beverly Hills*.

When the big three cried that they lost money on the Emmys, what they really meant was that for those three hours they didn't make what they considered to be an acceptable profit. They certainly didn't lose money.

Fox was prepared not only to match the network bids but to exceed them. Murdoch and Diller both saw the Emmys as a loss leader, meaning that they would spend more than it was worth because it would introduce new viewers to the network and bring attention and credibility to Fox. Fox bid $1,125,000 per year for each telecast, plus $200,000 to conduct the judging. It also agreed to broadcast the Hall of Fame for an additional license fee of $250,000 per telecast. Fox said it would carry all of the awards and guaranteed it would also spend a substantial amount promoting the shows.

Fox's willingness to pay a record license fee was part of the secret agenda developed at the top of the Fox network in the earliest days. Murdoch, Diller, Kellner, Ancier, Johnson, and others knew it was going to be a long, slow climb to establish the network. The one chance they had to find a short cut to success, it seemed, would be to grab certain high-profile programs.

The first show they had gone after was a new version of "Star Trek," which had started as a TV show and then, while Diller was at Paramount, gone on to success as a series of movies. At Paramount Diller and Frank had looked at "Star Trek" as the basis of a new program service they wanted to start, but when that fell through, the show concept moved onto the big screen. Four *Star Trek* movies had been made with the original cast. Now, at the urging of Ancier and Wendle, Fox wanted to bring it back as a TV series with a new, younger cast—sort of an offspring of "Star Trek."

There were a number of meetings to explore the concept. In the end, Fox had only been willing to guarantee that it would buy thirteen episodes of the new "Star Trek," whereas Paramount wanted a guarantee of at least twenty-two episodes. It was also using Fox's interest as a wedge to get other offers, including one from NBC, which was definitely interested in the new "Star Trek." Inside Paramount there was also considerable concern about helping a competitor. As the Fox network grew, there would be fewer hours available for Paramount and other TV syndicators to sell shows to those stations. Mixed in with this were the emotions from the changing of the guard from Diller to Frank Mancuso that were still fresh in the minds of many involved. The press was constantly comparing Diller, Mancuso, and Eisner, since all three had started from the same studio and then gone their separate ways.

As negotiations reached their most-delicate stage, Diller was quoted in a nationally syndicated column by Marilyn Beck denigrating Mancuso's abilities. Diller later claimed he was misquoted and called Mancuso to apologize, but the damage had been done. There was no way Paramount was going to give Fox that particular show. Instead, Paramount decided to do the new "Star Trek" itself and sell it into syndication.

Paramount did agree to pick up the deficits on a new show for Fox, however, which turned out to be "Duet," a romantic comedy done by "Family Ties" producer Gary Goldberg's company (which was based at Paramount).

Next Fox had gone after the Disney studio's weekly movie for television, which was then on the ABC network. Facing competition from the highly rated news magazine show "60 Minutes" on CBS, the Disney Sunday night movie had not been performing well. ABC was considering dropping it. When Fox executives heard about it Diller got on the phone to Eisner. Fox would pick up the movie at the same license fee ABC was paying and run it as their programming on one night, probably Friday evening.

There had been a meeting on a Sunday afternoon in late 1986 at Eisner's large West Los Angeles home. All of the key Fox executives, including Murdoch, had sat around Eisner's living room with the top Disney executives.

After considerable discussion, Disney opted to take an ABC offer to cut the show back to one hour and keep it at that network on Sunday evening. Disney did agree to work on another new show, however. It was "Down and Out in Beverly Hills."

The third big event Fox had gone after was Monday Night Football, which had become an institution on the ABC network. For years it had been the network's anchor on Monday night, but recently the ratings had sagged a bit. In early 1987, when it came time to negotiate a new contract, ABC dragged its heels with the National Football League. It wasn't prepared to increase what it paid and was even talking about ways to reduce its costs. ABC was threatening to drop the Monday night game altogether if it didn't get its way. ABC's position was that CBS and NBC had all the football they wanted on the weekends, so the NFL really had no choice.

Then along came Fox. Murdoch had learned while running a TV network in Australia how valuable it was to have major sporting events. He knew sports fanatics would find even an obscure UHF channel if their favorite team was playing. It also would allow Fox to add another night of programming—Monday—instantly, expanding its ad sales and giving it a tremendous tool to promote other shows.

ABC entered the bidding offering around $6 million per game for the rights to show each of the sixteen Monday night games during the regular season. Fox started at over $7 million a game for three years and soon raised its offer to about $8 million a game, an astoundingly huge, $384 million commitment for a fledgling network. Murdoch himself was involved from behind the scenes and told his negotiators not to blanch over the amounts. He would happily pay.

Unfortunately, one of the NFL owners most involved in the negotiations was Arthur Modell, owner of the Cleveland Browns. His public complaint about Fox was that in Cleveland, he couldn't even get their affiliated station on his TV set because its signal was so weak. He felt strongly about this and told his fellow owners that it would downgrade the NFL's most valuable product, its games, to have them on Fox. There also appeared to have been some personal bias involved. Modell was a close friend of Marvin Davis and had even served on the Twentieth Century–Fox board when Davis was owner. He was aware of the feud that had developed between Davis and Diller and wasn't about to help his pal's enemy if he could avoid it.

ABC, which in the face of the Fox threat decided it really did want the Monday night football games after all, came back to the NFL with a new offer. It would pay more for the Monday games, and its affiliate, ESPN, the all-sports cable-TV network, would buy a separate package of Thursday and Sunday night football broadcasts. In total, the ABC package worked out roughly equal in economic terms to what Fox was offering. And, after all, it was ABC, a *real* network making the offer. The NFL quickly agreed to deal with ABC and ESPN. Fox was once again left at the altar.

Later there would be accusations of improper antitrust activity by combining the ABC and ESPN bids, and it would become the subject of a long investigation by the Federal Trade Commission. Fox was right, but it still didn't get the Monday night franchise.

If it had gotten it all, Fox would have been on Friday through Monday, a four-night network. It would have grown much bigger much more quickly, and that would have helped promotional efforts. Instead, Fox was left to battle it out night by night with whatever programs it could come up with.

At least Fox had the Emmys, a coup even if the other three networks were making it known that they wouldn't cooperate as usual with promotion, with entries, with serving the stars on the night of the show, or by running weak programs during the show. In fact, all three would roll out blockbuster programming when the time came.

So, even flushed with winning the Emmys, Fox had some immediate problems to solve, particularly in the areas of promotion and advertising. Brenda Farrier reported first. She rolled off a list of promotional projects in progress, plans for meetings with affiliate promotion directors, and other details involved in advertising, publicizing, and promoting the new operation. She tried to be upbeat about the numbers from a study of how many people were aware of the new network, but clearly the expensive launch had only begun to seep the name Fox into the public consciousness.

That wasn't the bad news, however, the short, dark-haired Farrier told them in her surprisingly strong voice. Spot studies indicated that it might take much longer than they had originally estimated to break through the national clutter of advertising and competing programs. It appeared that the best advertising tool was on-air promotion on a strong station. In Washington, D.C., for instance, where the Fox affiliate was already strong, Fox was delivering the six percent of viewers it had expected. What was bringing down the national average were all of those cities with weak UHF affiliates, where the on-air promotion reached almost no one because they had so little an audience to start. Where they had tried print and radio ads, the impact had been depressingly mild. It seemed that somehow, the entire station had to be lifted up to a higher community profile before the Fox shows would have any chance at all to be sampled. It was going to be a gradual process requiring a lot of resources.

To illustrate the problem, Farrier described a test they had run. They selected two medium-sized cities of about the same size, both of which had a UHF station as a Fox affiliate. In one they did no promotion at all. In the other they did an all-out media blitz on the radio and in the local newspapers, as well as heavy on-air promotion on the UHF affiliate station. When the ratings came in the following week, they were essentially the same in both cities. It seemed as if it made no difference how much Fox spent or what it put on the air. The only thing that mattered was that people associated that station with junky shows and reruns. They turned to the network affiliates for the best shows during prime time.

That was even more depressing in light of the huge cost of the prime-time launch. Diller jumped in to ask Farrier how things were going in setting up a new advertising department. The week before, the Fox leadership had decided to part company with Chiat Day, the creative advertising agency used for the launch. Farrier reminded those at the meeting that the consensus was that Chiat Day had been spending too much money and hadn't been responsive enough to the constant demands from Fox for more material and adjustments in what had already been prepared. Privately, Farrier told close associates that the agency couldn't seem to handle the Barry Diller style of constantly tinkering with every ad and promo up to and past the final deadline. When new ideas were needed, the agency wanted to discuss when and what it would cost, while Diller wanted answers immediately. When the network brought ideas to the agency, the creative people seemed to feel threatened, which made everything even harder. The final blow was that Chiat Day, after the launch, assigned relatively low-level personnel to the Fox account, some of whom seemed to have no knowledge of the TV business and no real understanding of who was who at the network. In particular, one woman at Chiat who had begun when Scott Sassa was at Fox never seemed to grasp that Farrier was now in charge. So Farrier had let her know in the way that mattered most: Fox pulled the account and brought it in-house, where Diller could make as many changes as he wished, no matter how late they were in the process.

Now Farrier was promising that they would do it for less, and get it done on time. There was to be no more behind-the-scenes laughing at "those bozos from the advertising agency." There was too much work to be done.

Ancier began questioning how Farrier was preparing for the upcoming meeting with affiliates, when a variety of promotional and on-air spots were to be shown. Farrier took a deep breath and maintained her self-control. Deep inside she considered both Ancier and Wendle to be not only a problem, but also the most severe critics of her professional judgment. They blamed her because the advertising wasn't drawing in enough viewers to sample the programs they created.

Wendle had recently left the programming department to take over the post–Joan Rivers "Late Show," which was trying to operate with a different host each night. It was turning out to be a much more difficult task than any of them had imagined, as each host made very different demands of the production staff. When Rivers had made demands, they were met because it was essentially "her" staff. Now "The Late Show" staff itself was in charge, and often there was hostility felt toward one-night hosts who tried to make a lot of budget-busting demands. At the same time, it was very difficult to get top people to host at all. Not only was the show's reputation in ruins after Rivers, but ratings had been steadily dropping since her departure. In retrospect, Rivers wasn't looking so bad after all, although none of those assembled in Diller's conference room was quite ready to admit it.

There had been another subtle change in the few weeks since the prime-time schedule started on Sunday night. In the early days, Fox had been run very democratically. Literally anyone, from the least-experienced staffer on up, was welcome to contribute ideas. Once they were on the air in prime time, however, the pressure had built. There was less time for discussion. More and more of the decisions simply were being made, usually by Diller, Kellner, Ancier, and Wendle. The company had stratified while still in its infancy.

Even among the top group there were increasing personality clashes. Ancier recalls that he and Wendle simply didn't have a lot of respect for Kellner's ideas on programming. They also were dubious about Farrier's ability to do the job in promotion and advertising. Their doubts were communicated with pointed questions, which added to the growing sense of isolation many mid-level Fox executives had begun to feel.

Some around the table already believed that Ancier was pushing for Kellner's job, and that Wendle would be pulled along on Ancier's coattails. It all came down to how Diller felt, since he was the ultimate center of power and the final decision maker in most cases. And Diller simply chose to wait and see who would be strong enough to survive.

David Johnson, the pragmatic head of marketing who also played a key role in selling advertising and dealing with affiliated stations, spoke next, and he had even worse news. Results were in from the first advertising sales in prime time. Due to a major miscalculation, they weren't very good. They were far below what had been budgeted. The problem, explained Johnson, is that they had begun to sell after the two-tiered network sales process was completed. The first tier is the "upfront," a period in late summer and early fall when the networks sell a large portion of their ads for the year based on guesses of how programs will perform in the ratings. Think of it as a sports team selling season tickets, but holding back some for those who want to buy at the last minute or to use as "make goods," ads given for free when rating guarantees are not met. In TV, the last-minute purchases are made on the "spot market." The ad agencies and network buyers, almost all located within a few blocks of one another in midtown Manhattan, do a telephonic mating dance that ends in a negotiated price for whatever ad spots are left. Now Fox realized that it had started selling for its first quarter of programming too late; consequently, it had missed out on both markets. This was going to put a huge dent in the annual budget.

Johnson delivered his assessment like a marine officer going over battle plans. His words were clipped and authoritative but frequently interspersed by sarcasm and a bit of anger hidden just below the surface. In his starched white shirt and narrow yellow power tie, Johnson was totally in control, but he seemed increasingly weary with being one of the few adults in the Fox kiddie crusade.

As for planning for the Saturday night launch in two weeks, there would be some advertising and affiliate promotional support, but it would be less than what they'd hoped for. If the launch was to plunge ahead, the network would just have to work harder to catch up on the run.

As the meeting progressed, both Diller and Murdoch knew that it was very questionable whether or not they should go forward with Saturday night as planned. They knew it would be enormously expensive to pull out at this late date, and they were concerned about affiliate reactions. It was like a new marriage that needed to develop trust. Since some affiliates already had begun promoting the Saturday night launch for the end of May, there was a real chance that it would hurt their credibility—and ultimately the affiliate-network relationship. Still, both Diller and Murdoch were far more concerned about the possibility of continuing without being completely ready. It wouldn't help anyone, neither the network nor the affiliates, if they failed because the shows weren't right or the promo-advertising mechanism wasn't functioning. It was a difficult decision.

Diller turned to Ancier for an update on how the program development was coming. Garth began by announcing the hiring of another former NBC executive, Alan Sternfeld, who would help with planning, scheduling, and programming strategy. Ancier then quickly began to go through some of the shows and problems they were encountering. As he spoke, he was supported by comments from Marion Davis, a strong-willed but soft-spoken woman with a pretty Asian face and short black hair who, along with Ancier, had the most experience in programming a network.

Davis (no relation to either Martin Davis of Paramount or Marvin Davis) had been brought into Fox by Kevin Wendle but had quickly become closer in attitude and philosophy with Ancier than any of the others. She had found herself in the tricky position of overseeing shows without the authority necessary to really make changes. One of those shows was "Mr. President," starring George C. Scott, which was meant to be a kind of "Father Knows Best" in the White House. She soon found herself caught in the battle between producer Gene Reynolds, who wanted the show to be politically charged, and executive producer Ed Weinberger, who wanted it to be more of a traditional comedy with stories dealing mainly with the family of the chief executive. "You had a situation of almost too many riches [in creative personnel]," says Davis. "When too many people try to work on a project, unfortunately it doesn't always work. You need that one creative vision. That's what caused problems. There were two bosses and ultimately no one was in charge."

Davis had grown up in New Mexico and then attended Yale, graduating in 1981. She got a job with a small New York City advertising agency and later, through a friend at Cable News Network, was introduced to Kevin Wendle, who was then producer of the six o'clock news at WABC-TV in New York. A short time after, when Wendle left the news to produce a late night music video show for channel 7, he hired Davis as a production assistant on the program. Since the staff was small, Davis got to do a little of everything, from writing scripts to producing segments.

When Wendle left for Los Angeles, Davis went to work on another local show in New York. Wendle kept calling from Los Angeles and telling her she should move west because that was where the real opportunities were waiting. She finally did go west for a short stay and did a special project for NBC. She then returned to New York and took a job at CBS producing segments of the news show "West 57th Street." Four months later NBC offered her a job developing dramatic shows, and so Davis moved back to Los Angeles.

A little over a year afterward, Wendle moved to Fox, and he called Davis and asked her to move as well. She felt she still had a lot to learn at NBC, but the Fox opportunity offered even greater challenges and a chance for greatly expanded duties. "Fox was like a blank page," says Davis. "You could go in and put whatever imprint you wanted on this blank tape. There's something intriguing about that." However, what Davis found when she arrived was an understaffed programming department and a whole group of shows in various stages of development.

As Ancier and Davis told the others at the meeting with Diller and Murdoch that day, program development was a patch quilt system that was breaking down all over the place. The idea of letting the producers take charge had been good in theory, but ultimately it was the network's money and reputation that were on the line. Thus the young Fox executives were finding themselves in confrontations with experienced producers who had been promised a free hand but now were being reined in.

There were frequent battles with Patrick Hasburgh over the content of "21 Jump Street," and they still hadn't settled on whether "Werewolf" would be a thirty-minute or sixty-minute series. Scripts were being written both ways.

They had finally cast Patty Duke as the lead in "Karen's Song," one of the Saturday night shows, and scripts were now being rewritten to make her character a bit more appealing.

Things were going painfully slowly on Disney's development of another Saturday night show, "Down and Out in Beverly Hills," and a meeting had been scheduled that would be attended by Diller and Eisner to try to straighten it out.

They even had run into a problem on "Married . . . With Children" over the use of certain language. Ancier said he was in the process of solving the problem that very day.

Diller finally cut Ancier short. It was clear that things weren't working as well or as fast as they had hoped in program development. Now, with the Saturday launch imminent, it seemed that there was a real question as to whether enough backup shows would be ready on time.

Both Ancier and Davis felt that the stockpile of backup shows was thin, but if needed, it could be done. Ancier charged that the real monkey wrench in the process was the promo machinery, which simply wasn't working well enough. Farrier retorted that it was the programming department that wasn't moving quickly enough to provide shows that would "create so much interest that they draw viewers in," as Diller often demanded.

Diller glanced toward Murdoch, who seemed to be thinking the same thing. The launch of prime-time programming on Saturday night would have to be delayed because of a myriad of problems. They would have to race to cancel print and radio advertisements and notify *TV Guide* editors of the change. Ironically, one of the few ads they would not be able to stop was in the *Boston Herald,* a newspaper owned by Murdoch's News Corp.

20

GARTH ANCIER'S SCOREBOARD

ON SATURDAY EVENING, July 11, 1987, the Fox Broadcasting Company carved out a bit of media history. A two-hour made-for-television movie called, "Werewolf" marked not only the delayed launch of Fox's Saturday night lineup but also the inauguration of a four-network economy in the United States, as determined by the primary company that measures who is watching what on American television.

For years the A. C. Nielsen Company, the dominant national-TV rating service, had refused all requests by producers wanting their shows cataloged in the Nielsen Television Index (NTI) along with the offerings from the three major commercial broadcast networks. Nielsen had simply shunted those shows into its Nielsen Station Index (NSI), which measures audience in local markets, or into the national "Cassandra" ratings for syndicated shows—those sold market by market instead of playing at the same time nationally.

Being treated as a syndicated show meant that commercial time was sold at a much lower price for each thousand viewers than if it were a network offering, which would command a premium price. While Fox was selling ad time at about 15 percent to 25 percent less than the big three, it was still asking for a much higher rate than syndicated shows. And while Fox wasn't a network—and didn't want to be declared one by the definition established by the FCC—it was anxious to be considered a network when it came to selling advertising time.

Jamie Keller and David Johnson led the Fox negotiating team that spent months in conversations with Nielsen executives. Finally Nielsen agreed to treat Fox as a network, which meant overnight ratings in major cities (for the two nights it initially was on) and overall national ratings issued in the same form and in the same materials that document the three larger networks. Fox, in turn, signed an expensive five-year contract to buy the research Nielsen provided.

There was some sentiment inside Fox that it was a mistake to demand Nielsen network ratings. The argument was that inevitably, at least in the early years, Fox shows would always be at the bottom of the ratings list. It would be disheartening to the company and to those it hired to produce shows. David Johnson's winning argument was that there was no other way to be seen as a major player in television, and eventually, when those ratings started to climb, Fox would be compared favorably to its own early Nielsen performance.

As it turned out, on July 11, Fox did better than even Kellner or Johnson had anticipated. The two-hour pilot show of "Werewolf" was a story of a young man, played by John J. York, who turns into a werewolf when angered. He is always being chased by an older man, played by Chuck Connors. The show was reminiscent of one of an earlier generation, in which an accused killer was on the run: "The Fugitive." "Werewolf" scored a solid 6.5 national rating. It actually beat both ABC and CBS in a number of big cities, including New York and Washington, D.C., and scored remarkably well across the country.

The next big question was how to sustain a weekly TV series about a werewolf.

Garth Ancier, who had strongly backed the show, could answer that question in two words: Frank Lupo.

As the creative force behind "Werewolf," it was Lupo who had woven some story ideas into the concept for the series. A native of Brooklyn, he had begun as a staff writer at Universal Studios in 1977 on shows such as "The Hardy Boys" and "Magnum P.I."

Lupo came into his own in 1981 when he joined producer Stephen J. Cannell to cocreate "The A-Team," an action show that

soared to the top of the ratings. It was also the show that first
brought Lupo into contact with Kevin Wendle, then a programming executive at NBC.

Later, when Ancier and Wendle were making up a wish list of
producers who they wanted to work at Fox, Wendle urged Ancier
to add Lupo's name. Later Ancier would be criticized for sticking
so closely to his list of NBC-style producers, but he never wavered.
Explains Ancier:

> I believe that making serious television programs is something you
> learn over a period of time. You learn from mentors. You learn from
> producing shows under more experienced people. And then you
> may have your hit in the future. But it only comes because you've
> been under some masters.

Ancier didn't mean that someone off the street couldn't come up
with a good programming idea. He meant that he doubted that that
person could then execute the idea on screen with consistent quality
week after week.

> If Joe Schmo walked in the door and said I want to do a show about
> a lot of people who work in a garage, it could be a major league
> embarrassment or it could be "Taxi" from Jim Brooks, a brilliant
> character study that runs for five years and wins awards. It is not just
> the idea.

At the heart of the Ancier philosophy was the belief that if you
want to compete effectively with the NBC's and CBS's, then you
have to draw from the same talent pool. That doesn't mean, however, that you do the same thing. Rather, you take the best people
and get them to do something special, something that most likely
would appear only on Fox. To get them to do that, you make a
commitment in advance to buy a substantial number of episodes of
whatever show they produce. While ABC and NBC had both made
similar deals on occasion, Fox was the first to do it with so many
different producers for so many different shows.

To attract the top producers, who were in constant demand, Fox
made an implicit promise of greater creative freedom, a chance to
be more daring in language and content and, for the most part, little
network interference in the day-to-day production process. It was
an easy promise to make in the early days of the Fox network, since
there were few executives to do much interfering, and many of

those who were around were too young and inexperienced to challenge the Hollywood veterans.

Ancier and Wendle met with Frank Lupo and his producing partner John Ashley, a native of Tulsa, Oklahoma, who had met Lupo when they both worked for Stephen J. Cannell. They talked about a number of different ideas. They told them they wanted to give the producers a thirteen-show commitment, in advance, and that ideally it should be a show that the other networks would never go for. They were also targeting it to fill one of the toughest time slots in broadcasting at the time, opposing NBC's mega-hit series "The Golden Girls" on Saturday night.

Out of several ideas, "Werewolf" seemed the most appealing. It would be inspired by the ancient primal fear of the half animal, half man but be told in an exciting, contemporary fashion.

One major obstacle remained: Barry Diller simply couldn't be convinced that the concept could be extended to a weekly series. To satisfy him, Ancier and Wendle arranged a face-to-face luncheon with Lupo in Diller's office. Of the first group of shows, it was the only one Diller had to be convinced about.

With Ancier and Wendle pacing impatiently upstairs, Lupo sat at a small table set in Diller's office. Diller's secretary brought in a simple catered lunch and cups of steaming coffee, and then left them alone. Lupo wasn't about to be intimidated. He gushed enthusiasm for the new series and countered every question with an appropriate answer.

Finally Diller challenged the producer to provide some sample plot lines. Lupo smiled broadly and began to reel off a string of ideas that had been percolating inside his head for weeks. He wanted to keep the violence and actual scenes of the creature to a minimum but still gain maximum effect. That would make it better for television and keep the costly special effects to a minimum.

"This guy only changes into a werewolf when the moon is full," said Diller, "so does that mean we only have a show once a month?"

"The moon is always full somewhere," responded Lupo. "You just can't see it."

"You've got a point," admitted Diller, "and you've got a show."

It was Lupo and Ashley's idea to begin each show with a disclaimer saying that "Werewolf" might be too intense for some children to watch.

Fox had just hired a consultant, Don Bay, to operate as a standards and practices division for the new network. That made him the official censor. Although Fox wanted to be more daring, it still had to protect the federally issued licenses held by its TV-station affiliates, which meant keeping some rein on the proceedings.

The new standards and practices consultant was extremely upset about "Werewolf." He kept writing memos about it, which led Diller to question what was going on. He told Ancier to check it out. Recalls coproducer Ashley:

> They called and said, "Hey, guys, is this show too scary?" We said, "It's not a violent show, but it is intense. Yes. It absolutely is an intense show. If you have any qualms, before you build up more concern in your mind, let us screen the show for you." So one morning very early we brought Kevin, Garth, and Marion to our offices in Century City and screened the in-progress picture. They walked out and said, "It's terrific. We have no problem. Don't worry about Don Bay."

"Werewolf" quickly became the most successful Fox show on Saturday night, although that wasn't saying much. Fox had picked Saturday as one of two nights on which to start mostly because it came right before Sunday, the night with the highest number of TV sets in operation. It didn't make economic or promotional sense to be on just one night a week, so the concept arose of the Fox weekend. The big miscalculation was in thinking that *any* show could work on Saturday night. Fox was set up to sell advertising based on an appeal to a young, affluent, urban audience—people who tend to be away from home on Saturday night or, if they do stay in, often watch a movie on their VCR.

Saturday night's audience is primarily older, and those were the people who couldn't even find Fox. Older viewers are less likely to try new things, or to understand how to tune in a UHF channel.

For Ancier, salvaging Saturday night would become a kind of crusade. As the first wave of shows failed, he looked desperately for ways to counterprogram, to bring the Fox audience back to the TV set.

The first thing Garth Ancier had done when he came to Fox was to arrange for his office to have a wall-sized billboard charting the program schedules of the networks. At NBC, Brandon Tartikoff, his mentor, had a similar board with the schedules of ABC, NBC, and CBS. Ancier's was exactly the same but along the right-hand side of each listing was another column—a space for the Fox shows.

He wanted the same producers and the same quality as an NBC, but he also wanted shows that were different. He would study that chart for hours, figuring out how to counterprogram, where the networks were weakest, and what kinds of shows would work in various time periods. A student of television from childhood, he would think about what had worked in the past and how it could be repeated, with updated variations, into the future.

It was exactly that thinking that led to the show that would become Ancier's biggest success and Fox's biggest hit, "Married . . . With Children."

Now, with the first Fox shows just hitting the airwaves, Ancier sat in front of the big multicolored program board in his office, moping as he waited for the producers of "Married . . . With Children" to arrive for a meeting. How was he going to tell them, after making endless promises of creative freedom, that Fox was censoring a line in one of their first shows? How would he explain why the network that boasted no standards and practices department was bowing to the view of its standards and practices consultant. How would he tell the same producers he had fought to recruit that the hands-off policy they'd been promised was now being modified to be an occasionally hands-on policy?

As he waited, staring at the program board, Ancier thought about how his most important show had come together, and prayed now that it wouldn't blow apart.

From the start, Ancier had preached the need to develop a situation comedy that would become part of the American psyche. In modern television history, no form had proven more powerful when successful than the sitcom, just as no form had proven so difficult to get right.

At the time, the biggest hit in television was NBC's "The Cosby Show," a sticky-sweet family sitcom starring black comic Bill Cosby as a doctor and the father who always knows best. "Cosby" constantly preached better values, which inevitably led to a happy ending. On Thursday night, week after week it was the most-watched show in America, helping make NBC the most-viewed network. Both CBS and ABC had rushed to create copycat programs, but none had done as well as "Cosby."

Ancier had no qualms about copying the "Cosby" formula, but he did have doubts that it could work. He felt that it was so soft and sweet that it wouldn't remain in viewers' minds. It might work on an established network, where the audience from a popular show would be carried over to the newer program. However, Fox needed shows with enough drawing power on their own to attract the young, hip audience. Each program had to be so special that viewers would take the trouble to find the Fox affiliate on their TV dial, even if it was a UHF station with a weak signal.

Instead, Ancier dreamed about doing an updated version of "The Honeymooners," about a couple who battle but always make up, or an "All in the Family," the hard-edged comedy featuring a character named Archie Bunker, an unrepentant bigot and bully. Ancier believes that

> the best shows in the world were just funny. You don't sit and watch "The Honeymooners" and say, Why can't you be like Ralph . . . or Alice. . . . The best characters on TV have been obnoxious, rude. But now you've got to be so straight-laced and TV is here to teach. Well, TV ain't here to teach. School is here to teach. TV is here to entertain.

As he thought about it, Ancier remembered Ron Leavitt and Michael Moye, a pair of writers he had worked with at NBC on a hard-edged hit sitcom called "The Jeffersons," about a kind of black Archie Bunker. Leavitt was white and young and hip, and Moye was black and young and hip.

The only problem was that Columbia Pictures Television, the production company that had the two under contract (and would have to back their show with millions of dollars in production deficits that could be earned back only in the syndication aftermarket), didn't want to hear about them working for Fox when they could be developing shows for the big three networks, which would lead to bigger profits in the aftermarket. At the time, it was far from clear that shows on Fox, with its smaller audience, would have any great value in syndication.

When Ancier first called Leavitt and Moye, his pitch was simple: "Do anything you want, but make sure it's different and funny. Do something that would never be on the other networks, something a little more daring, more biting. Fox is here to give you the chance to do things you can't do anywhere else."

"We'd always hated the typical family on television," recalls Leavitt. "It just makes us sick, basically."

Moye adds that the three networks

> all hired the same independent research people. They could basically type up one set of notes that would apply to every show ever made. That's why all sitcoms look alike. They have a little spat and then

make sure at the end that you hear the words, "Just kidding." Or "I really do love you." You can set your watch to that. You know the hugging is coming about thirty-seven seconds before the credits start to roll. I always hated that, because I've never seen a family act like that.

Michael Moye, a black man of medium build with longish curly hair, had the introspective air of a college professor. A self-described loner, Moye was born in Connecticut but grew up in North Carolina, where his father worked for Winchester, the company best known for making firearms. In 1977 Moye was majoring in marine biology at the University of North Carolina when he won a comedy playwriting contest sponsored by Norman Lear, the legendary writer and producer who created "All in the Family" and many other hit shows. As part of his prize he was flown to Hollywood, where he wrote for one of Lear's shows, "Good Times," about black teenagers. He also began contributing scripts to "The Jeffersons," "Different Strokes," and other shows produced by Lear's Embassy Communications.

Leavitt, a tall, gregarious Caucasian with a thick head of black hair, long face, and prominent nose, was born and raised in Brooklyn. After his father died when Leavitt was very young, he suffered through a series of stepfathers before leaving to attend the University of Miami. After about a year Leavitt was thrown out for academic nonperformance. He took a series of odd jobs around southern Florida and began writing scripts, just to see if he could do it. One of the scripts was for a show called "Busting Loose," which he mailed off to the producer. In 1977 he was offered a job by that producer. He and his wife moved to Los Angeles and he began hanging around, contributing ideas to the senior writers. It lasted sixteen weeks. He moved on to write for "Happy Days," and then went to Embassy to work on several different shows.

It was there that Leavitt and Moye established an instant rapport. "We both independently had a dislike of traditional sitcoms," says Moye, slipping into a high nasal voice. "Let's handle AIDS this week, nuclear waste next week and make sure people get all their dogs and cats spayed the week after. Then we'll do a funny one."

"Our feeling was first and foremost to entertain," says Leavitt. "We like to be funny. We think that's what a comedy should be if it's called comedy."

Despite their success, both also felt outside of the show biz mainstream. "We have no suits and ties and we don't hang around with the Hollywood hoi polloi" Moye explains. "We had another thing in common—a disdain for people who think they're doing Molière [the French actor and dramatist] out there."

It was Leavitt and Moye who convinced Embassy to let them do a show for Fox. "They're kind of afraid of us," Moye laughs. "It's like the gifted child they can't control."

Moye first came up with the idea of two married people who are totally embittered toward each other and life says Moye, "The anti-"Cosby" backlash was starting to grow. The hot new comedians were people like Sam Kinneson, who screams at his audience, and Roseanne Barr, a heavyset woman with a sarcastic tone. It really just became, Gee, what if Sam Kinneson married Roseanne Barr?"

"What we didn't want was to look at Fox as the fourth place to sell," Leavitt recalls. "We didn't want an idea everybody else rejected. We wanted something we could only do on Fox. They deserved to be the outlet you go to because you want some creative freedom."

Ancier and Wendle immediately grasped what the coproducers wanted to do, and they sold it to Diller. Ancier says he

> knew they were very talented writers with a blue-collar sensibility that was really delightful. I loved that they would get away from the huffiness of a "Dynasty" or "Dallas" [popular nighttime soaps]. They were going into something with a little edge, a little lower-middle-class fun to it. Because television should be fun.

The basic cast, chosen by Leavitt and Moye, was the Bundy family: a husband who is an unsuccessful shoe salesman, Al, played brilliantly by a stage actor named Ed O'Neill; Peg, a housewife who hates to cook and clean, played with savage aplomb by singer-turned-actress Katey Sagal; a sexpot teenage daughter named Kelly, played by the fifteen-year-old busty blond, Christina Applegate; and a wiseguy preteen son, Bud, played by David Faustino. As foils there were the prissy, newlywed neighbors, played by Amanda Bearse and David Garrison.

Leavitt explains that the show

> was always meant to be a man-woman thing. . . . It was called "Married . . . With Children," because the children were, like, there. It was a different way of people getting along. Man against woman. We gave Al Bundy a lot of raps about what has happened

to men. Once it was good to be a guy. Men were kings. Now we're just a pussy-whipped nation. He doesn't understand what happened.

In reality, much of the relationship between Al and Peg Bundy, the snide bickering and backhanded love, came directly out of Leavitt's own relationship with his wife, another Brooklyn native. Like Peg, she doesn't like to cook for her husband at home too often because he might get used to it. Says Leavitt:

We've heard about people in therapy since they were fifteen because they would watch "Father Knows Best" and their family wasn't that great. . . . We figured we'd show them a real family and save them some money. They don't need a psychiatrist. Nobody's happy out there.

Leavitt and Moye certainly weren't happy when they discovered that Fox had penciled out one of their favorite lines in one of the very first scripts. It was an episode titled "The Period Piece," in which the show's three female characters all suffer from premenstrual syndrome, or PMS, simultaneously. In one scene Al is complaining to his neighbor, Steve, about women. "Women can shoot their husbands and get away with it," says Al. "It's this period, PMS thing." Then Al looks back over his shoulder at Steve and very philosophically added, "I think PMS really stands for Pommel Men's Scrotums."

Fox said it was just too visual a description, and it was cut from the script. "We were really upset and pissed off," recalls Leavitt of the day they met with Ancier to complain.

"You told us to be free," Leavitt told Ancier. "Now you tell us not to be free. Which is it?"

Ancier looked at them sheepishly and tried to explain. "If it wasn't the first show, or second show. But . . ."

Leavitt and Moye stormed out that afternoon. They talked about just walking away from the whole thing. They thought about going to Diller, but quickly decided that that was a terrible idea. They finally decided that as bad as it was, it would only be worse at NBC, CBS, or ABC. "It came down to, We love the line, but it is the first show," said Leavitt. "If it happened now [two years later], we definitely would have fought for it longer."

As it turned out, it was one of the few times Fox ever tampered with "Married . . . With Children." That show and "21 Jump Street" quickly became its two most successful series.

21

THE DARK
BEFORE THE DAWN

EVERY EXECUTIVE AT Twentieth Century–Fox and the Fox Broadcasting Company lived with a small box on or near his or her desk. It was about the size of a toaster. In a physical sense it was an intercom with a digital readout on the front that identified the caller. In a psychological sense, it was an instrument of terror. At any moment of the day it might buzz with a message that Mr. Diller was calling. The executive would drop everything and rush to the box. Suddenly Diller's voice would pour out with a gush of orders, ideas, and questions. He would seldom begin by saying hello or finish by saying good-bye. He would simply take care of business and demand whatever information he was seeking. If he was unhappy, he might be yelling over the box. At best it served as an electronic chain that Diller could rattle whenever he wished.

Often it left the executive on the receiving end quite rattled. "You see his name," Brenda Farrier recalls, "and your heart stops."

In early summer 1987, Farrier was seeing Diller's name on her intercom frequently. She was deeply involved not only in trying to promote and advertise shows but also in helping to create an overall image for the network and maintaining relations with the affiliates scattered around the country.

It almost always seemed like an impossible job. She was averaging twelve- and fourteen-hour days and working many weekends. In a few short months she had hired nearly thirty people to work in her areas of responsibility, but the work load still grew much more quickly than the available help.

Farrier's nature was to stick with the job. She believed that the new network could succeed, if it could survive long enough for its programming to develop, its advertising to penetrate into every market, and its weak lineup of affiliated stations to mature. If all she had to do was her own job, she could have stuck it out.

Instead, Farrier found herself constantly in the middle of confrontational situations, something she really hated. As much as she admired Barry Diller, she often felt that he fostered those confrontations because he believed it drove people to do their best work. Perhaps it did, she had to admit, but it also wore good people down.

She also felt that she wasn't really appreciated, which made it difficult to keep up the pace. She enjoyed getting excited about what she did, but it seemed that each time she did, she was criticized by Wendle or Ancier or someone else. She found her confidence shaken and her ability to generate excitement about her work diminished.

She always felt she worked well with both Barry Diller and Rupert Murdoch, but she, more than anyone, saw how different these two men were. Murdoch would send her a packet of clippings containing promotions he liked from the Australian newspapers. Most were bold, strong statements. Many looked "busy" on the page, with various kinds of artwork, graphics, and bits of information. She knew they were just the kind of advertising Diller would call "unfinished." He always leaned toward advertising that made a bold statement in a simple, clean, powerful way. Diller liked uncluttered but dramatic statements that were visually arresting but rarely busy.

Even though Barry Diller sometimes embarrassed her at meetings in front of others, she still felt it was a privilege to work with him. She knew from their Paramount days that underneath his tough exterior there was a human being who was extremely passionate about his work—a part of him that few people ever got to see. She felt she just wasn't seeing enough of that side of Diller in her dealings at Fox. Instead, as the new Fox shows failed to live up to expectations, one after the other, she saw Diller driven to push everyone around him even harder.

As the hot-weather months progressed, Farrier found that she had to force herself not to be afraid to see Diller's name on the front of the intercom. She knew from long experience that as soon as one of his underlings began to fear him, Diller lost all respect for his worker. They might as well be dead. Inevitably, they were soon gone.

By August, Farrier just couldn't take it any more. Using the excuse that her new husband wanted her to move east, she handed in her resignation. Diller was truly surprised and sorry. When he yelled at her and demanded constant last-minute changes, he wasn't being mean to her, he said, it was just his way of operating. He had brought her in because he thought she understood. She told Diller that she did understand, she just couldn't handle it anymore.

In her place Diller appointed one of her severest critics, Kevin Wendle.

For most of the prior six months—since shortly after Joan Rivers's departure—Wendle had been the executive in charge of "The Late Show." He had survived, even though the show had become a fiasco.

Fox's concept after Rivers departed was to use a different host each night. Wendle believed they would be able to recruit a star, who would then work with the show's permanent staff to recruit his or her friends as guests. To make the star feel at home, he arranged for special foods and other little touches. He even offered them a masseuse to help them relax. To handle the logistics, Wendle assigned a different young producer to each night of the week.

Wendle recalls that it took only eight shows to realize that the plan was unworkable.

What we found out was that most people really weren't very good at hosting. Number two, most people weren't interested in doing it because they weren't good at it and they didn't want to look bad. Number three, unlike what you and I might think, most stars don't have a lot of other friends who are stars they can call up. So our thinking turned out to be pretty faulty.

The constant change in guest hosts was jarring to the audience, too. One night the guest host would be Martin Sheen, with all serious guests, and the next night it was blond bombshell Suzanne Summers, with musical and comedy acts. Nobody knew what to expect, so they stopped caring. The already-low ratings plunged.

Then "The Late Show" staff booked Frank Zappa, the rock singer and unorthodox pundit. When they asked him who he wanted for guests, he came back with a list more appropriate for "Meet the Press." The Fox producers told Zappa they wanted an entertaining variety show, not a bunch of serious talking heads. "Mr. Zappa simply didn't want to appear on anything that came close to what we wanted for 'The Late Show,' " says Wendle.

At the same time, the staff was in near revolt. Under Rivers it was understood that the host was in charge. Under the new system, with no permanent host, the staff felt that *it* was in charge. When Zappa came in refusing to book any musical guest and demanding that Fox use handheld cameras for the taping, they felt it was too much. They convinced Wendle to drop Zappa altogether.

It was as if a nuclear bomb had dropped. Zappa, who had already been announced, was a gentleman about it, but the critics tore into Fox savagely, suggesting that it was interfering with any effort to produce a serious TV show at a time when what they were doing was already terrible.

"When we zapped Zappa it was as if the press woke up," Brad Turell recalls. "It opened the floodgates to disastrous press. Every paper in the country was suddenly calling 'The Late Show' the TV version of a train wreck."

Inside Fox, both Diller and Kellner knew they had to speed up the search for a permanent producer, for someone who could bring a whole different approach to Fox's late night efforts.

Kellner already had had conversations with two New York–based producers, both associated with NBC's "Late Night with David Letterman." He had first approached Letterman's longtime producer Barry Sand about producing a special they were doing in New York with a controversial Big Apple disc jockey, Howard Stern. Sand wasn't interested. About three months later Kellner had had conversations with Sand's assistant, Robert Morton, about becoming the producer of "The Late Show." He, too, decided to pass.

Then, in late spring 1987, with "The Late Show" produced by Kevin Wendle beginning to resemble the Titanic leaving the dock, Kellner flew to New York again. He had breakfast with Sand and told him that Fox wanted to hire someone, as Kellner put it,

to explore their imagination and creativity and develop a whole new kind of show. We didn't want to fall into the trap of doing a Johnny

Carson or David Letterman show. Or anything that had been done before. We wanted someone to take on a new challenge, and we were willing to pay that person well for it.

What actually happened after that remains the subject of conflicting stories. Sand didn't return calls, and Morton declined to answer any questions directly. Letterman denied that he had any involvement. The version making the rounds in Hollywood was that Letterman was looking for an excuse to get rid of Sand and replace him with Morton, who is one of Letterman's best friends. Apparently, Fox didn't know that. When Morton went to Letterman and told him he had a fantastic offer from Fox, Letterman suggested that Morton give that job to Sand and stay with Letterman as his producer.

Sand then took the Fox job, with a $1 million contract for one year, and almost total creative freedom. In mid-August, Sand became producer of "The Late Show," but only for as long as it took to get his new program ready. He immediately began to assemble a second staff, which left the existing staff feeling left out and demoralized.

Among the various guest hosts, Kevin Wendle liked comic Arsenio Hall best. His humor seemed to appeal to everyone. He was quick witted but never biting, and he seemed equally adept at star interviews and issue questions.

Fox stopped all promotion for "The Late Show" as it awaited the new Barry Sand product. Even so, with Hall as host, the ratings steadily built. When Fox finally let Arsenio Hall go, there was a feeling that Fox was losing something special. It was only the promise of Barry Sand's new show that made it unimportant. Kellner told anyone who would listen that something very, very special was coming.

However, Ancier saw what Sand was developing, and he became skeptical. He also saw Kellner becoming very deeply involved. Both Ancier and Wendle decided to back off. This was Jamie Kellner's show. They would let him take the credit—or the blame.

Kellner told Diller it would be a whole new kind of show that would mix news and information and comedy into an entertaining package. Sand decided to name it after the building at KTTV in Los Angeles where "The Late Show" was produced. He called it "The Wilton North Report."

There was a sense at the weekly Tuesday morning network staff meeting late that August that things were finally getting better. To these young executives, hiring Sand was like calling in the cavalry just as the Indians are about to win.

There was also a growing sense that the upcoming Emmy Awards show in late September would be a boost. And, best of all, "21 Jump Street" on August 23 actually had finished the night, on a national basis, ahead of the competing program on ABC. It was the first time that a Fox show had finished anyplace except last in the ratings.

The weekly staff meeting was held in the large ground-floor conference room a few doors down from Barry Diller's office. By 10:00 A.M. the staff, mostly young and male, was sitting around the long wooden table sipping coffee, chatting, or paging through the pile of memos and research notes stacked neatly at each place. Noise from the busy Twentieth Century–Fox studio lot filtered through the tall glass windows as Jamie Kellner took his place at the head of the table. At the last minute Diller rushed in, followed closely by Rupert Murdoch, who had arrived the night before for his monthly visit.

At the three major networks, each department generally has its own meeting—if they meet at all. At Fox, all of the executives gathered regularly to discuss everything and comment on anything. While decision making was increasingly concentrated in a small group, including Diller, Kellner, Ancier, and Wendle, the weekly meeting was the one place where everyone could speak out. It was Diller's way of letting the more ambitious and aggressive executives push the others on to greater achievement.

Murdoch, as was his habit, sat quietly listening to the presentations as Kellner called on each department head around the table. Murdoch took notes, mostly keeping his thoughts to himself.

It wasn't that Murdoch had nothing to say. On occasion he would contribute, and his comments were always astute and to the point. His problem was that under Barry Diller's contract, Murdoch was limited to the role of advisor and consultant. And, contract or no contract, he didn't like to ruffle Diller or any other key executive unnecessarily.

However, Murdoch had plenty on his mind as he listened. The Metromedia stations and the network represented only a small part of his activities. The previous December he had completed a transaction in which he sold his TV interests in Australia and bought the largest, most powerful newspaper chain down under—the same one his father had once run. His new newspaper holdings gave him about 60 percent of the newspaper business in the entire country, not only building his political power but also insuring a huge flow of profits for many years to come.

That spring of 1987, Murdoch had purchased the American publishing house of Harper and Row for $300 million, at least $100 million more than any other bidder had offered. It was a price that had astounded the financial community, most of which didn't understand the leverage his Aussie base gave him in acquisitions. Murdoch also envisioned merging Harper and Row in some way with another publisher he partially controlled in England, boosting both properties.

The cost of all of this activity was to increase the News Corp. debt from less than $100 million in 1985 to over $400 million in 1987. Murdoch's yearly interest payments had jumped from under $50 million to well over $200 million.

At the same time, he was losing millions on Sky Channel, his satellite television venture in Europe. It was supposed to be the English language service for the entire continent as well as the United Kingdom. The lesson had been that in German and French and other non-English-speaking countries, the audience for such a service was far too small to make it economical.

As he sat listening to the glowing, upbeat reports of his Fox executives, Murdoch quickly compared their reports to the financial reports on the company, which showed that the new network was losing around two million dollars a week—almost double what had been projected.

The speaker at that moment was Andrew Fessel, the network's youthful head of research. He stood in front of an easel, lifting page after page to illustrate through statistics and charts Fox's success in attracting audience. Tall and solidly built, with short dark hair that never seemed to stay in place, Fessel spoke in a steady monotone as he tracked the performance of the four networks the previous weekend.

Barry Diller didn't really like research. He didn't trust it and rarely believed in it. He trusted his own instincts. However, he had to put up with this one type of research, audience measurement, because it was the scorecard used by everyone in the industry, especially the advertising community. While the other networks used all kinds of sophisticated research to determine the fate of their programs, Diller called that sort of thing "voodoo." He frequently pointed out that "All in the Family" and many other hit shows had not done well in initial research. Asked about a show, or shown a reel of tape, there are some things that a group of suburbanites cannot predict.

Fessel had been among the first employees hired after the core group of executives. The clean-shaven, thirty-four year old with an oval face and intelligent blue eyes still had been working at the Arbitron rating service in New York when David Johnson, Jamie Kellner, and others began calling him with questions. A native of New Jersey, Fessel had graduated from New York University and gone directly into research at ABC. He worked his way up through the ranks before leaving to join Arbitron as a regional sales manager. He never liked sales as much as research, though, so he was immediately receptive when David Johnson called and offered him the challenge of joining Fox.

Now Fessel was putting the best possible face on bad news. The Saturday night shows were a total disaster, and Sunday was performing at half the level promised to advertisers, he admitted. The good news was that they were drawing in lots of young adults, exactly the audience Fox wanted and needed. Fessel was going through category after category to show how well Fox was doing—teens, young adults, eighteen- to forty-nine-year-old women; eighteen- to thirty-six-year-old men . . .

As Fessel finished, Rupert Murdoch cleared his throat and got Kellner's attention. The table, full of young, eager faces, turned toward him. Murdoch's expression looked as if he had just taken an evil-tasting medicine. In a cool, controlled voice he said he had a question:

All of this demographic information is one thing but when do you cut the bull and begin to get the numbers as well? When do you stop looking at *who* is watching, and start selling *how many* people are watching? You can't go on making programs for narrow audiences. To succeed, Fox must reach out to large numbers. When does that happen?

Diller immediately sensed the change in Murdoch's mood. He also realized that he was right. They were kidding themselves. Identifying how many young women watched wasn't the answer. They needed a much larger share of the market to succeed. Diller knew how much they were losing every week, and he knew that something had to be done.

After the meeting, Diller set the wheels in motion. It was time to act. Within a short time Fox canceled two of the weak Saturday night shows—"Karen's Song," starring Patty Duke as a woman having an affair with a younger man, and "Down and Out in Beverly Hills." Diller also decided it was time to make sure that at least one night was working and making money. After consulting with Kellner, Ancier, Wendle, and others, they decided to move "Werewolf," the only show performing at an acceptable level on Saturday night, to Sunday. And they moved the weakest of the Sunday shows, "Mr. President," to Saturday. They also ordered a complete retooling of the show "Second Chance," rather than just canceling it. Ancier had argued that it had strong characters with solid appeal to young people but was a flawed program concept. Instead, he said, they could bring it back as "Boys Will Be Boys," with a more simple, funnier set of story lines.

Murdoch and Diller still agreed on one thing. It was worth pouring millions of dollars into the new network to make it work, but only if they could see progress as they went along. It was now time to make Sunday night jell while they tried to fix Saturday.

Fox had to correct its course before it became the joke of broadcasting. There were already some restless affiliates complaining that their old movies did better than many Fox shows in attracting audience. If something wasn't done soon, the network would start losing affiliate clearances. And then no amount of money would be able to save it.

22

THE AFFILIATES
ARE RESTLESS

THE COOL, PLEASANT evening of January 5, 1988 featured one of those made-to-order southern California sunsets that paints the sky with pastel ribbons of color. It was as if Barry Diller had ordered his art department to come up with the perfect twilight sky as a backdrop for his guests, who were arriving at Soundstage 14 on the Twentieth Century–Fox back lot aboard motor coaches. As the smartly dressed men and women disembarked they found themselves in an outdoor plaza made up to look like Rick's Cafe in the classic movie *Casablanca.* Walls of off-white alabaster led to an interior courtyard and long mahogany bar, next to which a black piano player entertained with old show and movie tunes. Tables against the back and side walls were laden with appetizers—silver trays of little roast beef sandwiches, lox and cream cheese on minibagels, small hamburgers, cherry tomatoes stuffed with cheese, and hunks of asparagus wrapped in ham.

Behind a canvas curtain, Barry Diller paced nervously around the dinner tables awaiting the guests. He checked to make sure each table had a bowl of red tulips and was set properly, with shiny black plates, crystal glassware, bottles of red and white wine, and glossy red plates of freshly prepared sushi. Every napkin, drinking glass, salt-and-pepper shaker, and fork had to be exactly in place. With so much else going wrong, Diller was determined that every element of this evening work as planned.

The guests, moving around the *Casablanca* set, which originally had been constructed for a scene in the television show "Moonlighting," were truly VIP's to Diller. They were the station owners, general managers, program directors, and others gathered for the week in Los Angeles from television stations around the nation that carried the Fox network programming on weekends and late at night. They came to town each year for the INTV convention. Those who had thrown their lot in with Fox stayed on this one extra day for meetings at the Century Plaza Hotel, adjacent to the Fox lot, and for this final affiliates' dinner.

It was Barry Diller's nature to push intensely for perfection, whether it involved an advertisement or a special dinner. After his experience with the Emmy Awards three months before, his drive for perfection intensified. It was as if he wanted to make up for all of the mistakes the new network had made and for the unqualified embarrassment the Emmy show had been. Despite the millions of dollars spent on promotion and production, the big event had gone awry and taken a terrible drubbing from the critics. It had fallen far below Fox's projections in terms of the number of viewers that it would attract.

The failure hadn't been from a lack of effort. Diller and the other Fox executives had picked an experienced event producer, Don Ohlmeyer, as producer. With a background in sports, news, and entertainment programming and even one previous Emmy show under his belt, he seemed an excellent choice.

Ohlmeyer had convinced Fox that the emphasis should be on comedy and that the approach should be to cover the thirty-ninth annual Emmys as an event rather than just run it as a TV show. That meant not only showing the award being won but also trailing the winner backstage through the pressroom. It meant not only showing the glittering crowd seated but also covering their arrival as a news event. It meant creating segments during the show that gave glimpses of TV behind the scenes, and even with entertainment segments, building them as part of the flow of events. It meant replacing the usual production numbers with long pretaped biographical segments on the key nominees and tributes to TV's past masters, such as Jackie Gleason.

Under its contract with the academy, there were minimum amounts that Fox had to spend promoting the Emmy Awards show.

Fox had far exceeded those minimums. It also had lined up a number of affiliated stations (mostly ABC network affiliates) to carry the show in areas where Fox wasn't represented. The Fox-owned stations had done well selling advertisements, as had the network itself. There was even the drama of Joan Rivers making her first appearance since her husband's suicide.

As it turned out, there was some comedy in the show, but it wasn't always because of the script. David Letterman, a multiple Emmy winner, used the podium to poke fun at Fox, which had just "lured" away his producer, Barry Sand.

The *Los Angeles Times* Pulitzer Prize–winning TV critic, Howard Rosenberg, reported that some of the biggest laughs came from Phylicia Rashad, the mother on "Cosby," and Alan Thicke, the father on "Growing Pains," who were acting as backstage reporters. "Those backstage segments," wrote Rosenberg, ". . . were unintentionally hilarious. 'I'm here in the green room,' Rashad whispered melodramatically at one point. 'Ooooooh, what excitement.' "

The perception was that Fox had lost control somewhere along the way. Award acceptance speeches became marathons of verbose emptiness. When it was finally over, the clock showed that the program had run four hours instead of three, an almost unforgivable sin by usual TV standards. There were immediate charges that Fox had wanted to get in more commercials and to block the affiliated stations carrying the show from returning to their regular network fare.

The *Hollywood Reporter*'s TV critic, Miles Beller, said the Emmy show "reached home screens as a painfully overlong and largely empty kudos production, marked by yawning stretches (on both sides of the screen) and soggy filler."

While there were mixed reviews the day after the show, as each day went by, the memory seemed to become more sour. This was particularly true after the ratings came in showing that Fox had produced the lowest-rated Emmy show in the thirty-nine-year history of the event, with less than 14 percent of the TV sets in use tuned to the show. The ratings were half what they had been a year earlier on ABC, and they were a full third less than Fox had guaranteed advertisers, meaning that Fox would have to provide free ad time to make up for it, at enormous expense to the new network.

Rick Du Brow, the veteran TV editor of the *Los Angeles Herald Examiner,* wrote a story two days after the show under the headline: "Emmy show earns no awards." Du Brow said that "Fox clearly was not yet ready to handle the event" and called the show itself a "fiasco" and "a mess of a program."

A few months afterward, Richard Frank would lose his effort to be reelected as president of the TV academy, at least in part because Fox had been allowed to telecast the Emmy show.

While Fox had enjoyed a few bright spots that fall, including the cult popularity among America's teenagers of "21 Jump Street," Fox had continued to run into problems. The second Saturday night schedule of shows had fared even worse than the first, forcing the more rapid development of replacements. On Sunday night, ratings for "Tracey Ullman" and "Duet" continued to be very low, and "Werewolf" had steadily slipped since the switch from Saturday to Sunday night.

There also had been some messy personnel matters. Initially, Diller had provoked competition between Ancier and Wendle, but it had seemed to get out of hand. The two men, who had arrived as best friends, now spoke only when necessary, according to Ancier. In contrast to the early days, when they had supported each other in almost every way, Ancier and Wendle were constantly sniping at each other in meeting after meeting.

Wendle, who had hired new promo executives from NBC and done a good job reorganizing the promotion and advertising areas after Farrier left, approached each show and project with the enthusiasm of a cheerleader. He was Mr. Positive, always ready to invite the world onto the Fox bandwagon. He pushed hard for alternative programming that would make Fox distinctive.

Diller appreciated the complete turnaround in the advertising and promotion department after Wendle took charge. For the first time materials were getting out on time and affiliate grumbling about lack of consultation on promotion had stopped. It was during this same period that Fox's ratings finally began to rise. Wendle clearly deserved a share of the credit.

Ancier, on the other hand, had a more conservative programming philosophy. He wanted to do the same things as the other networks but be a bit more daring and innovative. Ancier was highly critical of almost everything, taking a more negative view of events. Often Ancier was right, but Diller, Kellner, and others found Wendle's approach easier to take.

Wendle himself professed to feel terrible about the breach:

[Garth] was very good to me in the programming department and really was a mentor. After the transition, I was in a position that no longer reported directly to him, yet I was still involved in programming meetings. What would happen, I think, is that before, we would get together and have our own disagreements about a program in a room with ourselves. Then, when I was out of the department, we would get together in the big room downstairs and that would be when Jamie and Barry would want to hear everyone's opinion, and when I dissented once or twice, I think Garth felt betrayed. It really was once or twice. It created a lot of tension.

Garth also suffered from a wave of unwanted publicity when a so-called true story about him came out in *Gentlemen's Quarterly*. Under a byline that later proved to be a pseudonym for Ben Stein, a former Nixon speech writer who had become a Hollywood pundit, writer, and occasional actor, *GQ* described a lunch meeting at the Ivy Restaurant in Beverly Hills attended by Ancier, Diller, Murdoch, and some others. It said that Diller and Murdoch were both lambasting Ancier because of the network's poor performance. Finally Ancier said he felt ill, went to the men's room, and passed out. When he didn't return to the dinner table, according to the magazine, Barry Diller went to the men's room, pounded on the door, and screamed repeatedly for Ancier to open the door and come out. Finally Ancier was discovered passed out, and an ambulance rushed him to a nearby hospital.

It made for some fun reading in Hollywood, but much of it was inaccurate. What it did do, however, was make it obvious that for all of his brilliance in programming development and strategy, and despite his youthful, appealing charm, Ancier was really an extremely fragile personality trying to cope with some personal problems.

In an interview days after the magazine hit the newsstand, Ancier admitted that there was some truth to it.

I did faint. First of all, Barry Diller was not even there. It was Rupert and me and two other Fox executives. It wasn't lunch, it was dinner. We were there talking about "Current Affair" [a Fox TV-station-group show] and how to make it better. We never talked about ratings or any of our prime-time programming.

. . . I had been tired. Rupert usually asks you out to dinner late in the day and so I was sort of along for the ride. I was very tired. I ate a very heavy meal. I kept my jacket on in the unair-conditioned Ivy on a hot night, eating hot soup gumbo and everything inside, in a corner. I just really got very hot and started to feel faint and excused myself from the table and walked away. I did try to get to the men's room. I just wanted to get myself together, get some fresh air. I passed out there in the hallway [near the men's room].

What's ridiculous is that Barry wasn't there, and the entire article was about Barry screaming at me. . . . I did go to the hospital. I was taken by ambulance, but I never checked in beyond the emergency room. They had me there two hours to observe me because I passed out. Then they released me.

The article had started a round of stories in Hollywood, some of which were about Ancier also having passed out while working at NBC. Ancier admits that he does get dizzy at times and that it probably is due to the long hours he puts in. He also denies that he used a lot of prescription drugs, but says he does regularly take a mild tranquilizer called Zanex, usually after the workday, at the recommendation of his psychiatrist. He says he has been in therapy from "a young age" and has always been open about it with his friends and colleagues because he has nothing to hide.

Ancier explains that

when I was very young and at NBC I realized it was difficult for me to deal with all the pressures upon me and a lot of emotional things coming from my childhood. Basically, this is not uncommon. People have trouble in business when they are carrying some baggage from their childhood. It's not any serious baggage. It's just how you relate to your parents. And being younger and working with older people, I found a parental sort of relationship develops. And it mixes in your subconscious. And the rivalry with other executives. It becomes like the whole family is duplicated. It can affect anyone. It's just part of growing up and being in a job with some responsibility at a young age.

The mounting tension between Ancier and Wendle took some of the heat off Jamie Kellner. In the first months after Fox's prime-time shows went on the air, Ancier and Wendle had appeared to be going after Kellner. This was widely seen as an attempt by Ancier to get the job of president, with Wendle moving up to head of programming.

Kellner may look like the boy next door, but he proved to be as tough as a leatherneck. Beneath the handsome exterior was a tough infighter who wasn't going to be pushed aside. If anything, he had survived his own series of tests that fall.

First there had been the arena football debate. Brad Turell, head of publicity, had learned about arena football, which was a professional football game played indoors on a small field with a smaller-than-regulation team. It was conceived to be perfect for TV, with a wide-open game—a lot of passing and risky plays—colorful field, and uniforms. The problem was that TV networks were interested only if the public was, and nobody in the United States knew much about arena football. Turell felt that Fox could fix that, and he enlisted Kellner's enthusiastic support.

Fox research had indicated that on Saturday night, young people aren't home and women dominate the TV set, watching shows like "The Golden Girls." Arena football, it was argued, would play to the disenfranchised male audience.

Aside from Saturday night prime time, Fox also could do some games late at night on weekdays. There would be a different live game for each time zone. Eventually they might be moved into prime time. If it worked, Fox would also own about one-third of the league, which could be very profitable.

Kellner argued that Fox could make arena football its own and develop a following.

Other Fox executives, including Ancier, who didn't follow football in any form, and fellow programming executive Alan Sternfeld, felt that Fox wouldn't benefit by being associated with what was, in essence, a minor-league operation. Sternfeld said that it wasn't for Fox to pull arena football up by the bootstraps. What Fox really needed was something to pull *it* up, something like having the Monday night NFL games.

As one of the few Fox executives with real major-network experience, Sternfeld frequently found himself at odds with the Fox network leadership, especially Kevin Wendle. In meeting after meeting, Sternfeld would be the minority voice arguing against what the rest, including Diller, thought should be done. When Diller pushed for an expansion to a third night featuring a mix of theatrical movies and made-for-TV movies, Sternfeld argued strongly that it would be better to expand to Monday night with series programming. His point was that Friday was the most lucrative movie night of the week for the independent stations affiliated with Fox, so it would be the last thing they'd want to give up. He said that movies, even made-for-TV movies, never would build the audience loyalty Fox needed, whereas strong series programming would. Sternfeld pointed out that Monday night had one of the highest levels of viewership all week and that since it followed the only two nights Fox now programmed, it would allow them to do promotion all weekend as a set up for what was coming. Eventually Diller and the other Fox executives would agree that Monday was better, but it was to provide little satisfaction to Sternfeld.

A native of the Long Island area of New York, Sternfeld had gone to Brandeis University, graduating with a degree in English in 1973. He then spent two years in the greenhouse business, which later became a symbolic analogy to what he did in TV:

> For instance, when we were planning what to market for Mother's Day, we would have to begin planning a year in advance; and we would have to figure out how to use every inch of space. In TV, you also commit a year in advance, and then you must find the writer, producer, and others needed to create the show. All of which can be reduced to simple logistics, just like planning a greenhouse operation.

When the Arab oil embargo of 1975 made the cost of heating and operating a greenhouse prohibitive, Sternfeld took a job in the public relations department of the NBC network in New York City. That led to a job with (LBS), a television syndicator, selling shows to independent stations. He left there to work as a media-advertising-time buyer for Young and Rubicam, one of the largest advertising agencies in the world. Then, in 1979 he returned to NBC as a programming executive specializing in the economics and financing of TV shows.

Sternfeld's wife, Martina Finch, was an actress. One day he called Marion Davis, whom he had known at NBC, and asked her about a job for his wife on an upcoming Fox show. "Forget her. How do we get you?" Marion Davis replied. "Throw some money at me," laughed Sternfeld, "and we'll see."

From the time he arrived at Fox in mid-August 1987, Sternfeld felt closest to Garth Ancier. They shared a belief that strong producers make the best programs and that TV shows have to be nurtured over a period so that they will constantly grow as the audience discovers them. Sternfeld felt that Diller's mentality was far more influenced by the movie business. He would compare Diller's intense interest in the ratings each week to a movie executive's concern over weekly box office results. The difference was that a single weekend could make or break a movie, while a TV show needed time to develop. Sternfeld also felt that Diller expected to be able to fix a show's weaknesses quickly, which wasn't realistic. When Sternfeld voiced his feelings, he sensed that Diller thought he was just being a pessimist.

Sternfeld came to believe that while it was true that Diller would not tolerate "yes men" who tried to please him, he also wouldn't tolerate "no men" who constantly disagreed with him.

Sternfeld also bumped heads frequently with Kevin Wendle, who was always championing "alternative" programming that would be unique to Fox. Sternfeld felt that it was much more important to find programs with mass appeal, shows that would draw in a large, wide audience. That didn't include "Tracey Ullman," no matter how many awards it had won.

To head off arena football, Ancier and Sternfeld rushed the development of a series based on the movie *The Dirty Dozen,* and some subsequent TV-movie spin-offs, as an alternative way to attract a Saturday night audience. If they were going to go after men, he preferred Fox do it with a story-form series that could be scripted and controlled.

The debate was suddenly interrupted on October 19, 1987, when the American stock market collapsed, recording a five-hundred-point drop in the Dow Jones Industrial Average, the worst in the post–World War II era. Along with many others, the stock market value of News Corp. fell sharply both in the United States and on the Australian exchange. Worldwide, there was a sudden need for belt tightening. The public markets no longer were waiting to pour money into any investment.

One of the things that fell by the wayside at Fox was arena football. The push began to get "Dirty Dozen: The Series" into production.

Kellner also had survived the loss of David Johnson, who had been the mastermind behind the network's affiliate and advertiser relations. The rumor around Fox was that Johnson was fed up with being caught in battles between Diller and everyone else—Murdoch, Kellner, Ancier, Wendle, and others. He felt that not enough promotion and advertising money was being spent, but nobody seemed to listen to what he was saying. He decided that life was too short to work in a company where the boss constantly pitted one executive against another.

Johnson said that he had arrived at his fiftieth birthday and taken inventory of his life. He realized that the most exciting part of his job—creating the business plan, bringing in the first advertisers, and signing on the core group of affiliates—was done. "I imagined myself in an office maintaining it, and that made me want to do other things," says Johnson. "I left because it had become a pro-gramming-driven company and that's not what I do for a living."

Fox had also recently forced out its first director of advertising in New York and had lost some executives in affiliate relations, leaving Kellner as the only one many of the advertisers and affiliates still knew at Fox. It made him more important than ever, but it also put a lot more work on his desk and pressure on him.

Still, in the fall of 1987, Kellner also found himself right back in the middle of a difficult programming situation. Given that he was the executive who had recruited Barry Sand, Kellner felt a personal involvement in the development of the new late night show. As the projected starting date of late November grew closer, Kellner spent more and more time trying to help shape and create what would be called "The Wilton North Report."

Normally the programming executives, not Kellner, would have been involved in the development of the new show. However Ancier, Sternfeld, and Wendle didn't like what Sand was doing and had pulled back from any involvement. So instead, it was Kellner who became the day-to-day executive most involved with the show. It was one time that Ancier was happy to let Kellner play a role in programming. As Ancier said to Sternfeld, "God invented the eleven-foot pole for things that you wouldn't touch with a ten-foot pole. This is one time I wouldn't even touch it with an eleven-foot pole." In reality, though, with his powerful contract, Sand had too free a hand for anyone to make much of a difference.

Kellner also was trying to deal with growing complaints from many of the Fox affiliates. At first most of the small independents had given Fox a chance because they felt it was a way to deal with the high costs of programming and to develop more of an identity for their stations. The trouble began with ratings that were lower than expected and a two-month delay in the start of Saturday night, after many of them already had begun promoting it. Says the general manager of one small station in the South:

> We told them they better get their act together. They were making too many last minute changes. That's not healthy for an indepen-dent. As it is we're usually not the first choice for the audience. So when we promote something, we need to deliver it. What works against an independent is change.

Other affiliates were growing even more impatient. In Daven-port, Iowa, Gary Brandt of KLJB-TV, channel 18, already had pushed the Fox late night show past midnight. The Fox Saturday night shows were getting "hash marks" in his rating books, which meant that the rating service could not even find 1 percent of the viewers watching the station. "Saturday night was a joke from day one," Brandt recalls.

Fox pushed Brandt to identify his station more closely with the network in promotions. They told him that other stations were experiencing a "halo" effect, which meant that their identity as a Fox station was spilling over and helping them in other ways, by creating a more solid identity in the community.

"I had a real serious problem believing that Fox would be around in three or four years," says Brandt. "I'm the Quad Cities Station and I decided to stay that way. I'd rather play it safe."

Brandt was being offered an increasingly attractive lineup of shows being produced initially for the syndication market, including "Star Trek: The Next Generation." He saw that they would get him higher ratings than the Fox Saturday night shows and decided to put them in as replacements. He told Fox he would run their entire Saturday lineup sometime after his late news.

Fox told him to run the shows as scheduled. "I said these other shows will do three times as well for me in audience and ad revenue," Brandt says. "The economics of staying with Fox just don't work out."

Brandt, a crusty fellow with a strong, independent streak, began to feel that the Fox executives really didn't know what they were doing. According to Brandt,

> They came out with all these grandiose plans but they had analyzed the marketplace incorrectly. They all came from a network background. Nobody had independent-station experience. They made decisions based on the network pattern which I felt were incorrect for an independent.

Fox told Brandt to either run Saturday night on the same day and date as the rest of the network or face disaffiliation. He reminded Fox that his contract allowed him to dump the network and that he was seriously considering doing so. It became a war of words—and nerves.

Fox faced similar situations all over the country. Fox executives felt that if they started allowing each station to decide when it would play the Fox shows, they would be a syndicator, not a program service trying to become a network. They had to draw the line. In December 1987, Fox notified KLJB that it would be dropped as an affiliate if it didn't do as the network wished.

Brandt studied the numbers and ratings and wished Fox luck. KLJB became the first station to be disaffiliated by the Fox Broadcasting Company. It set a bad precedent and helped heighten tension as the affiliates came to Los Angeles the first week of January 1988.

The biggest problem of all, however, was the affiliate, audience, and critical reaction to "The Wilton North Report." It had been scheduled for launch on November 30, but the night before it was to start, Barry Diller saw a run-through of the first show and sent it back for more work. He told Sand that what he had seen was not only unfunny, but also mean spirited, and too many jokes seemed to be about people's physical appearance. "The Wilton North Report" finally premiered on December 11, 1987, a day that was to live in infamy for the fledgling Fox network.

From the start, "Wilton North" was savaged by newspaper critics across the nation. Ratings were disastrous and getting worse. It was poorly done, amateurish, and often offensive.

Sand had said repeatedly that he wanted it to be like nothing else on television—and indeed it was. It was worse. He was trying to do humorous commentary on the news of the week as well as various off-beat, reality-based comedy stunts. For hosts Sand tapped two morning disc jockeys from Sacramento—Phil ("I'm the tall one with the mustache") Cowan and Paul ("I'm the shorter one with glasses") Robins.

Sand hired eleven writers and then named himself head writer. The writers, including hip magazine publisher Paul Krassner *(The Realist)*, complained that Cowan and Robins—"the Boys"— weren't funny, weren't hip, weren't good on TV, and were too conservative in their views. Sand said that he would stick with them, however, and that it was up to the writers to put funny words in the hosts' mouths.

It never worked. As Barry Sand was later quoted as saying when the first reviews came in: "If it wasn't my show, I'd be laughing at me."

"The Wilton North Report" had been on for three weeks by the time the affiliates gathered in a large conference room at the Century Plaza Hotel on January 5 for a day of meetings. Diller and Kellner told Murdoch, who had flown in for the gathering, that they knew there was a potential for a revolt by the affiliates.

But Murdoch had his own problems to deal with. Almost every

day for two weeks he had been page-one news all over the nation. In late December, just as Congress was about to break for Christmas, Senator Edward Kennedy, the Massachusetts Democrat, had slipped a rider onto a bill being sent to the White House for signature. It prohibited the FCC from giving anyone a temporary waiver from the media cross-ownership rules that say that no person or company can own both a TV station and a newspaper in the same city. It was obvious that Kennedy had had Murdoch in mind. Murdoch was now trying to get permission to hold onto his TV station in Boston and his newspaper, the *Boston Herald,* which frequently opposed Kennedy and his politics.

The animosity between the media mogul and the powerful senator really went back to 1980, when Kennedy challenged President Jimmy Carter, who was running for reelection. Murdoch's *New York Post* had not only supported Carter, it had used news columns to constantly blast Kennedy. With similar coverage in his hometown of Boston in the years that followed, Kennedy's dislike of Murdoch became well known.

Kennedy had acted in the middle of the night, with help from only one other senator. What he did offended many people, especially the conservatives who didn't like Kennedy very much in any case. The debate over what Kennedy had done raged in news columns and among editorial columnists of every political bent. Murdoch fanned the flames by having his papers, including the *New York Post* and *Boston Herald,* run daily articles supporting his position. It was just the kind of thing that happened all the time in Australia and England, where Murdoch also owned newspapers, but in America it was startling.

Two months later a federal judge would agree that Kennedy was wrong to act in a way that clearly singled out Murdoch as the victim of the new law. Murdoch won a moral victory, but he still had to sell the *New York Post,* which was losing money, and eventually put the Boston TV station into a blind trust until it could be sold.

With the Fox network losing around $2 million a week, Murdoch was in no mood to risk angering the affiliates that January day. Diller and Kellner explained their strategy to him. They would go to the affiliates and admit that they had made major mistakes. They would ask for their patience and their help to correct the situation. They would offer as proof some new programming they had purchased, and they would once again delay the start of the third night until the first two nights were working better. "Looking back, that was a real turning point for us," recalls Kevin Wendle. "We really began to understand the complexity of this company and the need for a real, honest partnership with our affiliates. We really opened up to them and asked them what it was they wanted from us."

Says Kevin O'Brien, general manager of the Fox affiliate in San Francisco and former general manager of the Fox station in New York City:

> I don't think the affiliates were angry, but they were very concerned. In particular, there was trepidation about the possible special treatment of some affiliates who didn't want to carry the Saturday night schedule while others felt trapped into doing so.

As the day progressed, many of the meetings became heated. The general manager of the affiliated station in Pittsburgh stood up in one meeting and shouted angrily at the Fox executives, charging them with ineptitude.

Some affiliates, however, supported Fox. Martin Colby, the general manager of Fox affiliate XETV, channel 6, in San Diego and chairman of the affiliates' board, stood up and pleaded with his fellow station managers to give Fox more time. "Without Fox," said Colby, "we will be returned to the limbo area we all came from, which is certainly something none of us want. Fox is investing money in research and development and it will pay off."

Finally, late in the day, the discussion turned to "The Wilton North Report." There was almost unanimous agreement: *nobody* liked it. 'Wilton North' was a terrible disappointment, especially because it had been built up by Fox as great," recalls Colby.

The Fox board of governors then met and voted to take "Wilton North" off the air after only three weeks. Murdoch listened quietly, his eyes full of deadly seriousness. After the board vote, he turned to Diller and said two words: "Cut it."

That was the end of the short-lived "Wilton North Report." Amid another blast of negative publicity, Fox pulled the plug and began running reruns of old versions of "The Late Show," including practically every show Joan Rivers had made.

Kevin Wendle was immediately anxious to get Arsenio Hall back to do "The Late Show," but he was in production on a movie with his pal Eddie Murphy at Paramount and was being managed by Murphy's management team. They turned Fox down. A few weeks later, Paramount announced that it would offer, in syndication, a new late night talk show starring none other than Arsenio Hall. It went on to become one of the biggest syndication hits of the 1988–89 television season.

There was even a feeler put out by some Fox executives to Joan Rivers's lawyer to see if she would be interested in coming back. No way, Fox was told. Shortly afterward, Rivers announced a deal with the Tribune Company, whose stations compete with Fox in almost every major U.S. city, to do a talk show for them during the day beginning September 1989.

Fox did have some good news to announce to the affiliates that January. They had made an unusual deal to acquire reruns of "The Gary Shandling Show" that had run previously on the Showtime pay-TV service. It also was picking up a show called "Family Double Dare" from Nickelodeon, a cable-TV service for kids.

For grown-ups Fox announced plans to go forward with "Dirty Dozen: The Series" and two new shows—an updated version of "Charlie's Angels," from producer Aaron Spelling, and "City Court," about young lawyers, to be spun off from "21 Jump Street," by Patrick Hasburgh.

On Stage 14 at Fox that evening, the affiliates were entertained by the introduction of a parade of Fox series stars and then the premiere of a new series of videos and commercials featuring those same personalities. Built around the theme of "Fox Weekend," the upbeat music and smiling faces invited viewers to join the Fox family of programs. The enthusiastic applause, said Kellner, was proof that Fox had accomplished its mission. A little humility, a greater effort to listen, the hype of some promising new programming, and a lot of affiliate hand-holding had defused talk of a revolt. Fox would indeed get more time to make good on all of its promises, although it was now clear that time was limited.

By two weeks after the affiliates' meeting, when Fox executives met with TV critics and reporters from around the country, Kellner was completely upbeat once again about the future:

Fox has been good for every constituency that touches this industry. Millions of viewers have been offered and have taken advantage of a new choice. Advertisers have been afforded a new national advertising medium and the vast majority have taken advantage of it. And the creative community—producers, actors, writers, production people—has found a new outlet for its creative talents. And I would say the three networks, faced with new and growing competition, have been stimulated to just be better, to run leaner and to make better programs.

I support that any member of broadcasting's old club would look askance at the emergence of competitors like Fox, because we represent, perhaps as well as anyone, an era of unprecedented change. And if networks examine their own histories, they may see something which for them is just a little bit ominous about Fox.

Indeed, even with Fox's problems, the older networks were being forced to take the new network's growth into account. Little did Kellner, the Fox affiliates, the press, or anyone else know that the revolution had just begun.

23

FOX HUNTS CRIMINALS, CAPTURES RATINGS

MICHAEL LINDER, THE producer who was the driving force behind the show that became Fox's first breakout ratings hit, was sitting in front of a bank of blinking television monitors in an editing room at WTTG-TV in Washington, D.C., on February 11, 1988. It was that afternoon that he first knew it really was going to work. Little by little, the blond, broad-shouldered forty-two-year-old producer had come to believe that the new half-hour television program he had helped create for the Fox-owned television station group, "America's Most Wanted," had the potential to become a powerful and important show. Now, with one phone call from the Federal Bureau of Investigation, Linder knew that his instincts about the program's potential had been right. The first fugitive ever profiled on the show, David James Roberts, a prison escapee who had been convicted of rape, arson, robbery, and multiple murders and had been on the loose for months, was captured only four days after the first show had aired.

Linder grabbed a phone from the editing console and quickly dialed another editing room on the other side of the continent, at KTTV-TV, the Fox-owned station in Los Angeles. Stephen Chao, vice president of programming for the Fox TV-station group and

Twentieth Century–Fox Television, picked up at the other end. Chao was also studying scenes for upcoming episodes of "America's Most Wanted."

"Hey Stephen!" Linder shouted into the receiver. "We got somebody!"

It was the beginning of more than just another television show. That first capture of a criminal featured on the show catapulted the Fox show onto the front pages of America's major newspapers and made the news on the rival networks' evening news programs. The ratings were up sharply the following Sunday night, when the Fox show presented more of "America's Most Wanted," and from there they just kept building. "It became a phenomenon from then on," says Linder.

Actually, it became a phenomenon in more ways than one. It was the show that marked the turnaround of the fledgling Fox Broadcasting Company and its rise toward credibility and profitability. It was the show that changed the economics of television programming, proving that it wasn't how much you spent on a show but rather the appeal of that show for the audience that mattered. And in terms of programming trends, it was the network show that revolutionized American broadcasting by ushering in the era of what the critics would call tabloid TV.

After two successful years on the air, Linder still bristled when his show was called tabloid TV and was described by the media and others as the forerunner to such programs as "The Morton Downey, Jr., Show," a short-lived talk show featuring a brash, loud-mouthed host. In fact, another Fox-produced show, "A Current Affair," had been the first tabloid TV–style show to make a splash. However, it had originally aired only on the Fox TV-station group, and then had been sold into the independent syndication market by Twentieth Century–Fox Television. So what "America's Most Wanted" really proved was that a hard-hitting, reality-based show could be a network success, and, Linder fought being grouped with "A Current Affair" and its many competitors. "We have tried and fought to get out from under that blanket," says Linder. "It was never our intention to be tabloid anything. We see ourselves as a public utility and an adjunct to police work."

Barry Diller quickly saw "America's Most Wanted" as Fox's salvation. With only a week's notice to Linder, he put it onto the Fox network in the crucial 8:00 P.M. time slot on Sunday night, bumping "Werewolf." That first week it was second in ratings only to "21 Jump Street," nearly doubling the audience that had watched "Werewolf" the week before. Within a month it was the Fox network's highest-rated, most-talked-about show.

Says Thomas Herwitz, the thirty-two-year-old vice president of the Fox Television Station group who played a crucial role in developing the show:

> It was very successful and it got a lot of press. It was really just the kind of show Fox Broadcasting had wanted to do. It was perfect for Fox because it was different than anything else on network television, it could regularly attract attention, it could make everybody feel good in several ways, and the affiliates liked it.

It also cost less—a lot less—than any other show on Fox or any other show on any network in prime-time television at that time. While "Married . . . With Children," "Tracey Ullman," and other half-hour scripted shows cost in excess of $400,000 for each half hour of production, "America's Most Wanted" cost only $125,000. It couldn't be rerun or sold into the lucrative syndication market, as the others could—although some individual segments of the show were used again whenever a capture was made—but Fox could produce it at a cost that instantly turned a money-losing time period into a profit center.

"I love this show," Barry Diller exclaimed one day a few months after it had become the network's biggest hit. "It's such good television. It's fun. It's different from anything else. And we own 100 percent of it."

"America's Most Wanted" became the catalyst that made Diller, and much of the American TV industry, rethink the economic model that drives television. As Diller explained it, from the very early days of network TV through the early 1980s, constant increases in the number of advertisers and advertising rates per minute made it possible to keep increasing the amount of money spent to produce TV shows. He explains:

> Up until [1985] you had double digit increases in advertising revenue every year so it was an easy business. You could make hundreds of millions of dollars worth of mistakes with that kind of compounded growth rate. I remember ten years ago at Paramount we had five shows in the top ten, and one of them, "Happy Days," came up for renegotiation, and we killed ABC. We were able to raise the license fee from $220,000 a half hour to $340,000. I said then, "This can't continue. It defies any logic." And it did.

It happened three years ago. Ask the head of Bristol-Myers, who I talked to this morning on something else. He said to me, "Anybody who thinks advertising is growing in this country is a fool." It's not growing because there are no new advertising categories. Advertising is going to grow from now on exactly in line with the nation's gross national product, and that's it.

Television, says Diller, had to mature as a business.

They have to make money on the corners. And that means putting pressure on costs. It's now a matter of taking market share away from somebody else, not of just riding the market expansion. That means you have to cut your cost of production or you become irrelevant. It's a process that is going to take place over time.

It was all suddenly very clear to Diller. You take away a show that cost $400,000 per half hour for two runs, which you don't own and which isn't performing, and you replace it with a show that costs $125,000 per half hour for one run, which you do own and which is performing brilliantly. At one fell swoop you go from being a loser to a winner. And you reduce your dependence on the great producer of the more expensive show who is demanding creative control. You make the show's *concept* the king.

"After a year I have learned that we go at our peril by copying the three television networks," says Diller. "We began by trying to copy their best. It was a mistake. It was the wrong way to go."

It was okay to have programs that were different from what networks usually offered, Diller is quick to add, but not too different.

You can't go too far. That's also dangerous. I don't think "America's Most Wanted" is really innovative or on the edge. It's very basic. . . . If we go too far toward "Tracey Ullman," which is innovative and on the edge, we're dead. We have to offer shows that have a reason for being. There's no reason for another television service unless it is an alternative. We must be interesting, provocative, compelling, fresh, and, hopefully, by the way, right in the center court, as big as *Star Wars* was in the movie world. It was fresh. It was a home run. It was as fresh as "Tracey Ullman," but it had appeal to everybody, and "Tracey" is limited in its appeal. That's what we should be. That's the only hope for Fox Broadcasting. Otherwise we're irrelevant."

It was at this point that Diller's thinking begins to turn away from the philosophy that formed the base of Garth Ancier's thinking. Although he was a late convert to "America's Most Wanted," Ancier was willing to try new ideas, new forms. But he continued to feel that the long-term security of the network would lay in sticking with the top producers, in trusting them to come up with the next generation of hits. That meant making expensive commitments—in advance—to carry whatever series they created. It was to become a constant source of irritation between Ancier and Diller, whose change in opinion was quickly mirrored by Kevin Wendle. The new line at Fox was that it was fine to use less-experienced producers—just as Diller favored giving executives responsibility "a year too early"—but only after a pilot show had been made.

Ancier constantly argued that just because someone can make a good pilot after months of intense effort, it does not mean that they are capable of creating a dozen or more shows under the pressure of weekly production. Those kinds of results, Ancier told anyone who would listen, only came with experience.

Ancier had a new ally in Jim McKay, an Australian who was brought in as a senior development executive, but Ancier was still losing more battles than he was winning. As Diller and Murdoch both moved toward the more attractive economics of reality programming, especially in time slots like Saturday night prime time, where the audience was small to start out with, Ancier's push for story-form shows became less effective.

It also became the subject of gossip in Hollywood, where the perception was that "America's Most Wanted" represented a setback for Ancier. After all, it hadn't come out of his department, but rather had been developed at a different test kitchen, the Fox TV-station group. That was just as Barry Diller had envisioned. He saw the network, the studio, and the station group all as places to grow shows, which then could flourish on the network or in syndication.

To Diller it made perfect sense. Fox had inherited a run-down studio facility in Washington from Kluge in the Metromedia deal, and producing there, even after an investment to modernize the plant, meant working at a far lower cost and without the unions and union work rules that applied in Los Angeles.

Diller saw it all as one system, feeding different parts of the machinery as needed. He had been just as intimately involved in developing "America's Most Wanted" as he was in any other Fox

Broadcasting show; only the input had come from his left hand rather than his right hand.

A closer look at how "America's Most Wanted" was developed shows why it became the program that changed television. It actually began as a thought from an executive at Rupert Murdoch's News Corporation.

Stephen Chao, the Los Angeles–based Fox TV development executive with ties to Murdoch, had gone to New Orleans in February 1987 to attend the annual convention of the National Association of Television Program Executives (NATPE), the largest annual gathering of U.S. broadcasting and programming executives. It is a marketplace of shows, old and new, that are available to stations outside of the network system. Chao was there with Jim Platt, a New York City–based News Corp. executive, to look for programs that could be acquired either for the U.S. stations or for the Ten Network in Australia, which Murdoch also owned at the time.

In the course of discussing many different programming ideas, Platt mentioned that they had been running a series in the *New York Post* about criminals being hunted by police and other law enforcement groups, such as the FBI. Platt mentioned that there were TV shows in other parts of the world, including Australia, the Netherlands, and the United Kingdom, that publicized such criminals to help in their capture. Platt asked Chao if it couldn't be done in the United States as a national show.

Chao remembers thinking to himself later, What a stupid idea. Still, he tucked it away in the back of his mind before he returned to Los Angeles, where he had moved recently to develop TV shows for Fox.

Stephen Chao had been raised in Boston and attended Harvard University. After graduating in 1977 he moved to Florida, where he worked for the *National Enquirer,* a very popular sensationalistic tabloid that is sold at supermarket checkout counters.

Chao returned to Harvard in 1979 and got a master's degree in business. Then he got a job on Wall Street at a brokerage firm working on movie tax-shelter partnerships. One of the executives he pitched was Rupert Murdoch. In 1983 Murdoch hired Chao to evaluate acquisitions for him in New York City. Chao crunched numbers for the purchase of *New Woman* magazine, Twentieth Century–Fox studios, and the Metromedia television stations.

"At that point I said, Acquisitions are nice, but I'd love to be a television producer and move to Los Angeles," recalls Chao, a lean, intense Chinese-American with black hair, olive-tinted skin, and the eyes of a wise old man.

When he returned from NATPE in early 1987, Chao plunged ahead with a show he was developing called "Dr. Science," which was intended to be educational as well as entertaining. He also was working with Michael Linder, then a documentary producer based in Japan. Linder had been asked to come up with a series of documentaries for Fox to produce. He had just flown in from Tokyo for further discussions on a documentary marking the tenth anniversary of the death of Elvis Presley.

The problem was that nothing was working. "Dr. Science" just wasn't as good as had been hoped, and the musical rights to the Elvis documentary were turning out to be difficult to obtain and much more expensive than they had ever anticipated. Linder, disappointed, returned to Japan.

Chao, a born overachiever, needed something to produce. He couldn't face the prospect of "another dry hole."

In the meantime, Platt had sent Chao clippings about his concept for a crime show, showing that similar shows had been successful all over the globe. "So I said, 'Hell! I'll get this fugitive show going,' " recalls Chao.

Chao called Linder in Japan and asked, "Michael, how about a show about catching criminals?" Linder was reluctant. After all, he was gearing up to do "serious" documentaries. He didn't feel that such a show would have the weight and importance of a documentary. Still, he agreed to discuss it further.

Linder, who had grown up in Illinois and Wisconsin, began his career in radio. He became a reporter for WNEW-FM in New York City and then moved into TV news at KCBS-TV in Los Angeles, where he worked in 1979 and 1980. Next he moved into producing segments of various magazine-style TV shows, including "Entertainment Tonight" and "Eye on L.A.," a local WABC show in Los Angeles. He won a local Emmy for his work on an anniversary special at independent station KTLA in Los Angeles. He also did consulting work in home video, produced an exercise video with Arnold Schwarzenegger, produced a short-lived ABC network series, and did dozens of other local TV specials.

On a trip to Tokyo for "Eye on L.A.," Linder fell in love with Japan. With American television going through a transition after the sale of all three networks within a one-year period around 1986, Linder decided to move his base of operations to Tokyo, where he produced programs for the Japanese government and worked free-lance on U.S. projects.

His friend David Simon, who had been the program director at KTLA when Linder won his Emmy, had moved to Twentieth Century–Fox Television and introduced Linder to Chao. In April 1987 Linder agreed to go to Washington and produce a pilot for the crime catchers' show, which was to be called "America's Most Wanted."

Chao recalls that Diller was adamant that the show be produced somewhere in the east, not in Hollywood. The place that made most sense was Washington, because Fox figured that the key to pulling it off would be getting the cooperation of the FBI. Chao asked a Fox station-group executive in Washington, Tom Herwitz, to make the initial contact with the nation's top law enforcement agency.

Herwitz had joined Fox only the year before, after a long career in government. He had most recently been the assistant to the chairman of the FCC, Mark Fowler, during the period in which Fowler had moved American broadcasting into an era of broad deregulation.

Herwitz went to see Buck Revell, the number-three man at the FBI, which was in turmoil. After a number of bureau directors in the post–J. Edgar Hoover years, the latest director was moving to head up the CIA. This meant a period of months when no one would be in charge at the top of the agency. It was a tough time to get high-level decisions made.

Herwitz explained their plan to use actors to re-create the events leading up to a crime and the crime itself. He said they intended to focus on the most wanted criminals and to provide a toll-free telephone number for tipsters to call. He told Revell that if the FBI refused to cooperate, Fox probably would not do the show at all.

Herwitz recalled that Revell was cautious about getting involved, although he generally liked the idea of enlisting the public's help in catching criminals. He responded that the top FBI brass would have to think it over.

Finally Revell came back and said the FBI would cooperate by making information available about criminals—all information that was available to the public in any case. He said the FBI wanted final approval over the show in return. Herwitz explained that that would be difficult and was not really in the agency's best interests.

"You want ultimate deniability," Herwitz told him. "You don't want this to appear to actually be your show."

In fact, Herwitz had already been to see the Drug Enforcement Administration, the Customs Bureau, the Secret Service, and others. He knew that Fox intended to take cases not only from the FBI but from police departments all over the nation.

After being promised that it would be done in a tasteful way and that they would be allowed to observe all phases, the FBI agreed to help, at least on the pilot.

Next Fox had to decide on a host. Chao, Linder, and Herwitz all began making suggestions and gathering audition tapes and pictures of candidates. There were actors associated with crime shows and, in some cases, actual crimes. There were politicians, former policemen, former U.S. attorneys, and more.

"We decided early on we didn't want just an actor or a news person," recalls Herwitz. "We wanted somebody who crystallized the idea of the show, who every viewer could empathize with and say, 'He's just like us.' "

Herwitz knew about John Walsh, who had come to public attention by leading a crusade to help others find lost children after his own son, Adam, had been abducted and murdered in 1981. Walsh and his wife Reve had helped to enact the passage of the Missing Children's Act of 1982 and the Missing Children's Assistance Act of 1984, which established a National Center for Missing and Exploited Children. Their incredible efforts were dramatized in the 1983 NBC television movie "Adam" and a 1986 sequel, "Adam: His Song Continues." The shows had led to the recovery of sixty-five missing youngsters and made Walsh a national figure.

His efforts also led to the establishment of the Adam Walsh Child Resource Center, a nonprofit group that provides education on child safety and works for legislation. Walsh also had been presented with numerous awards.

What his work on behalf of missing children did not do was equip Walsh to host a weekly television show. "However, John had a dynamic look, was very believable, and had a strong voice," says Linder. "Most importantly, he had this vortex of energy that grew out of his obsession with all the things 'America's Most Wanted' is all about. He had taken tragedy and made it something positive."

The pilot was shot in the second half of the summer of 1987 and was completed around Labor Day. Out of hundreds of candidates, Linder had selected to profile David James Roberts on the first show, for several reasons. First, because the show would air only on the seven Fox-owned stations, he needed a felon who might be in one of those seven cities. Roberts, Linder reasoned, was probably in the Chicago area, where Fox is seen on WFLD. He also chose Roberts because his three murders and other crimes were such clear-cut violations of everything decent. In one case he had burned down a house with his victims inside as he stood outside listening to their screams for help and mercy.

Linder flew with a TV crew to Indiana to re-create that incident, which had happened fourteen years before. To the police and residents of the small Indiana town, however, it was as fresh as if it had been yesterday. They provided Linder with complete cooperation and helped him secure an old farmhouse on the edge of town that could be burned down for the re-creation of the crime. "I started to see that this show could have real impact in a small community that had been touched by such a crime," says Linder. "It was a pattern that was to continue."

That fall the pilot was shown to Barry Diller and some other Fox executives. Diller loved it. He ordered that nine more episodes be prepared to run on the station group sometime the following year. The pilot was to sit around for eight months before it aired in a time slot that, in Washington, D.C., replaced reruns of "The Wonderful World of Disney."

Roberts, meanwhile, was working in a hospital in Staten Island, New York, as a resident coordinator in charge of helping the homeless. Under the name Bob Lord he had appeared on TV in New York, been photographed with Mayor Ed Koch, and become a well-known advocate of the rights of the homeless. None of those who knew him as Bob Lord, however, had any idea that he was really an escaped convict.

Roberts was sitting in the hospital watching television when a promotion came on channel 5 for a new show airing that night, "America's Most Wanted." He saw his picture flashed and went into a panic. He packed up his belongings and started to run.

It was too late. Within a few hours after the first show aired, twenty-four people had called the toll-free number to identify Lord as Roberts and to give his location. The FBI sent its entire New York City–area force of agents to find him. Roberts was arrested four days later, on February 11, 1988.

After that the ratings rose and police help poured in from all over the nation. Frustrated law enforcement officers with cases long unsolved came begging for help, and quite often "America's Most Wanted" was there for them.

Diller, realizing he was riding a powerful new force, unleashed "America's Most Wanted" on the Fox network on April 10, and the list of captured felons quickly grew.

So did the list of copycats. As happens so often in TV, when one program hits, everyone else wants in on the action. NBC came up with "Unsolved Mysteries." The following year at the NATPE convention there were a dozen other "reality" shows that dramatized crimes and helped find criminals.

But Fox had the franchise. Linder says that

> the show has continued to grow. It started just with reconstructed crimes. Now it has become an anthology series about criminal personalities. We try to discern as much about a fugitive's background as possible, or about the victims. It really has become a deterrent to crime. We're very proud that we're the ones who are able to provide that ounce of prevention that matters.

24

SUMMER OF DISCONTENT

IT WASN'T ALWAYS easy to get Barry Diller's attention, but once he became involved in a situation—be it a big decision like deciding the fate of a program or a minor matter such as the menu at an upcoming Fox event—he usually would stay on top of it until it had been resolved.

This hands-on approach to even the most minor detail was both Diller's greatest strength and greatest weakness. Attention from the highest echelon could have a positive effect on the outcome of a problem, but it also drew Diller away from the bigger issues and sometimes threw a monkey wrench into the decision-making process. One point was certain: since Diller's hands-on style often cut across the normal organizational lines of authority, Fox executives were always looking over their shoulder. This magnified Diller's already-awesome power within his organization. Anyone who worked for Diller soon came to realize that the real power was concentrated at the top. That left them to scramble for knowledge of what Diller wanted, to jockey for position close to him, and to fight with others in the company for whatever share of the power that Diller might bestow on them.

At Paramount, where he grew steadily in stature alongside his fellow executives, Diller's natural strength was kept in check by others who considered themselves his equal. At Fox, where Diller arrived with his giant reputation already intact, his powerful personality made him seem as awesome as the burning bush Moses found on top of Mount Sinai. His word was law.

As one former Fox executive puts it, the running gag was that working for Diller was like putting out a fire on the Alaska oil pipeline. If you got too close, you'd be burned to death, but if you moved too far away, you'd freeze.

As perceptive as he was unpredictable, Barry Diller was an enigma to almost everyone. Except to Barry Diller himself, that is.

"What people don't understand about me, and I think about Mr. Murdoch," said Barry Diller nearly two years after the Fox network first went on the air, "is that what we do is on the table. It's sometimes noisy but it's without artifice and it's very direct. It's very clear. There's no back channel, second agenda, or much subtlety. There just isn't."

While what Diller said was true, it didn't change the problem faced by those who worked with him. It was true that he didn't create long-range strategies and then manipulate events to fit his plan. If he had, it would have been easier to follow what he was doing. Instead, Diller used his position of great strength to make decisions very quickly, usually based on his own experience and instinct. Often Diller was the only one with a broad enough knowledge to understand why he did what he did. By the time all of the implications were clear to those around him, Diller would be on to the next thing, the next decision, the next course correction. His executives constantly had to scramble to keep up.

This steady, occasionally ruthless "editing" process, as Diller liked to call it, had helped Fox achieve more in a few months than anyone, even Diller, had imagined possible in the early, difficult days of the Fox Broadcasting Company. The examples of rapid progress abounded, beginning with steadily rising ratings. The first Emmy show had gone badly, but by the second a new producer had been found and the reviews and ratings were much more upbeat. Many of the assumptions that the network had started with had been proven false—particularly the need to depend on star producers. So Diller had quickly moved on to new ideas that did produce the desired results. Those employees who couldn't, or wouldn't keep up, were left by the side of the road watching his dust.

One of the biggest questions had been how to deal with the

majority of Fox-affiliated stations. Many had weak signals, tradition-
ally low ratings, a poor position on the TV dial, and lacked good
promotional staff. Some were almost unknown in their own com-
munities or were perceived to be where only the oldest, poorest
programming might be found. All of these were reasons why the
stations couldn't deliver enough audience to make Fox a success.
So Diller, Kellner, and others at Fox devised Operation Bootstrap.

This was a special unit of experienced executives who went to
one city at a time where Fox had a troubled affiliate. For a week or
even a few weeks, they worked with the station to improve their
publicity, promotion, and public profile. In some cases Fox spent
its own money or shared the cost with the station to run advertisements in local newspapers and on radio promoting both Fox and
the station. It was expensive, but it brought results. In some markets
the ratings for Fox shows—and the affiliates' programming in general—rose sharply.

It was money well spent, in both Diller and Kellner's opinion.
They had to get the national average ratings up in order to continue
the growth of the network. The original idea, before the network
had gone on the air, that Fox could pay the same license fee as the
big three networks with a smaller audience because of lower overhead had not proven true. So Diller had come up with a new
economic model based on lower-cost programming—shows like
"America's Most Wanted"—that fit Fox's circumstances. Finally the
red ink started to dry up. Step by step Diller pushed, pulled,
molded, and trimmed until the fledgling program service began to
look and feel and act like a real television network.

Diller's unsystematic, instinctual approach was tough on people.
Says Diller:

> When you're in the hothouse environment that we've been in you
> use the material that you can and shape it the best way possible at
> that moment without doing too much damage to the whole body.
> That's got certain consequences at different times. The fact of the
> matter is, everybody [at the top-management level of Fox] has lived
> through the process. I think some are better for it and some aren't.
> That's just the way things go. I think [they're] mostly better for it.

For some people there were times when it was hard to tell
whether it was for better or worse. Consider the dilemma faced by
Garth Ancier at the beginning of July 1988. A few weeks earlier

Ancier had celebrated a series of changes in the management and structure of Fox Broadcasting, including his own promotion from president of programming to president of Fox Broadcasting Company Entertainment.

At Ancier's suggestion, Kevin Wendle had been brought back into the programming department, while continuing to oversee publicity, promotion, and advertising. Officially Wendle had been promoted from vice president of advertising, publicity and promotion, to senior vice president of entertainment, reporting directly to Ancier—or at least that's what it would have said on the organization chart if Fox had had one.

Ancier recalls that

> for six months I'd been asking if I could have Kevin back in programming. Because Kevin is a great organizer. He gets things done. He's not a visionary, but he had great organizational skills. You need a person who when you say, "I need this done," gets it done. Especially because I don't like dealing with the administrative paperwork all the time. I really don't do it that well. I only want to put shows on the air. That's what I do well.

Ancier's happiness with the new order was short-lived. It seemed to him that from his first day in his new position Wendle acted as if he were the new wave, rather than reinforcement. Ancier began hearing from outside producers that Wendle made references to "the new regime." Wendle, with Diller's full support, made certain that all of the other programming staff reported to him and through him, and that nobody went to Ancier or Diller without his knowledge. He even physically separated most of the programming staff from Ancier, grouping their offices down a long hallway close to his own.

In a business where relationships are everything, it upset some program suppliers and pained Ancier, who felt as if everything he had worked to build during his career, and especially during the two difficult years at Fox, was slipping through his fingers. No matter what Ancier said or tried to do, he couldn't seem to get control over the department he was supposed to be running.

Wendle steadily maintained that he was just doing his job.

> I really wasn't doing anything more than I had been doing before. When I was in the program department the first time, remember that I reported to Garth, and the department reported to me. So I was

running day to day. When I returned to the department, I simply resumed that role. The difference was that I had a much stronger relationship with Barry.

Wendle also had a much more adversarial relationship with Ancier. Wendle, Ancier felt, wasn't there to support him, but to replace him.

Ancier never enjoyed confrontation, especially with Diller, but by early July he felt he had no choice. When he tried to exert his authority with Wendle, his protests were simply ignored. Wendle did as he pleased. If pressed, Ancier says, Wendle would tell him that he should consider leaving Fox, because Diller really didn't like him anymore. It seemed to Ancier that Wendle had a different agenda. Ancier finally decided to discuss with Diller his status regarding Wendle.

"We have to clarify this," Ancier said to Diller as they sat in the front room of Diller's office. "This is silly. What's going on here? I'm the president of the division and I'm not being included in supplier meetings?! People in town are asking me what's going on. All of a sudden people with whom I've had a long relationship don't see me in meetings."

"Kevin doesn't have those relationships," Diller responded. You need to give him some space to develop those relationships. . . . We want to give Kevin his chance. We want to see what he can do."

"What does that really mean to me then?" demanded Ancier.

"You'll be included when it's appropriate," said Diller.

"What am I supposed to do?" Ancier wanted to know. "What are my responsibilities?"

"Just tell people you're busy and you'll be involved where it's appropriate," repeated Diller.

"But what does that mean?" asked Ancier again.

"It means you'll go to your office and say you're busy," said Diller. "It means you will work on special projects. You will develop shows for other parts of the schedule, for daytime, for late night. Specials."

"It means Kevin really is in charge."

"We're going to give him his chance."

For Diller the spur-of-the-moment decision to support Wendle over Ancier was wrapped up in the dynamics that were changing Fox and the entire TV world. In Diller's mind, Ancier was still the guy who fought for the old NBC way of doing things, who had been critical of reality programming, who too often was pessimistic about new ideas. Wendle, on the other hand, was always supportive of new plans, especially if they represented an alternative form of television that Fox could call its own. Wendle was also a born optimist. Diller had listened to him talk for months about what he could do if only he were in charge. So Diller had decided to give him his opportunity. Diller's intent wasn't to be mean. It was just another course correction.

Diller explains that

> Part of the problem of having people who have not had very much experience—and it's part of the continuing problem of operating that way—is that it's very rocky to get through. You're doing different things to both test the people and the organization. You move the boxes around and see where they end up and you go through some areas where, without question, you make mistakes. You do things a lot out of circumstance and timing and you do things at certain moments that you wouldn't ordinarily do. And the fact that you can't do them becomes a signal, which becomes the next circumstance.
>
> It really says one thing, which is that when you're doing the company, starting it, growing it, and operating it all at the same time, and you're doing it in a hostile environment, and the competition is trying to do you in, and the media is killing you, and the mistakes are gaping and ugly, and all sorts of things are happening, you're suddenly compromised at the same time that you're moving forward. You have all of these things going and it's much more circumstance and process than it is anything else. So what happens is, at certain times, especially in a very cooked period, you just take certain paths in the road.

It became Ancier's summer of discontent. He turned inward. He anguished over his current dilemma and relived many moments from the past trying to understand what had happened. He became moody and he brooded. Much of his energy had wilted along with his enthusiasm. Later he would look back on it as the worst summer of his life.

For those loyal to Ancier, it was painful to watch his agony, and as he withdrew, they felt abandoned. The perception spread that Ancier didn't protect his people in the political infighting; so when Ancier was under attack, few rushed to his defense.

At the same time, Wendle was emerging and growing as an executive and rapidly consolidating his power base. He wasted little time in exerting his authority as head of programming and sharply defining the role he expected each member of the department to play. Those who didn't want to go along soon found themselves isolated and, within a short time, out of Fox altogether.

The first to feel it from both Wendle and Diller was Alan Sternfeld. A ruggedly handsome, stylish thirty-five-year-old, Sternfeld had arrived a year earlier with a sense of mission. He had recognized immediately that most of those at Fox lacked what he called a "network mentality." That meant that they looked only at their own areas without taking into account how their actions would impact the long-term interests of the network. He had started out believing that it was only a matter of time before they would become educated in his way of thinking, what he called "broadcast management."

Instead, Sternfeld had suffered a year of frustration and disappointment. He was frequently in the minority on every decision, and even when he was proven right in the end, he won few friends in the process. Diller, who had been intensely interested in his views at first, seemed to fade in and out on what he had to say.

Sternfeld also quickly came to dislike the Diller management style. It didn't bother him that Diller pitted one executive against another, but rather that Diller seemed to feel that, when he ordered an executive to get something accomplished—boosting the ratings on Saturday night, for instance—it became that person's fault if it didn't happen. To Sternfeld, that attitude was foolish. He knew there were times when such a request simply could not be fulfilled. The situation, he felt, as much more complex. There was the lack of young viewers on Saturday night, the heavy use of VCR's, the powerful competition from the NBC hit show "The Golden Girls." Yet Sternfeld knew that Diller blamed him and Ancier for the failure to find solutions more quickly.

Sternfeld also had found himself in a running series of skirmishes with both Diller and Wendle over scheduling. To Sternfeld, Diller's ideas were locked in a time warp circa his ABC days in the early seventies. What Sternfeld wanted was to think more in terms of *when* viewers would be dialing around looking for something to watch. He believed it would be best to move "Married . . . With Children" to 9:00 P.M., when all of the networks change shows; that way they could hook viewers with a strong show. Then, once they had missed the first half hour of the movie on the other networks, Sternfeld argued, there was a greater chance that they would stay with Fox throughout the night. Diller didn't agree, and he wouldn't discuss alternatives.

Early on in their relationship, it appeared that Diller had become suspicious of Sternfeld's programming instincts. For instance, on the night the first Emmy show ran on Fox, the episode of "21 Jump Street" that ran adjacent to it had not been one of the better episodes. Diller blamed that mistake on Sternfeld.

As time passed, Sternfeld's only ally seemed to be Ancier, and he was having problems as well. Sternfeld wanted to get closer to Jamie Kellner, but it never seemed to work out. He finally came to view Kellner as the old-fashioned version of a network president who operated under the strong hand of a powerful network chief (William Paley at CBS, David Sarnoff at NBC, or Leonard Goldenson at ABC). He was really president of sales, marketing, advertising, and affiliate relations, with little say in programming. He wasn't the real boss in any sense of the word. It was obvious to Sternfeld that even if he had Kellner's support, it wouldn't much matter unless Diller agreed.

Throughout it all, Sternfeld felt that Wendle was always sniping at him and suggesting that if *he* were in charge, he could certainly do a better job. To Sternfeld it was obvious that Wendle was desperately trying to be Diller, but lacking the boss's strength, charm, and experience, he was, instead, just transparently ambitious.

Sternfeld also had been caught up, along with Ancier, in the "Dirty Dozen" disaster, even though he had seen it coming and loudly warned all who would listen.

When "Dirty Dozen" was first being readied for production, the writer, Dan Gordon, had submitted a series of scripts for the first shows to be produced by MGM/UA Television in Yugoslavia. The foreign locale had been chosen because it would be much less expensive, and the Yugoslavian army could be rented for a fraction of what it would cost anywhere else to re-create World War II scenes.

Sternfeld and Ancier had both seen problems coming. The scripts were weak on character and heavy on action. Sternfeld felt that the original movie of the "Dirty Dozen" had worked because it was about a scruffy, disgusting group of individuals who had committed horrible crimes but now had one last chance to redeem themselves. In the movie, the roles were all played by character actors.

For the TV series, MGM/UA was following the usual TV formula of choosing handsome young male leads. They felt that that was what would draw in young adult viewers, especially women. Sternfeld pointed out that those were not the type of guys the story called for at all. MGM/UA went ahead anyway.

Even that might have been fixed if the scripts could have been developed more fully. Instead, by the time the first show was in production, the Writers Guild of America had started a marathon strike that shut down almost all TV production. The writer, Dan Gordon, now on strike, couldn't work on the scripts.

Fox shut down "Boys Will Be Boys" and some other shows for lack of scripts. However, MGM/UA refused to be shut down. They not only had sold "Dirty Dozen" to Fox, but they also had sold it around the globe to other TV services. They had a commitment to produce the first season no matter what, and they weren't about to let Fox off the hook.

It was Ancier who finally called David Gerber, the veteran head of MGM/UA Television, to tell him that Fox was not going to pay for any more shows. Gerber told him they had to go forward and that as far as they were concerned, Fox had made a deal and had to stick by it. Ancier said they were using a clause in the contract stating that in the event that something happened that was beyond the control of both parties—in this case, the writers' strike—the contract could be canceled.

MGM/UA went forward on production without Fox. It also filed a lawsuit against the Fox Broadcasting Company charging breach of contract and bad faith, demanding the original license fees, all costs, and some damages. Later on, after the strike, Gerber also would be censured by the writers guild for allegedly writing and rewriting those scripts during the strike.

At Fox there was a deep sense of gloom. "Dirty Dozen" was a flop, even with the targeted audience, and two other shows planned as replacements couldn't be produced because of the writers' strike. As interim programming, a show developed by Jim McKay was rushed into production. It was a spin-off from "A Current Affair," with more than a little of the format borrowed from "60 Minutes," called, "The Reporters." It was inexpensive to produce and quickly improved the ratings on Saturday night. Another show McKay imported from Australia and created an American version was called "Beyond Tomorrow," a showcase of futuristic ideas and inventions. It, too, improved the Saturday ratings, although it didn't do as well as "The Reporters."

Sternfeld, in the meantime, was feeling the heat for the continued failure of the story-form, narrative-series programming on Saturday. He knew he was in real trouble when he began getting calls from Kellner about things which in the past Diller would have called him directly.

Then Sternfeld scheduled a meeting to talk about some scheduling problems. He carefully worked out the time and date with Diller's and Kellner's secretaries to make sure they were free. When the time came, neither Diller nor Keller showed up or bothered to call.

Soon Sternfeld was hearing about meetings to which he wasn't being invited, meetings concerning items that directly involved him. By late spring 1988, he knew he consciously was being isolated from the rest of the company.

Then, in June came Wendle's rise in programming. Soon afterward, Wendle paid Sternfeld a visit. It was short and to the point. Wendle felt that Sternfeld was not on his team and that they weren't on the same wavelength. Wendle made it clear that he felt it would be best if Sternfeld went elsewhere.

For Sternfeld, it was relief. His reputation, established at NBC, was still very good, so immediately there were other job offers. Leaving Fox was like escaping from a sort of prison. Within a few weeks he announced that he was joining GTG Entertainment, the company started by TV industry legend Grant Tinker and the Gannett newspaper company.

While Sternfeld went relatively quietly, Marion Davis's last days were marked by more obvious disagreements and bad feelings. A very pretty, demure woman, Davis had been everybody's early favorite. In a company full of inexperience, she seemed to be a voice of authority. While she clearly had high standards, Davis at first also seemed to be a solid team player. As time passed, it was clear that she was mainly on Ancier's team, however, even though it had been Kevin Wendle who had been her mentor and recruited her first to NBC and then to Fox.

It hadn't taken long for disillusionment to set in. Davis, like Ancier, was a strong believer in hiring strong, experienced producers and giving them a free hand to do their best work. Since Diller had soured on the idea of making the producer the priority and instead wanted to concentrate on the show's concept, Davis had found her views losing favor along with those of Ancier. She had begun to see her old friend Wendle as a member of the other camp within Fox. In her mind, that made him disloyal to Ancier.

Davis also had lost points with Diller because she was the program executive on a whole string of failed shows, beginning with the painful George C. Scott series "Mr. President." Despite several efforts at retooling, it had never worked as a comedy or a drama and finally had been canceled.

In addition, Davis had been in charge of a show called "Family Man," which Fox had ordered from Universal Studios but never aired. It was the kind of standard-issue, soft family comedy that might have worked on NBC if run right after a hit like "The Cosby Show" but that on Fox was simply too little, too late to be usable. The completed episodes were later sold off to ABC at a loss; ABC happily ran them during prime time with little impact on the ratings.

The other show Davis had supervised was "Duet," the "next generation" romantic comedy from Gary Goldberg, creator of such NBC hits as "Silver Spoons." In reality Goldberg had never worked on "Duet" beyond setting the deal and the concept. It had been turned over to Ruth Bennett and Susan Seager, two of his best writers. The show had become a kind of living workshop. Week by week it moved away from the original central characters and premise—a love story about two nice people—to concentrate more on the couple's saucier friends, a bitchy woman and her overly sweet husband (played by Chris Lemmon, son of movie star Jack Lemmon).

Despite all of the changes, "Duet" had never attracted a very large audience. After Fox picked up "Gary Shandling" in early 1988, "Duet" had been pushed all the way to the end of the schedule, where it was often preempted by the local affiliates' news show or run later at night. Fox kept renewing it with orders for small numbers of episodes, but the story, like the ratings, was never as good as Fox had hoped it would be.

In the spring of 1988, Davis came up with a new programming idea, one of the big events Fox had been seeking. An English company, Elephant House Productions, had spent two years developing plans for a huge charity concert in London in association with Artists Against Apartheid and the antiapartheid movement. It was to be a celebration of the seventieth birthday of Nelson Mandela, the imprisoned South African activist, featuring many of the top contemporary acts in pop music, including Phil Collins, Whitney Houston, George Michael and the Bee Gees.

The concert would run for about fourteen hours. Fox made a deal to run an edited six-hour version. Jamie Kellner felt that Fox had made it clear that it was interested in what came to be called

"Freedomfest" mainly because it was a musical event, not because of the political overtones. In particular, Fox specified in advance that it would refuse to carry anything that even vaguely advocated violence or revolution in South Africa.

The concert was an all-day event broadcast from Wembley Stadium in London. Marion Davis went from Los Angeles to London first to help set it up. Jamie Kellner, Brad Turell, and a producer hired by Fox arrived shortly before the event.

The events of that two-day period are the subject of considerable disagreement. Kellner and Turell say that Davis seemed to think she was working for Elephant House instead of Fox and that she got the company into hot water by telling them too much about what parts of the concert the network planned to use and what it intended to cut.

Davis felt that Fox tried to rush in and grab all of the credit for what Elephant House had spent two years putting together. She also got caught up in a fight, which was blown out of proportion by the English media, over whether the cuts being made by Fox were for programming content or were a form of political censorship. At the suggestions of censorship, several of the performers made statements denouncing Fox as well as anyone else who didn't support their views.

There was also a question as to what degree Fox was being influenced by one of the major advertisers, Coca-Cola. Kellner contended that he made all the final decisions, but the Coke representative was allowed to sit next to him in the editing room and make suggestions. Davis and others felt that Coke was allowed to exert too much influence. Kellner commented on the situation a few weeks later:

> Did [the Coca Cola rep] influence me? Probably. I was sitting there watching the entire thing. He was with me, as were a couple of others. . . . However, I don't think it would be fair to say he was in any way editing the program. I tend not to be influenced. We finished the final edits with no one else but me there. If he was actually editing, he would have stayed for the whole thing.

There were other battles and hurt feelings, but the bottom line was that by the time the concert was over, both Kellner and Turell were angry and unhappy with Davis. Kevin Wendle, back in the United States, had gotten the impression that Davis not only wasn't a team player but, at a time when she should have been on top of things, was out of control personally.

Davis, who felt she was always in control, spent a couple of weeks on vacation in Europe before returning. She arrived back in Los Angeles shortly after Diller had told Ancier that it was time to give Wendle his opportunity to run programming. She was told upon her return she would no longer report directly to Ancier, the head of the department. Instead, she was to report to Rob Kenneally, a new vice president brought in by Wendle to replace Jim McKay, who had returned to Australia.

Davis knew that it was time to go, and Wendle made it clear to her that he agreed, although he strongly denies having fired her.

> She really wasn't fired. Her departure had much more to do with the fact, with my returning to the department, and Rob coming in, that she was not interested in reporting directly to Rob, who reported to me, who reported to Garth, when previously she had reported directly to Garth. She was also frustrated by her own inability to get projects going here. She decided this was not the kind of company she wanted to work in.
>
> I had a conversation with her, I said, "Do you really want to do this or not?" And she said, "I really don't. I'm unhappy." Listen, she's very talented and I want to protect her. She wasn't fired and she certainly wasn't fired by me.

Kellner, too, insists that Davis was not fired, despite the fact that that was the general impression throughout the company.

> I came back [from Freedomfest] with concern, but certainly didn't recommend that she leave the company. She worked very hard over there. It became obvious [that] certain things got confused, but everyone deserves a second chance as far as I'm concerned. She decided she didn't want to stay on.

Whatever the ultimate reasoning, the loss of Davis, following closely upon the departure of Sternfeld, left Ancier even more isolated. The Hollywood creative community was becoming aware that there had been a real changing of the guard.

In his darkest hour, Ancier could take some comfort. Brandon Tartikoff called him from NBC and invited him back to produce a show. And Jeff Katzenberg and Rich Frank at Disney began feeling

Ancier out about going there to develop programming for all of the television networks. Soon Disney made its offer firm. But it wanted an answer.

Ancier, who was only about one year into a four-year contract at Fox, went to Diller and asked to be released so that he could go to Disney or take some other job. Diller told him it would be a mistake to rush off—that things could and would change again. After all, this was Fox, where the only thing anyone was certain of was that Barry Diller was in charge.

And Diller's decision was firm. Ancier might have felt that he was in cold storage, but Fox still needed his services. There was another night of programming to plan and ideas about how to expand into daytime and make a return to late night programming.

No, Barry Diller wasn't about to let Garth Ancier go. At least not yet.

25

A LITTLE CULTURAL
REVOLUTION

WHEN GARTH ANCIER learned that Rupert Murdoch was in Los Angeles at the end of summer 1988, he decided it was his opportunity to try and do something about his intolerable situation. If anyone could help, or at least give him some sane advice, Ancier felt it was Murdoch. Although their association had been brief and almost always buffered by Barry Diller, Ancier respected Murdoch greatly and felt that it was mutual. This was one time, however, that Ancier had no intention of telling Diller he was going to see Murdoch. He wanted it to remain top secret. He immediately phoned and asked for an appointment. Word was quickly relayed that Murdoch would be happy to see him in his office on the main floor of the executive building.

When Marvin Davis had owned Fox, he had taken the biggest, most central office in the building, even though he was rarely present for more than one or two days a week. Murdoch, however, opted for a much smaller, more modest space, allowing Diller to take the larger office. After his first few months, Murdoch also decided it was silly for him to have a full-time secretary in Los Angeles to take calls and sort his mail. Instead, he began bringing his secretary from New York or using another company secretary who would be available for his brief stays in Los Angeles.

The office might have been small, but Murdoch's empire continued to grow rapidly. During the second week of August, Murdoch sent shock waves through publishing circles when he announced a deal with Walter Annenberg for News Corp. to acquire Triangle Publications, its most important U.S. acquisition since Metromedia. Among other things, Triangle owned and published *TV Guide*, the largest-selling weekly magazine in the United States, with a circulation of 17 million, and one of the largest in the world. Other properties included the *Daily Racing Form* and *Seventeen* as well as a large magazine- and newspaper-distribution system. It made Murdoch, in one giant step, the largest (in revenue) publisher of consumer magazines in the United States.

Even more astounding was the price of $3 billion, which was at least $1 billion more than any American company thought Triangle was worth. Of course, what a few sophisticated observers realized was that no U.S. company had Murdoch's advantages. He could move the ownership of *TV Guide* offshore, where instead of being a tax drain for years to come, it would be an immediate asset that could be borrowed against and leveraged for even greater gains. Murdoch did undertake the sale of some assets to bring down his massive debt, including a Fox office building in Los Angeles, his stake in *Elle* magazine, and, later, a group of travel-industry publications. Still, the important thing was that he had moved News Corp. into the rarefied atmosphere of the very largest, most powerful companies in the world, with annual revenues of over $7 billion annually.

Not everyone was overjoyed. Andrew J. Schwartzman of the Media Access Project, a Washington, D.C., public interest group, told the Associated Press that he was concerned that Murdoch would use *TV Guide* to favor Fox TV stations and Fox network shows. Murdoch quickly rejected these accusations. He wasn't paying all of that money to turn *TV Guide* into a house organ; that wouldn't be very smart. And Murdoch was smart when it came to acquisitions.

Instead, Murdoch decided to quickly shift the emphasis of *TV Guide* toward an even more consumer-oriented point of view, which meant heavier use of stars and famous faces, more personality stories, and fewer articles about the inner workings of the television industry.

His mandate not to favor the Fox network in *TV Guide* was to insure continued support from all of the networks; but it certainly didn't mean that he was any less enthusiastic about the new network. In numerous meetings Murdoch had made it clear that FBC took priority over all other entertainment properties, meaning the Fox station group and Twentieth Century–Fox. If anything, Murdoch was feeling better near the end of the summer of 1988 about FBC because a number of factors had combined to raise the ratings and stem the huge losses, which had totaled almost $100 million the year before.

The strike by screen and television writers that had done in "Dirty Dozen" and shut down many other shows had become an undisguised blessing for Fox. At first it had seemed as if the strike would last only a short time. Then it had dragged on week after week, finally forcing a delay in the start of production for the new fall television season. The result was that the three major networks had to scramble for any kind of programming while depending mainly on reruns.

Fox Broadcasting, too, had had to shut down most production and rely on reruns. The difference was that only a very small percentage of the American TV audience had ever seen the shows on Fox, so even in rerun they seemed fresh and new. In fact, bored by what the other networks had to offer, millions of viewers began searching for an alternative and found themselves watching Fox. All of the shows were boosted, but none quite as much as "Married . . . With Children," which suddenly became a nationwide cult hit. "America's Most Wanted," which had replaced "21 Jump Street" months earlier as Fox's most popular show, was now surpassed in the ratings race by "Married . . . With Children."

Fox's strike shows, "The Reporters" and "Beyond Tomorrow," were also able to continue producing new episodes throughout the work stoppage because they weren't dependent on guild members. In the case of "The Reporters," the on-air correspondents wrote their own stories; and "Beyond Tomorrow" was produced in Australia, out of the guild's jurisdiction.

Suddenly Fox found itself in the enviable position of having the few new shows available plus lots of older, underexposed shows. Ratings rose steadily on both Saturday and Sunday nights, and Fox advertising rates moved right up along with them.

Murdoch was on the phone when Garth Ancier arrived for their meeting. He waited in the cramped outer office where Murdoch's secretary sat, until the light on the phone switched off. Murdoch came out to greet Ancier, shaking his hand warmly and leading him into his small, comfortable office. Murdoch waved a hand toward the couch, where both of them found seats.

Ancier, looking thinner than Murdoch had remembered him, began by telling the chairman of News Corp. that he had the greatest respect for him and a lot of personal loyalty. He said he understood that Murdoch, both by design and under his contract with Diller, didn't run the Fox network, but he felt he had to tell him what was going on. "Look," said Ancier softly. "This is really not working out. I don't know what to do. The situation's become unbearable."

It was painful for Ancier to even say the words. He really did admire and respect Murdoch. He had found him to be completely fair in all of their dealings, and, even rarer, Murdoch was a man who could separate personal emotions from business dealings. He remembered a conversation he and Murdoch had had a year earlier. Murdoch had told Ancier that he was proud of the fact that he had employees who had worked for him for thirty years or more, and that he and his employees had always taken care of one another. Ancier had immediately thought about Diller, whose associations tended to be considerably shorter. Ancier thought about what that said about the styles of these two highly capable men.

Murdoch said he knew that the office politics had gotten out of hand and that the situation between Ancier and Wendle concerned everyone. Murdoch told him that he also recognized that a lot of the difficulty stemmed from the fact that Ancier tended to be the realist delivering the bad news, while Wendle was always the booster, putting the best face on every situation. And clearly there were times when Diller and others at Fox just didn't want to hear about grim reality. They just wanted to believe that their ideas could work—and of course, they could. It just took time and patience, something in very short supply at Fox.

Ancier was relieved to hear that Murdoch had a clear view of the situation. They also talked about Barry Diller. Ancier told Murdoch that he would even consider spending the two years or so of his contract working in other areas of News Corp., because he really enjoyed his association with Murdoch.

Murdoch, his dark hair slicked back, the sleeves of his white shirt rolled up, was low-key and soft-spoken, but the gravity of the matter showed on his face. Murdoch said that he felt that Ancier had the best judgment in the building about television and that he hoped that Ancier wouldn't make any rash decisions. Murdoch said that he knew about the Disney offer, but unless Ancier was being asked to run one of the major networks, Murdoch felt it would be in Ancier's best interest to stay at Fox for now. Murdoch made it clear that he personally wanted Ancier to stick around.

Ancier wasn't sure what would come of the meeting, but he returned to his office feeling much better. At least he knew that Murdoch had confidence in him, even if others at Fox didn't.

Murdoch left Los Angeles the next day and Ancier went back to work, developing some new concept shows for Fox and meeting with some producers about new ideas. Later that week, Barry Diller returned to Los Angeles after a three-week absence. A few days later, Diller called a meeting of all of the key programming executives, including Jamie Kellner, about some matters on which he wanted to be updated.

Throughout the summer, Ancier says, Kevin Wendle had been telling him what he could do, who he could meet with, and which areas he should concentrate on. Wendle says that was not the case, but to Ancier, it was as if there was a fence around him and it kept moving closer, constantly shrinking his area of mobility.

Early in the programming meeting, Ancier says Wendle began to complain that he was overstepping his bounds. Ancier says that Wendle had learned that he had met with Bernie Brillstein, an important personal manager and producer, whose firm represented several stars of Fox shows, including Gary Shandling. It had been Brillstein who had originally advised Edgar Rosenberg and Joan Rivers not to leave "The Tonight Show" for Fox.

According to Ancier Wendle said that he had not cleared Ancier to meet with Brillstein and that he didn't want him doing it anymore without clearing it with him first. In fact, he really didn't want him meeting with the important suppliers of prime-time shows at all. Wendle felt that that was now his job.

Wendle said later it wasn't that he didn't want Ancier meeting with Brillstein or other program suppliers. Wendle was upset that when such meetings were held, Ancier wasn't informing him and other key programming department executives about what had been decided, which made him and the Fox programming department look like it wasn't functioning in sync. Wendle said he just wanted the department to operate with a unified face to the world.

What Wendle didn't know was that Diller had been doing a lot of thinking about how Wendle had performed that summer. While the programming department had run smoothly, it hadn't developed many viable new properties that were ready to become series on Fox. Although they had developed twenty new projects, despite a writers strike in Hollywood, Diller wasn't satisfied.

Wendle also didn't know that Diller had gotten a phone call from Patrick Hasburgh complaining that Ancier, who knew what he was doing and who handled creative people well, was no longer at meetings, and that in his place was Wendle, whom he liked dealing with less. Hasburgh had had many run-ins with Wendle during the early days of "21 Jump Street."

It also appeared that Diller had been talking with Murdoch about the way things were going.

When Wendle had finished his litany of complaints about Ancier, Diller just glared at him for a long moment.

"Barry," said Wendle, "I want you to reprimand Garth for taking that meeting."

Diller continued to glare, fire burning in his blue eyes. Jamie Kellner and the others in the room were all dead silent. "Why do you bring this up now?" Diller demanded of Wendle. "Why in front of all these people? You are not the president of the entertainment division. He [pointing at Ancier] is. You report to him."

Wendle says he just wanted the lines of authority more clearly defined so they could all work better as a team. "My sense is Barry was saying, 'It's not in your interest to spell this out,' " says Wendle. Even so, Wendle says he felt the important thing was to do what was right for Fox's programming department, and ultimately to benefit the Fox network.

Diller, who became obsessive when something important that has long been festering in the back of his mind finally rolls out, just kept on and on putting him back in his place.

Then Diller turned to Ancier. He told him that it was all his fault, that he had not kept his underling in his place, that he should have taken more control of his own department.

Ancier felt like asking Diller how he was supposed to control someone who went around him, directly to the chairman, but instead he just listened, satisfied that order had been restored in his universe, at least temporarily.

To Diller, it was simply the right thing to do.

What happened is that you had two people who were ambitious and could be destructive out there being competitive with each other. It didn't last very long. It was destructive. I wasn't happy about it. I went away for three weeks and it was only when I came back that

I saw it. The day I came back it was over, literally. I remember the meeting I attended. . . . I came back and attended one meeting where there was this attitude showing and I said, "This is it, folks. You go upstairs and settle this. How dare you come into this room and talk to us about these issues. You go upstairs and work them out yourselves and come out of it with a way of operating between yourselves. . . . You can't [be allowed to] hurt this company. You straighten this out. Don't look to Kellner or me to straighten it out, or we will."

Diller had given Wendle his chance and Wendle had done well in getting the department organized and running smoothly, but now more balance was needed. Like most of his decisions, Diller didn't really decide in advance to once again change things around; it had just happened because that was what was needed to keep things on an even keel.

Diller explained later that

you can't chronicle it as if it was an attempt on somebody's life, so to speak. For a long time these two people didn't work for each other. One worked someplace else. He didn't have anything to do with programming. He was in advertising and promotion. Then, because we had a weakness in the structure of our programming department, because we really didn't have much of a structure, because we were just moving along hand to mouth, he came back in. And he brought that operation back into greater order. But there's going to be a lot of conflict when that happens. And there was. It dealt itself out. Some of it was destructive. Some of it was constructive. Now it's back in balance. You look at the program department now and the people who are in it, and look at where it was nine months ago, and tell me if there isn't a difference.

With both the Fox ratings and advertising revenue up and costs down, it was true that Fox had come a long way in those months; but it was the total sum of several years of work.

Says Diller:

We've come up much faster than anybody would have had a right to predict, and I think the important thing for Fox Broadcasting Company, and the really dramatic struggle, is not in some small-time power struggle but in what has actually happened. As I say, if there were casualties, then there would be some drama there, too. But all we did is we grafted one department to a totally different department and had a little cultural revolution which lasted about four or five months. That then settled down and now it's not as if there is any different authority.

When the confrontation between Ancier and Wendle was over, things ran more smoothly, although neither of them could ever return to the innocence of those early, heady days, when the network was first becoming a reality. Diller, who had barely spoken to Ancier in weeks, began discussing every programming issue with him again. While Wendle still had his personal audiences with Diller, whenever anything was decided, Diller made sure that Ancier also was involved.

There was still a mountain of issues to confront, and the basic philosophical rift between Diller and Ancier still existed. Diller no longer trusted the star producers; and he wanted Fox out of the advance-series-commitment game completely. Diller felt that if the program concept was strong enough, any young, smart producer could carry out the assignment. He wanted to alter his philosophy of hiring an executive "a year too early" to hiring a producer "a year too early."

Ancier, however, continued to battle for the top names in TV production. He still felt that the quality and experience of the talent would always be at the heart of any real success.

The rift surfaced again that fall in two important discussions. The first involved Patrick Hasburgh. After an association with Stephen J. Cannell, Hasburgh had left to form his own company. That meant that he was walking away from producing the next season of "21 Jump Street" and would not be available to create and produce an intended spin-off called "City Court," which would be a show starring young lawyers handling the cases first seen on "21 Jump Street."

As soon as he'd left Cannell, Hasburgh had been offered a number of lucrative opportunities. Production companies wanted him to base his operation with them; and at least two of the three major networks wanted him to do shows. The ABC network was willing to guarantee him an on-air commitment.

Despite his many battles with Fox, Hasburgh wasn't unwilling to do something else there. He began discussing ideas with Ancier and others.

Ancier told Diller and the others that Hasburgh was too big a talent to lose. He pleaded with them to allow him to guarantee

Hasburgh that Fox would air whatever series he created for them, with the usual consultations.

Wendle was vocally against it. He felt that it would set a bad precedent right after the network had told everyone else that there would be no more on-air commitments. According to Ancier, Wendle preferred that producers make a pilot first and then give Fox time to consider it.

None of them wanted Hasburgh, who was very sensitive about his relationships, to be aware of the battle in the inner councils of Fox. Finally they reached a compromise. Hasburgh would be given a commitment for a pilot, with the stipulation that it would get priority as an on-air series. They wouldn't let him go, but they wouldn't blindly guarantee him airtime, either.

The other emotional issue for Ancier that fall was a show called "Cops." It had begun a year earlier as an idea brought to Fox by producers John Langley and Malcolm Barbour. They had an agreement from the sheriff's department in Broward County, Florida (the Fort Lauderdale area), to send a crew out with actual officers on duty. Their concept was a series of shows that actually took the audience out on the streets with police in one of the highest-crime areas of the nation, where drugs and the constant influx of new people created one hot situation after another.

Diller and Ancier didn't know if it would ever make a series, but it was intriguing enough to green light a handful of pilot shows. When they saw them, they were instantly excited. When they actually aired some in New York and Los Angeles, the ratings went through the roof. During a five-night run in Los Angeles, "Cops" finished second in the time period, beating two of the three network affiliates.

Ancier, who had been slow in coming around on "America's Most Wanted," was a quick convert this time. He wanted "Cops" on the Fox Saturday night schedule immediately. He lobbied Diller, but Diller was hesitant. He still wasn't convinced that it would work as a weekly series. There were a lot of unanswered questions. Would they stay with one police department or move it around the country? Would it be a flash in the pan or would it sustain high ratings week after week?

Ancier argued strongly that if Fox moved quickly, it could create a kind of franchise in the reality-police-show genre. If not, it was such an easy show to copy, that everybody else in America would do the same kind of show and Fox would lose its edge. He told Diller that at least one local news show in New York City was already doing something similar, and when the "Cops" producers had contacted the Los Angeles County Sheriff's Department about riding with them, they had been told that the Los Angeles sheriff had already made a deal with somebody else.

When Diller still didn't agree, Ancier wrote a memo outlining his position and circulated it among the senior executives in the company.

More and more Ancier was like a man on the end of an electrical wire, always frazzled, on the verge of burning out. He had thrown himself back into his work at Fox and, despite the tension with Wendle, felt back in control. But it had all taken a toll. He no longer had the same enthusiasm. He began seeing his psychiatrist more often and was taking a higher dose of tranquilizers at night. One day seemed to slide into the next, and there barely seemed to be time to breathe.

Ancier told Diller that he was happy that they were working well together again, but he was still thinking about leaving. He felt as though he were inside a pressure cooker. It just wasn't fun anymore.

Diller, on the verge of announcing that Fox would add a third night of programming on Monday and would begin a monthly movie that eventually would become their fourth night, encouraged Ancier to hang in there for a while longer. Fox needed him, Diller said. He couldn't let him go.

Meanwhile, the writers' strike had ended in late summer but the uptick in Fox's ratings had continued. It appeared that a larger number of viewers had sampled what Fox had to offer, and many had liked it enough to keep coming back. On the night of 27 November 1988, Fox finally made the breakthrough they had all dreamed of since the days before Joan Rivers's show.

On that night, a Fox show received a perfect 10 rating. For the first time, a Fox show had a double-digit rating and had attracted 27 percent of all TV homes viewing at that hour. The show was "Married . . . With Children," which had suddenly become one of the hottest shows in all of television.

In January 1989, at the annual NATPE convention, Embassy Communications was proudly announcing that "Married . . . With Children" would be available soon in syndication. The company that had not even wanted to be in business with Fox because it was too risky was predicting it would get some of the highest advance payments in history for "Married . . . With Children." It appeared that Columbia would reap over $100 million in profits.

Columbia even used Fox's non-network status as a sales gimmick. Under federal laws then in effect, network-affiliated stations couldn't play shows from 7:30 to 8:00 P.M. on weekday evenings that had previously played on a network. That had allowed the independent stations in each market to have an advantage, because they *could* play such shows and would regularly program lucrative, highly popular situation comedies against the game shows and magazine shows the affiliated stations had to run. Columbia pointed out that since Fox was not officially a network, "Married . . . With Children" could play in that time period, providing the first real competition for the off-network sitcoms on the independent stations.

At that same convention, the first syndication sales were made on "21 Jump Street." Not only did it command prices as good or better than any off-network show, it also sold to the Tribune stations. It was taken as a sign by the industry that a show on Fox could do as well or better than a show anywhere else; and there would be no limits on who could buy a Fox show in the aftermarket.

In January 1989, Barry Diller proudly stood before his affiliates gathered in Los Angeles for the annual INTV convention and announced that the Fox network had broken into the black. After losing $99 million the year before, it had finished 1988 with a profit of $400,000. He said it might still go back into the red as it developed more nights of programming, but Fox had proven that it was for real. The affiliates, who made more money as the Fox ratings went up, cheered wildly.

A month later, Garth Ancier was in his office preparing for a trip to Chicago for the taping of a pilot for a new kind of talk show to feature a college professor. His phone rang and he saw on the message indicator that Barry Diller wanted to see him. Diller told him that he and Kellner had hired another executive, Peter Chernin, as the new head of programming at Fox. Ancier was invited to stay on as an independent producer of shows for Fox.

Ancier immediately felt that Chernin was a good choice for Fox. Chernin's experience had been primarily in alternative network or programming situations. Chernin had been highly regarded when he was head of programming at Showtime and had earned high marks during his tenure as president of the movie division of Lorimar. He'd left Lorimar when it was sold to Warner Communications and the movie division was shut down.

Ancier had asked repeatedly to be let out of his contract, yet his feelings were mixed. It was the end of an era for him—and for the Fox network. Said Ancier shortly afterward:

The accomplishment for all the people involved in Fox is that two or three years ago, I don't think you could have found more than 10 percent of the people in this town who thought it would work. People weren't making four-network schedule boards. Yet today, I don't think you could find more than 10 percent of the people who don't think it will work. To see that kind of radical shift in opinion over a two-year period is pretty good.

I was thinking, The next thing I'm going to do is going to be either in a network or studio. It's going to be something in the business. And in my office is going to be a schedule board. Everyone has a schedule board. Suppliers do. And the networks do. I was thinking, Should it have three slots or four slots? It was a radical idea putting four slots on when I first made up the board for my office at Fox. . . . Today, you'd be crazy to do a three-network scheduling board. Fox is going to be a factor in every night it's on the air. It may not be the dominant factor on every night, but it is going to be a competitive factor.

A week after Chernin's appointment had been announced, Diller, philosophical, said he simply believed that it was time for someone with different management skills. But he remained generous in his praise of the job Garth Ancier had done to get them that far:

The process was damaging him personally. It was brutalizing to him. It is an enormously demanding and harsh environment. . . . I think [Garth] decided a long time ago, sometime in the summer, that his business life had kind of went, to a degree, out of him. He tried to connect again, but it became apparent he had moved on. Along about January or February [1989] we said, "This is not going to change. He really doesn't want to do it." He had repeatedly asked us for his release. This was at our most difficult moment. We had to ask him to wait because we were too young and too vulnerable. Now we have dealt with it. Peter [Chernin] brings us what we need for today, and tomorrow.

The Diller philosophy of management is a clashing of styles and ideas. He takes young people and molds them, but he does it by constantly testing them. Young people by nature need a lot of support, but that is the one thing he usually will not give them. The result is a kind of test by fire. Some, like Ancier, burn out and move on to do other things. Others remain and grow because they have been pushed along faster than they would have gone in a different kind of atmosphere.

Says Diller:

I know when I arrived [at Fox] I had a big history. I think the effect that has on people sometimes isn't healthy. I can't wait until we get people to the point—and it's coming along—where they are comfortable enough, who have gone through the process enough, that they get to the point where they treat me the way I wish to be treated, which is certainly not as an exclusive force that has a frightening history to terrify the present. But somebody to whom you can come in and say exactly what you think, and do all of the lively things that are vital to a creative enterprise. That just takes time.

EPILOGUE:
THE HAPPY ENDING

ON SUNDAY NIGHT, July 16, 1989, a pair of half hour shows aired over the Fox Broadcasting Company's affiliated stations between 8:00 and 9:00 P.M.—"America's Most Wanted" and "Totally Hidden Video"—were the most watched programs in America. That meant they were viewed by more people, in more homes, than competing shows aired at the same time by NBC, CBS, ABC, or any other broadcaster transmitting over the air or via cable. It was the first time Fox had ever beaten all three of the established broadcast networks, but it was not the last.

A week later, on July 23, Fox did it again with a different half hour show, "Married . . . With Children."

"While it took the then upstart ABC many years to wrestle a time slot away from NBC and CBS," crowed a Fox network press release, "Fox was able to outrate all three major networks in three different time periods in just two-plus years on the air."

Even more impressive was Fox's share of the eighteen- to forty-nine-year-old viewing audience, the group most important to those who spend millions on television commercial time. In that category, Fox took first place over all competitors on Sunday nights for the entire month of July. As a story in *The New York Times* on July 18 put it: "Fox, in fact, is making the greatest strides of any network in that audience most wanted by advertisers."

What it meant was that Fox Broadcasting, just a few weeks before it launched a third night of programming, had become fully competitive with the three established networks on the two nights where it competed. Despite the lack of promotion time on weekdays, its relatively weak line-up of affiliated stations, a smaller program development budget, and the fickle nature of the audience, Fox was a success on its own terms.

It was even more amazing because Fox's success flew in the face of common wisdom. Only two years earlier, in August 1987, *Daily Variety* had headlined an article: "Dirges Sounding for Fox Broadcasting." The article quoted critics who were not only pessimistic, but openly derisive of Fox's prospects for success. "How can a new network hope to flourish," they asked, "when the established networks are hemorrhaging audience? How can any program service imagine it will be able to quadruple the number of people watching that station at that time of day?"

At the time, Barry Diller said they would do it by having a lower overhead, better promotion and marketing. He said they would take more risks and push the cultural barriers further in terms of language and content.

All of that turned out to be true, but the success of the Fox Broadcasting Company more than anything simply proved one of the oldest maxims in the entertainment world: the show is the thing.

Fox became a success, both in terms of perception and economics, because it came up with individual programs that were sufficiently seductive to draw audience away from established programming outlets. In doing so, Fox not only had to beat the competition, it also had to change the historic viewing patterns of the nation's television audience. The audience could no longer think only of the three established networks when it came to the primetime evening viewing hours as it had for four decades. Now there was a fourth alternative.

Since many of the Fox affiliated stations operated on the less popular UHF band (Channels 14 to 83), Fox's success also helped breathe life into that alternative technology. While many UHF stations continued to struggle, Fox became a beacon that proved that with good enough programs people would take the trouble to find their way across the dial.

Fox's plan was to go after younger viewers because they were most attractive to advertisers, but also because they were most open to experimentation. Offered attractive programs, they would take the trouble to find the Fox affiliated station on previously uncharted areas of the TV dial. It took longer than some at Fox expected, but it was achieved much more quickly than most outside experts ever imagined. Fox's "21 Jump Street" did bring teenagers back to the tube. Fox's "America's Most Wanted" did legitimize nonfiction "reality" television. Fox's "Married . . . With Children" did push the barriers of language, culture, and content further than what was happening on the established networks.

And not everybody liked it. Fox was forced to stand tall in the face of fierce criticism aimed at the two forms of TV that were its mainstay, reality programming and shows with content that offended a portion of the viewers. Beginning early in 1989, some advertisers began refusing to buy time on these so-called "reality shows," which included everything from talk shows like "The Morton Downey Jr. Show" to programs that re-created sensational events like Twentieth Century–Fox's syndicated "Current Affair." The ABC network canceled two specials that had already been paid for in reaction to the out-cry. But Fox stood by "America's Most Wanted," and so did most of its advertisers. And then it expanded its franchise with "Totally Hidden Video," a take-off on the old "Candid Camera" show.

Fox also took the heat from critics of the strong language and ideas in some of its shows, especially "Married . . . With Children." A Detroit housewife named Terry Rakolta became an instant media celebrity when she denounced an episode of the Fox show for showing too much sexy female flesh. She was following in the footsteps of a number of other would-be reformers, including Rev. Donald Wildmon, who charged that TV was overloaded with sin and sex, and lacked good moral values.

It was clear these protests put fear in the hearts of the established network programmers. The proof, according to TV critics, was that in the fall of 1989 NBC, CBS, and ABC offered the blandest crop of new shows in modern times.

While Fox was more careful about the content of its shows, including "Married . . . With Children," it clearly did not back down in the face of these would-be censors. In part, that was because the only way to attract the young adults that Fox was after was to give them shows with more edge than they could get on the other networks. To secure its franchise, Fox had to stand up to the pressure groups.

On the road to credibility and financial reward, Fox didn't just offer better or stronger programming either. It literally rewrote the economics by which network television had operated since the 1960s. It showed that non-story form TV shows like "America's Most Wanted," which cost far less to produce than the typical situation comedy, could draw just as many viewers—or even more.

Fox accomplished all of this at a time when television—especially network TV—was in a rapid state of change. The share of the audience viewing network television was steadily declining. The size of the audience viewing non-network alternatives, ranging from independent TV stations to cable TV services like ESPN and HBO was growing rapidly. And an increasingly large segment of the audience was turning off all of the broadcasters in order to watch programming on pre-recorded video cassettes played on their VCR (video cassette recorder).

As fast as its shows succeeded, Fox began looking for ways to build on its accomplishments. Murdoch and Diller didn't even pause to take a breath when Fox hit the breakeven point; they plowed all of those profits and more back into expanding and helping the new network to grow. That meant not just expanding to a third night of series programming, but also making plans to quickly launch a fourth night of programming once a month with a two-hour programming block (most often a movie). It also meant beginning to explore other parts of the day, and new kinds of relationships.

For instance, the Fox station group joined with the Fox network and some affiliated stations to develop its own block of programming for children in late afternoon. Fox began looking at the possibility of doing a news oriented show in the middle of the day. Fox came close to launching a pop music show for late at night, but pulled back when it couldn't guarantee consistently high quality.

Fox also expanded the frontiers of television marketing and promotion. It became the first network to really make use of cable television. It offered some shows, including the annual Emmy Awards, over cable systems in markets where its affiliated stations did not reach. Fox also joined with HBO in an unprecedented promotional experiment. Fox agreed to telecast three hours of HBO shows in the fall of 1989 over certain affiliated stations, marking the first time a broadcast network and a cable programmer worked together to offer a "preview" of shows available on cable TV.

The establishment of the Fox Broadcasting Company sent many other shock waves through the world of communications, some of which will not be fully felt for years to come. For the TV syndication industry, which sells shows after their network run (and some first-run programs), Fox's debut meant there was less time available on independent stations to place such shows. However, at the same time, Fox's success strengthened many independent stations, making them more economically viable and more likely to survive into the future. And that was good for the entire industry.

The established networks don't like seeing Fox become a permanent part of the broadcasting scene. There is no question, however, that Fox's presence forced them to re-evaluate their own position in the marketplace. Over time Fox's success will push the other networks to become smarter programmers and marketers, if only to assure their own survival.

Against all odds, Rupert Murdoch and Barry Diller turned their dream into a reality. In less than three years, all of the other players in the worldwide communications industry had to take Fox into account when making their own plans. Changes in technology and the political climate may have made the birth of the Fox network possible, but it was attractive programming that made it viable.

While Barry Diller and Rupert Murdoch stood proudly watching Fox grow, many of the others who were there for the creation moved on to new challenges.

On March 28, 1989, the Walt Disney Company announced that thirty-one-year-old Garth Ancier had been named President of Network Television Production. Ancier had been placed in charge of series development and production of television programming for the network division.

In mid-August of 1989, Kevin Wendle announced that he was leaving his executive position at Fox to become an independent TV producer with a special relationship with the Fox Broadcasting Company. He was immediately named producer of "Totally Hidden Video," one of Fox's most popular new shows. Wendle had gotten along with Peter Chernin, the new head of programming, but as the network grew and matured, he became itchy for other challenges. "Fox had really become a company up and running," said Wendle shortly after his resignation was announced. "I've always been most energized by start-ups. I like to get in and turn around something that isn't working. That's the most fun."

"Totally Hidden Video," uses secret cameras to capture people in real life that are funny or embarrassing. Wendle first became involved with the show when it was criticized for faking some episodes in what was supposed to be a completely unstaged show.

When the show became an instant hit, he saw an opportunity to use it as his vehicle to move back into producing on a full-time basis.

Ancier and Wendle also patched up their friendship. Wendle compared what happened to a "sibling rivalry." Wendle added that he and Ancier are now social friends again. "I think Garth has realized, with some distance," said Wendle, "that I wasn't the enemy . . . I think essentially Garth is a good person and I'm a good person. No one is out to kill anyone. It was just a competitive situation, but I think everyone played by the rules."

In retrospect, Kevin Wendle feels that Garth Ancier was quite justified in how he felt at the time. "He was having a lot of difficulty. In his mind, I became the bad guy. So he didn't want to spend a lot of time socially with me because in his mind I was more successful and that hurt. Now that period is over and he can see I wasn't intentionally out to hurt him. I think there's once again a trust between us and an understanding of what has happened."

Barry Diller continued running Twentieth Century–Fox, Fox Inc. (the TV stations) and Fox Broadcasting Company. Diller brought in a successful independent producer, Joe Roth, to replace Len Goldberg as head of the movie production operation, with a mandate to triple the studio's output of feature films in a short period of time.

During a News Corp. executive retreat in mid-1989, Diller broke his ankle in a motorcycle accident. He was briefly hobbled, but soon was back at his desk.

Rupert Murdoch continued adding to the News Corp. empire, along with an on-going restructuring. He spun off some of his publishing interests to reduce debt, and raised about $100 million by selling innovative shares of preferred stock in News Corp. through a subsidiary in the Cayman Islands. The preferred stock was innovative because it was based on the value of the company's holdings in Reuters, the European news service. That meant Murdoch could cash out of the investment, while keeping it.

Sky Television, Murdoch's DBS (direct from satellite to home TV) service in the United Kingdom began offering four channels of programming in February 1989, but it was not an immediate success. Consumers were slow to buy receiving dishes to pick up Sky TV, and to subscribe to the service. Experts placed first year losses at around $150 million. The Walt Disney Company made an agreement to operate The Disney Channel as part of Sky Television, with Disney becoming an investor in the venture. When Sky ran into start up problems, Disney's Michael Eisner pulled out of the venture despite a personal plea from Barry Diller to stick it out. Murdoch's News Corp. sued Disney in May 1989, but two months later an out-of-court settlement was arranged. Disney would not be a partner with News Corp. in Sky TV, but did agree to sell certain movies to the Sky movie channel.

Jamie Kellner remained President of the Fox Broadcasting Company. After the arrival of Peter Chernin as head of programming and promotion, Kellner's role was more sharply defined in the areas of sales, affiliate relations and administration. Under his leadership Fox achieved extraordinary sales results during the 1989 advertising "upfront," when the networks hold their annual advance sale of advertising time for the coming season. Fox more than tripled its sales from the prior year, grossing over $300 million in ad sales for 1989–90, providing solid evidence that the advertising community had accepted Fox.

Marvin Davis continued searching for a way to re-enter the entertainment industry, but by summer 1989 had not yet found it. He moved his permanent residence from Denver to Los Angeles, where his annual Christmas party became celebrated for its ambiance and turnout of famous faces. Davis continued to make millions in a wide variety of other investments in real estate, communications, and other businesses. He bought the Beverly Hills Hotel, where he had once stayed during his visits to Los Angeles from Denver, and then sold it one year later to the Sultan of Brunei for a profit of about $65 million. He purchased Spectradyne (a company that provides pay-per-view TV service, mainly to hotels) in partnership with the Prudential Insurance Co. of America for $635 million in March 1989. He attempted to acquire CBS Inc., Northwest Airlines, Lorimar, MGM/UA Communications, and the *Los Angeles Herald Examiner* without success. In July 1989, Davis led an investment group that opened a new deli in Beverly Hills called the Carnegie, after a famous New York restaurant. As this is written, he was also pursuing a takeover of United Airlines.

Marvin's son, John Davis, became his closest financial advisor, while remaining an active film producer. John Davis also engineered the purchase of three small TV stations from Lorimar for $23 million.

Sherry Lansing, in partnership with Stanley Jaffe, based at Paramount Pictures, became one of the most successful movie producing teams of all time. Their hits included *Fatal Attraction* and *Black Rain*.

Dennis Stanfill has quietly continued to operate several investment partnerships and remained out of the public eye.

C. Joseph La Bonte became President of Rebok, the maker of a line of athletic foot gear.

Norman Levy, who received a $1.5 million out-of-court settlement of his contract, became President of New Century/Vista, a film distribution entity. By mid-1989, after about three years of operation, New Century/Vista had not had any notable successes and had dismissed the majority of its employees.

Burton I. "Buddy" Monash rejoined Marvin Davis as an executive of The Davis Company, which is headquartered in the Fox Plaza office building.

Martin Davis continued to reshape Gulf + Western Industries into a pure communications and entertainment company. He renamed it Paramount Communications and made a brief, ill-fated hostile takeover attempt at Time Inc., just as it was about to merge with Warner Communications.

Joan Rivers became a hit on Broadway, continued working in Las Vegas, and in September 1989 launched her new daytime talk show produced by the Tribune Company. Rivers was awarded a star on the Hollywood Walk of Fame in July 1989. During interviews on that occasion, she softened her view of Fox considerably, saying they were contributing factors in the suicide of her husband, Edgar Rosenberg, but that she did not blame Fox or its executives for his death.

Kirk Kerkorian started a small luxury airline, MGM Grand Air, bought a hotel in Las Vegas. He also put his majority interest in MGM/UA up for sale again.

Herb Siegel remained Chairman of Chris-Craft Industries. Siegel and Steve Ross, Chairman of Warner Communications quickly became enemies due to different views of how to run Warner. Siegel attempted to oust Ross, but instead was isolated on the Warner board. When Warner was merged into Time Inc., Siegel made a great deal of money, but was frozen out of any role in the new corporation.

Marc Rich remains a fugitive from U.S. justice living just outside Zurich, Switzerland, where he quietly invests his considerable fortune.

Daniel Melnick continued producing motion pictures and entered into new partnerships with Carolco Inc. and producer Ray Stark.

Michael Eisner, Frank Welles, Jeffrey Katzenberg and Rich

Frank continue to lead the Walt Disney Company, which has achieved record results under their management.

Leonard Goldberg remained at Twentieth Century–Fox as head of movie and TV production until mid-1989, when he returned to independent production.

Alan Horn became a partner in Castle Rock Productions, which quickly had a major movie success with *When Harry Met Sally.*

Lawrence Gordon continued as an independent producer with a series of outstanding successes, including the movies *Die Hard* and *Predator.* In August 1989, Gordon was named head of Largo Entertainment, a company funded with over $100 million in movie production funds by JVC, the big Japanese electronics manufacturer. Gordon was given total and absolute control over movie production.

David Johnson consulted in Hollywood briefly after Fox, then moved back to Connecticut, where he was—in the summer of 1989—once again trying to put together investors to back him in a company that would purchase TV stations.

Brenda Mutchnick Farrier moved back to Connecticut and went to work as an executive at a home video company. In early 1989, she once again moved to Los Angeles where she worked as an advertising and marketing executive for a new company founded by former Paramount marketing head Gordon Weaver, which provided public relations, marketing, advertising, and related services to independent movie companies.

Scott Sassa rejoined Turner Broadcasting as Executive Vice President of the TNT network, an advertiser supported basic cable TV service which began programming October 3, 1988. TNT quickly became a rare cable TV success story.

Marion Davis became a production executive at the CBS television network.

Alan Sternfeld became a financial executive at GTG Entertainment, a company started by former NBC Chairman Grant Tinker and the Gannett Company.

In late 1989, entertainment industry rumors swirled that there might be a start-up of a fifth over the air broadcast network. Those said to be considering such a move reportedly included Paramount, MCA Incorporated, and the Tribune Company of Chicago. Why would anyone consider undertaking such a risky, expensive venture? They hoped to imitate the surprise success of the Fox Broadcasting Company.

INDEX

295